WRITTEN IN BLOOD

WRITTEN IN BLOOD

A Cultural History of the British Vampire

Paul Adams

The History Press

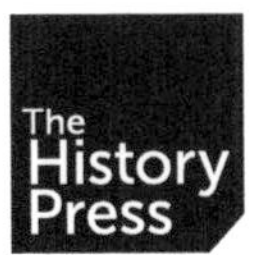

For Alan Frank,
the man who taught me about horror.

First published 2014
Reprinted 2021

The History Press
97 St George's Place
Cheltenham, Gloucestershire, GL50 3QB
www.thehistorypress.co.uk

British Library Cataloguing in Publication Data.
A catalogue record for this book is available from the British Library.

ISBN 978 0 7524 9715 0

Typesetting and origination by The History Press
Printed in Great Britain by TJ Books Limited, Padstow, Cornwall

Contents

Introduction and Acknowledgements 6

1 Gothic Beginnings and Victorian Vampires (1816–1873) 9

2 The Beast of Croglin Grange and Other Strange Happenings (1100s–Present) 21

3 Bram Stoker: A Benchmark in Blood (1847–1912) 46

4 The Undead in Britain: Vampire Fiction Before and After the First World War (1890s–1940) 61

5 The Vampire Murderers (1920s–2012) 75

6 The Mysterious World of Montague Summers (1880–1948) 88

7 A Silver Scream: The Road to British Vampire Cinema (1921–1955) 97

8 Lord of Misrule: The Rise and Fall of Hammer's *Dracula* (1956–1974) 106

9 Sex and Blood: Hammer's Legions and Beyond (1970–1988) 136

10 The Strange Story of the Highgate Vampire (1965–Present) 156

11 Undead Television: Vampires in British Broadcasting (1968–2010) 185

12 The Music of the Night (1960–2000) 192

13 In the Shadow of Stoker: Modern Vampire Literature (1975–2013) 197

About the Author 207

Bibliography and Further Reading 208

Index of Names and Titles 210

Introduction and Acknowledgements

Vampires. Blood-drinking spectres that inhabit a world of shadows in a hidden realm somewhere between life and death: seemingly impossible but tantalisingly real; dark but alluring, sensual and dangerous. Today the vampire is a cultural icon whose origins in a distant age of ignorance and superstition continue to make themselves felt. In July 2013, during the time that I was researching and writing this book, archaeologists working on a roadway construction site near Gliwice in southern Poland unearthed what was reported to be an ancient Slavic 'vampire' burial: the skeletal remains of several human bodies, decapitated with the skulls placed between the legs in the hope that the dead would stay dead and not rise from their graves to attack and infect the living. In Bulgaria the previous year, two medieval skeletons were similarly excavated in the Black Sea town of Sozopol. Both bodies had been nailed into the ground with iron rods. Similarly, the day before submission of the final manuscript, the audience at London's Royal Court Theatre were apparently shocked out of their seats at the gory goings-on in the National Theatre of Scotland's full-blooded stage production of Jack Thorne's *Let the Right One In*, an adaptation of the original Swedish vampire story by John Ajvide Lindqvist.

Looking back, it would seem that any writer of a work on a subject that rational thought and modern scientific study demands to be wholly nonsensical undertakes the task in the shadows of strange revelations that begin in some way to cloud the water. If I had been drafting this introduction in the mid-1990s, the then recent discovery (in 1994) of another skeleton, that of a middle-aged man in a Turkish cemetery on the Greek island of Lesbos, nailed through his neck, ankles and pelvis into his coffin with eight-inch metal stakes, would no doubt be playing on my mind. Similarly, for writers in the early 1970s, the frenzied media coverage of mass vampire hunts and exorcisms in a large Victorian cemetery in north London, just over 25 miles from where I am now writing, would be impossible not to mention and give support to those individuals who still believe and give a positive response to the familiar phrase, 'Can such things be?'

Like many people, my introduction to the world of the vampire came through film and television. At half past ten on Friday, 15 March 1974, wearing no doubt a British Home Stores dressing gown, I sat down aged 7 with my father and watched *Dracula Has Risen from the Grave*, then a relatively recent offering from Hammer Films and one which we will encounter in more detail in the pages that follow. 'Here comes the blood!' my father announced as the living room filled with the first strains of James Bernard's stirring orchestral introduction, and the television screen became a mass of Technicolor gore. Five months later, now in a caravan in Bognor Regis on a tiny black and white portable, Hammer and the Count returned for *Dracula: Prince of Darkness*, by which time my vampire education had moved up several gears with a copy of Alan Frank's recently published and lavishly illustrated, *The Movie Treasury: Horror Movies*. Despite much exposure to a vast array of cinematic and literary horrors over the years, the vampire remains a personal favourite, one that seems to step out of both the silver screen and books, and become something more than simple words and flickering shadows, walking effortlessly down through the pages of recorded history into the present day.

In this book I have attempted to give a concise account of the 'British vampire', a strange and compelling amalgam of literature, music, criminology, film, television and the paranormal. Vampiric activity has seemingly been recorded in the British Isles since the days of the twelfth century, when medieval chroniclers set down for posterity accounts of strange happenings and unquiet graves. To these historical reminiscences are added a selection of later happenings, some well known, others obscure, and many of which are still within living memory, such as the Gorbals Vampire, the Blackburn Vampire, London's infamous Highgate Vampire, and Stoke-on-Trent's Vampire of the Villas. The contribution of creative fiction to the world of the undead cannot be underestimated and many British writers have laid down classic works that comprise a formidable and powerful body of literature. As well as the classic writers of the nineteenth century, such as Le Fanu, Rymer and Polidori, I have devoted space to some of the modern masters of terror, including Ramsey Campbell, R. Chetwynd-Hayes, Brian Lumley, Guy N. Smith and Simon Clark, who have all developed, expanded and redefined the vampire novel from its beginnings in the opening years of the 1800s. One writer above all others, now over a century ago, single-handedly created the vampire as a twentieth- and twenty-first-century icon, and it is difficult not to write a work such as this without an examination of the writings of the Irishman, Bram Stoker. He is included here, despite his Dublin origins, due to the fact that his benchmark novel *Dracula* was both set and published in London, that Stoker himself worked for many years at the Lyceum Theatre off the Strand, and that Ireland did not become totally free from British rule until 1949, by which time his novel had changed the world of the undead forever. Similarly, Montague Summers, whose books remain a constant reference point for students and aficionados of the undead, is another character who would be noticeable by his absence.

As well as fictional horrors, the reality of the vampire in the mind of the murderer has resulted in several violent and tragic deaths which are touched on in a chapter looking specifically at the vampire murderer in Britain. Finally, with the medium of film and latterly television at the forefront of the vampire's public persona, both here in the UK and worldwide, I have devoted a not inconsiderable amount of space to the development of the vampire in British cinema, in particular the importance of Hammer Films in the re-establishment of Gothic horror in mid-twentieth century film-making.

Before we begin, though, I would like to take a moment to thank a number of people who have helped considerably in various ways with the task in hand: Peter Underwood, for his interest in the project and for supplying illustrations; Colonel John Blashford-Snell, for recounting his experiences of vampire bats in Darren Province; Tine Appelman, who assisted with reviews for Bram Stoker's *Dracula*; Darren W. Ritson, who provided the photograph of Croglin Low Hall; David and Della Farrant and Bishop Sean Manchester, for patiently revisiting their involvement in the Highgate Vampire case; Hammer Films historian Wayne Kinsey, who kindly supplied illustrations; Allan Downend and the E.F. Benson Society, who also assisted with illustrations, as did Rosemary Pardoe, Simon Ball, Stephen Jones and Paul Groundwell. I would also like to thank my old friend, Eddie Brazil, for his support and encouragement; Matilda Richards and Naomi Reynolds at The History Press, who have seen this book through to production with their usual efficiency; and finally my children, Aban, Idris, Isa and Sakina, who as usual have had to put up with it all.

Finally, it only leaves me to say that I hope you enjoy exploring the world of the British vampire in fact and fiction. Now, if you're ready, here comes the blood …

Paul Adams, 2014

1

Gothic Beginnings and Victorian Vampires

(1816-1873)

The British vampire was born appropriately enough under the wet grey skies of the 'year without a summer', a world of rain-lashed cemeteries, waterlogged graves and dark fearful imaginings over 450 miles from home. Across Europe this, to coin a phrase from American writer Richard Matheson, 'Brontean weather' caused crops to fail, which resulted in food riots and looting across England and France, marking 1816 as the time of the worst famine of the nineteenth century. A cumulative series of volcanic eruptions during the preceding four years, the most powerful of which took place at Mount Tambora on the Indonesian island of Sumbawa in April 1815, was the turbulent background to one of the most important and seminal events in the history of supernatural horror fiction, and which simultaneously established two of its greatest and most enduring franchises into European literature and beyond: the vampire myth and the world of the artificially created living dead. The fictional vampire was not new in 1816, but its various disparate strands found a focus and permanence at this time. In his book *The Monster with a Thousand Faces* (1989), Brian Frost suggests that the honour of the first example of an undead creature in a work of 'pure imagination' dates to the eleventh century and a piece of Anglo-Saxon poetry entitled 'A Vampyre of the Fens'. He then subsequently traces a chronological lineage of fictional blood-drinking and vampire activity that encompasses Sir Thomas Malory's late fifteenth-century *Le Morte d'Arthur*, Heinrich Ossenfelder's 1748 poem 'Der Vampir'; then from Gottfried Bürger's *Lenore* (1773) and late eighteenth-century de Sade – *Juliette* (1791) and *Justine* (1796) – through Goethe's 1797 *The Bride of Corinth* and on to early nineteenth-century works including Johann Tieck's *Wake Not the Dead* (republished in 1973 as *The Bride of the Grave*), Robert Southey's 1801 *Thalaba the Destroyer*, and Samuel Taylor Coleridge's *Christabel* (1816), at which point our present survey begins its bloody and patriotic course.

In the early part of 1816, two Englishmen – the noted Romantic poet George Gordon, the 6th Baron Byron, together with John William Polidori, a physician and writer employed at the time as Byron's travelling companion and secretary – took up residence in a large rented house, the Villa Diodati, in Cologny on the southern shore of Lake Geneva. Polidori, aged 20, and eight years his employer's junior, had been paid by the London publisher John Murray (who would later burn the manuscripts of Byron's memoirs in his office fireplace for fear that their scandalous contents would damage the poet's posthumous reputation) to keep a diary of their travels. Murray had successfully published the second volume of Byron's narrative poem 'Childe Harold's Pilgrimage' in 1812, but the two men did not get on. Before the year was out the young doctor had been dismissed from his lordship's service and after a brief and unhappy sojourn in Italy had returned to England.

Byron's high-profile affair with English socialite Lady Caroline Lamb (then married to Lord Melbourne, MP for Leominster, who subsequently held the office of Prime Minister in 1834 and from 1835–41) had been the talk of the country four years before. Its bitter conclusion resulted in her former lover's immortalisation by Lady Caroline's own hand, as the dastardly Clarence de Ruthven (pronounced 'Ruvven'), the titular anti-hero of the novel *Glenarvon*, published in May 1816 only days after Byron and Polidori had left the country for Switzerland.

Byron's presence in Geneva caused something of a stir amongst fellow English tourists, who took to spying on the occupants of the Villa Diodati through telescopes from across the lake. Their gossip mongering soon reached feverishly new levels with the arrival of Byron's former lover Clara 'Claire' Clairmont at another rented house nearby called Montalègre. Claire, then in the early stages of pregnancy with the poet's daughter Allegra, arrived with her stepsister, the 18-year-old Mary Godwin, and another poet, Mary's lover and soon-to-be husband Percy Bysshe Shelley. Claire, Mary and Shelley took to making regular visits to be in Byron's company, and it was amongst the neurosis of the Villa Diodati's candle-lit decadence during that 'wet, ungenial summer', as Mary later famously described it, that legends were born.

In his book *Vampyres: Lord Byron to Count Dracula* (1991), Christopher Frayling has demonstrated that Mary Shelley's posthumous recollections of the events of that time (included in an introduction to a third edition of *Frankenstein* in 1831, by which time Byron, Polidori and Shelley were dead) are not as accurate as its famous author would make out, but still it remains a monumental landmark in the history of supernatural horror fiction.

Confined by constant heavy rain to the rooms of the Villa Diodati for several days in mid-June, the assembled company amused themselves by reading aloud from a French edition of the *Fantasmagoriana or Tales of the Dead*, a collection of German ghost stories that had been published anonymously by Jean Eyriès in 1812 (a similarly nameless English edition appeared the following year). Inspired by the first story in the book, known as 'The Family Portraits', the group began an exercise to see who could write their own successful ghost story, the competition eventually taking several days to complete. Stultified with laudanum and on the verge of a nervous collapse, Shelley was unable to write a line and no details of Claire's contribution (if it ever existed) have survived. However, the teenage Mary Godwin famously delivered what amounted to the bones of a fully-formed *Frankenstein* that on publication two years later went on to become, in the words of H.P. Lovecraft, the twentieth-century American master of the weird tale, 'One of the horror-classics of all time', containing, as Lovecraft noted, 'the true touch of cosmic fear'.

Polidori was able to set down an account of incest and spirit-rising that was later published in 1819 as *Ernestus Berchtold*, while Byron took the opportunity to create a supernatural parody of his present situation, describing a tale of sinister happenings in a Turkish cemetery involving two travelling Englishmen on a sightseeing tour of the East. Having told the story aloud, Byron felt enough of the work to write out the opening pages but soon tired of the project and quickly cast it aside. At some point during his remaining time at the Villa Diodati, John Polidori was challenged to complete Byron's 'fragment', which he duly did: over the course of three days he reworked the basic plot, grafting on an ending that followed closely the conclusion that he himself had heard Byron relate to that strange company of 'sexual and literary outlaws' only a short time before. By the time he left Cologny under a cloud at the end of the year, the handwritten pages of what Christopher Frayling has considered to be 'probably the most influential horror story of all time' lay behind, forgotten and discarded in a drawer.

Polidori's *The Vampyre* found its way to England two years later and was eventually published in the *London New Monthly Magazine* on 1 April 1819. The anonymous manuscript, bundled with a gossipy letter about the rainy shenanigans at the Villa Diodati, seemed to imply that the entire story was from Byron's own hand and in this fashion it was enthusiastically embraced by the flagging *New Monthly*'s editor Henry Colburn, who threw caution to the wind and in what proved to be a successful coup, presented 'A Tale by Lord Byron' to the public at large, a bold decision that not only boosted the sales and literary reputation of the magazine (particularly as a suitable outlet for macabre and sinister stories) but also imprinted both the scourge of the undead myth and the singular character of the 'Byronic Vampire' firmly and indelibly into the unsuspecting human psyche.

Taking the character of Augustus Darvell, the mysterious traveller from Byron's own story, Polidori overlaid Caroline Lamb's *Lord Glenarvon* (and therefore Byron himself) to create the vampire Lord Ruthven, 'a nobleman, more remarkable for his singularities, than his rank' who, appearing unexpectedly in the midst of fashionable London society, a strange figure with dead grey eyes and a similar unnatural pallor, quickly becomes the object of much speculation and attention: 'His peculiarities caused him to be invited to every house; all wished to see him, and those who had been accustomed to violent excitement, and now felt the weight of ennui, were pleased at having something in their presence capable of engaging their attention.'

The licentious Ruthven, however, like the noble poet on whom he was based, is bankrupt and, in order to escape both his creditors and the soon-to-be revealed string of torrid affairs amongst a clutch of high-society women, plans to leave the country. Before he sails he is joined by Aubrey, a rich young gentleman who is tired with the London scene and desires to escape England.

As they journey to Italy on their tour across Europe, Aubrey witnesses the strange ill fortune that befalls all those that come into contact with the mysterious Ruthven: the young gamblers who are bankrupted by him at the casino, and the curse that seems to afflict any of those on whom Ruthven bestows his charity – '… for they all were either led to the scaffold, or sunk to the lowest and the most abject misery'.

In Rome, Aubrey watches as his companion attempts to seduce an Italian countess, but when a letter arrives from his guardians in England exposing the ruin of all the society women that have fallen under Ruthven's spell, Aubrey successfully prevents a union between the couple and, abandoning Ruthven, leaves for Greece alone. In Athens he falls in love with Ianthe, a young innkeeper's daughter who tells tales of vampires that haunt the countryside surrounding the inn. Aubrey dismisses such stories, but promises to return from an outing to an ancient temple before nightfall, as his trip involves passing through an olive grove 'where no Greek would ever remain after the day had closed, upon any consideration'. However, Aubrey lingers in the ruins and it is dark before he attempts to make the return journey. Caught in a storm, the Englishman shelters in a mud hut deep in the woods where he is attacked by an unidentified assailant. Aubrey survives and is rescued by a party of torch-wielding villagers but amongst the trees the men find the body of Ianthe, the first vampire victim in the history of English literary horror:

> He shut his eyes, hoping that it was but a vision arising from his disturbed imagination; but he again saw the same form, when he unclosed them, stretched by his side. There was no colour upon her cheek, not even upon her lip; yet there was a stillness about her face that seemed almost as attaching as the life that once dwelt there:- upon her neck and breast was blood, and upon her throat were the marks of teeth having opened the vein:- to this the men pointed, crying, simultaneously struck with horror, 'a Vampyre, a Vampyre!'

Stricken with fever, Aubrey is confined to a bed at the inn where he is discovered by Lord Ruthven, who has followed him to Athens. The two men continue on together but in the mountains are attacked by brigands and Ruthven falls, mortally wounded. On his deathbed, he challenges Aubrey to withhold any information about the happenings on his return to England: '"Swear!" cried the dying man, raising himself with exultant violence, "Swear by all your soul reveres, by all your nature fears, swear that for a year and a day you will not impart your knowledge of my crimes or death to any living being in any way, whatever may happen, or whatever you may see."' Aubrey eventually complies, at which point Ruthven slumps dead. In the morning, the dead man's body has disappeared and Aubrey, now '[w]eary of a country in which he had met with such terrible misfortunes' sets out to make the return journey home alone.

Back in England, Aubrey is busily preparing to present his 18-year-old sister at a reception for her formal entry into the London society scene. Among the many guests in a crowded salon, he is horrified to again see the apparition of the sinister Lord Ruthven, who takes his former companion by the arm and gives a chilling reminder of his 'year and a day' oath. The young man collapses and is taken away in a carriage. In the days that follow, Aubrey is haunted by visions of the sinister vampire and his health fails; the horror is almost complete when, after his sister announces her engagement to the Earl of Marsden, the tormented hero sees in a locket about her neck 'the features of the monster who has so long influenced his life'. Powerless to act, as the wedding is scheduled to take place on the very day the oath expires, Aubrey sinks further into insanity and is confined to bed by a physician. In an attempt to delay the union, he writes a letter to his sister warning her of the danger but it remains undelivered and the marriage goes ahead, after which the couple leave on their honeymoon. On the stroke of midnight, Aubrey, now on his own deathbed, relates the entire series of events to his sister's horrified guardians and expires immediately afterwards. The revelation, however, as Polidori notes with grim finality in his closing lines, has ultimately come too late: 'The guardians hastened to protect Miss Aubrey; but when they arrived, it was too late. Lord Ruthven had disappeared, and Aubrey's sister had glutted the thirst of a VAMPYRE!'

Neither Byron or Polidori would live to see the later manifestations of the literary phenomenon that between them they had unleashed. Henry Colburn's sudden and incorrectly assigned publication of *The Vampyre* took both men by surprise and was the cause of much annoyance, although its immediate success was something that could only be marvelled at. The tale was published in book form soon after it appeared in the *New Monthly* – still credited to Lord Byron – and it was only in later printings that the correct author's name was amended on the title page.

The following year, French writer Cyprien Bérard wrote the first vampire novel, *Lord Ruthven ou les Vampires*, an expansive two-volume work using material extracted directly from Polidori's narrative. A little over thirteen months following its release, the first stage adaptation of Polidori's *The Vampyre* had taken place when Charles Nodier's *Le Vampire* was presented at the Théâtre de la Porte Saint-Martin in Paris on 13 June 1820 to much acclaim.

Byron had sent John Murray the incomplete manuscript of his own Villa Diodati tale shortly after *The Vampyre* had first appeared in print and it was published the same year – without the author's permission and much to his chagrin – as *Fragment of a Story* (and subsequently using the name of the titular character Augustus Darvell) tacked onto the end of his narrative poem 'Mazeppa'. Less than five years later Byron was dead at the age of 36, slain by a fever while fighting on the side of the revolutionaries in the Greek War of Independence. 'Poor Polidori', as Mary Shelley subsequently described him in her introduction to *Frankenstein*, had already preceded his former employer to the grave. Suffering from depression and saddled with gambling debts he committed suicide with prussic acid at his residence in Great Pulteney Street in London on 24 August 1821 – he was 25 years old.

European commentators on vampires pre-Polidori described their undead foes as loathsome creatures of the fields and the farmyard: rancid, swollen, peasant corpses gorged on the blood of both animals and humans alike; educated, urban vampires from the middle or upper classes were conspicuous by their absence. Robert Morrison and Chris Baldick, in their introduction to the Oxford University Press edition of *The Vampyre*, published in 1997, reiterate what modern researchers such as Anthony Masters, Basil Copper, Christopher Frayling, Tina Rath and Kim Newman have described both before and since. 'The historical and mythological importance of Polidori's *The Vampyre*,' they note, 'lies in its ... elevation of the nosferatu (undead) to the dignity of high social rank. By removing the bloodsucker from the village cowshed to the salons of high society and the resorts of international tourism, he [Polidori] set in motion the glorious career of the *aristocratic* [original emphasis] vampire'. In this respect, future British and non-British vampires such as Le Fanu's Carmilla and Stoker's Dracula, as well as Anne Rice's Lestat (*Interview with the Vampire*, 1976) and Stephen King's Mr Barlow from the 1975 novel *Salem's Lot*, share a macabre lineage that begins with the seemingly effortless appearance of Lord Ruthven on the rain-soaked shores of Lake Geneva so many years before.

In 1995, the late English journalist and writer Peter Haining (1940–2007), a prolific editor and compiler of horror, fantasy and crime anthologies, published *The Vampire Omnibus*, a wide-ranging collection of tales involving a gregarious presentation of the vampire myth spanning nearly 100 years, beginning with an excised passage from *Dracula*, through inter-war tales by Gustav Meyrink (*The Land of the Time-Leeches*) and Henry Kuttner (*The Vampire*) and on to later twentieth-century contributions from writers such as Clive Sinclair, Ray Bradbury, Theodore Sturgeon and Richard Laymon. In his anthology, Haining rescues from obscurity a little-known story 'The Skeleton Count', written by the early Victorian author Mrs Elizabeth Caroline Grey. It appears to now hold the title of the first extended vampire series in English, a trophy wrestled from the hands of a contemporary writer James Rymer.

Published in the appropriately named penny dreadful paper *The Casket* in the autumn of 1828, Mrs Grey's narrative concerns the adventures of the Ruthven-like Count Rodolph of Ravensburg, a German nobleman whose diabolical pact with the Devil in order to gain the power of eternal life results in him being doomed to spend the hours between sunset and sunrise transformed into a living skeleton.

Sub-titled *The Vampire Mistress*, this early instalment sees the Count employing necromancy in order to bring the dead body of a local teenage beauty, Bertha Kurtel, back to life. Unfortunately for Rodolph, although successful, the ritual transforms the restored Bertha into a vampire who proceeds to menace the inhabitants of a nearby village. A young child and one of the village maidens are attacked, an outrage which raises a mob of torch-wielding menfolk led by the local blacksmith, who storm Ravensburg Castle at dusk and succeed in dragging the unfortunate creature back to its grave:

> Then a sharp pointed stake was produced, which had been prepared by the way, and the smith plunged it with all the force of his sinewy arms into the abdomen of the doomed vampire. A piercing shriek burst from her pale lips as the horrible thrust aroused her to consciousness, and as her clothes became dabbed with the crimson stream of life, and the smith lifted his heavy hammer and drove the stake through her quivering body, the transfixed wretch writhed convulsively, and the contortions of her countenance were fearful to behold. Thus impaled in her coffin, and while her limbs yet quivered with the last throes of dissolution, the earth was replaced and rammed down by the tread of many feet.

Given the summary execution denied to Lord Ruthven by John Polidori, Mrs Grey's Bertha Kurtel appears to hold the honour of being the first traditional vampire slaying in the pages of English literature and as such provides the template for countless writers and film-makers through the years. As for the 'Skeleton Count' himself, Haining notes that he suffers a similar fate when, after a raft of supernatural adventures with such titles as 'The Vampires of London' and 'Der Vampyr!', Rodolph is finally tracked down to the ruins of Ravensburg Castle where another mob of villagers succeed in imprisoning him in a coffin and a final stake is driven through his heart. Elizabeth Grey, a former teacher, was the author of several mystery novels and melodramas whose route to popular writing came via the London publisher Edward Lloyd (1815–90) for whom she initially worked as secretary and later as editor-in-chief of his penny dreadful series of magazines, to which she also contributed several stories. She died in 1869, aged 71.

More familiar than Count Rodolph of Ravensburg is another British penny dreadful bloodsucker, Varney the Vampyre, who first appeared in August 1845 and whose chronicling, again at the hands of Edward Lloyd (who provided the famous alternate title *The Feast of Blood*), ran for an astonishing 109 weekly episodes before being subsequently published in its entirety in book form in September 1847. Today credited as the work of the prolific London-born hack writer James Malcolm Rymer, the author of over 100 full-length books – all written between 1842 and 1866 – whose works include many sensational serials including *Ada the Betrayed*,

Newgate, *The Lady in Black*, and *The String of Pearls* (the latter remembered for its introduction of the character of Sweeney Todd, 'The Demon Barber of Fleet Street'), the eponymous vampire of the title is Sir Francis Varney, the scourge of Bannerworth Hall. Varney is an undead aristocrat who may have had his real-life inspiration in the career of Sir Edmund Verney, a Royalist politician killed at the Battle of Edgehill in 1642, although the villainous Richard Varney from Sir Walter Scott's *Kenilworth* (1821) is also an interesting literary possibility. What is clear, as Christopher Frayling has noted in *Vampyres: Lord Byron to Count Dracula*, is that the republication of Polidori's *The Vampyre* in an illustrated penny edition in 1838 most likely provided Rymer with the stimulus for his long-running undead saga. However, the authorship of *Varney* was for many years attributed to the pen of another of Lloyd's popular weekly authors, Thomas Preskett Prest (*c.* 1810–59): several twentieth-century commentators, including Montague Summers, Basil Copper, Peter Underwood and Anthony Masters, all credit the character to him and it was not until the early 1960s and the discovery of Rymer's personal scrapbooks containing reviews of his work that the error was discovered. Internal evidence within the writing of this and another serial, *The String of Pearls*, corresponding to financial problems in the early months of 1847, also point to Rymer being the true creator of one of the genre's most important and influential literary characters.

Making his entrance in suitably dramatic fashion during the height of a violent hail storm, Varney begins his gruesome career of bloodletting, the object of his fiendish desires being the long-suffering Bannerworth family and several other interested parties that make up a rich soap-opera cast of mid-nineteenth-century characters. As well as the Bannerworths themselves – the widowed Mrs Bannerworth, her sons Henry and George and their attractive sister, Flora – they include the local physician, Dr Chillingworth; an old family retainer, Mr Marchdale; the doomed heroine Clara Crofton; Charles Holland; Flora's fiancé as well as a cheeky sailor, Able Seaman Jack Pringle (loosely based, according to historian Dick Collins, on British seaman Sam Weller); Holland's uncle, Admiral Bell; and in a much later episode, Count Pollidori and his daughter, the Signora Isabella. Much of the action in the early part of the serial takes place in and around the Hampshire mansion of Bannerworth Hall, a fictional building which may have had its inspiration in the real-life haunted manor house at Hinton Ampner (nine miles east of Winchester on the western edge of the South Downs), an account of which first appeared in Sir Walter Scott's *Letters on Demonology and Witchcraft* published in 1830.

As the popularity of Varney's bloodcurdling and barnstorming adventures increased, Rymer was obliged to pile on the wordage until eventually in its complete form the saga reached Tolkien-like proportions (the modern Wordsworth Editions reprint runs to a total of 1,166 pages) and was littered with such lurid and sensational sounding chapter headings as 'The Stake and the Dismembered Body',

'The Vampire in the Moonlight', 'The Bone-house of the Churchyard of Anderbury' and 'The Horrors in the Night'. As well as traditional elements of vampire lore, such as bodily stakings in coffins and the decapitation of undead victims, Rymer introduces original and interesting elements into his writing, such as Varney's ability to be restored to life by the rays of the full moon, and in the story's closing pages ('Varney gives some personal account of himself', reproduced in an edited form in Haining's *The Vampire Omnibus* as 'The Vampyre's Story') the incident of a first-person narrative enters a vampire tale for the first time, with great dramatic effect:

> I sprung upon her. There was a shriek, but not before I had secured a draught of life blood from her neck. It was enough. I felt it dart through my veins like fire, and I was restored. From that moment I found out what was to be my sustenance; it was blood – the blood of the young and the beautiful.

In these vampiric confessions, Rymer dates Sir Francis Varney's origins to the time of Oliver Cromwell and reveals how the curse of vampirism was bestowed upon him as revenge for the accidental murder in a fit of rage of his own son: 'Be to yourself a desolation and a blight, shunned by all that is good and virtuous, armed against all men, and all men armed against thee, Varney the Vampyre.' Although the speed and pressure of writing created a somewhat chaotic chronology of chapters and characters in some parts of the story, it would appear that given his contemporary setting in the mid-1840s, Rymer's undead anti-hero was something in the region of 200 years old at the time of his first resurrection.

James Rymer's shilling shocker writing career continued post-Varney for several years although his output dropped around 1853 following the death of his first wife Caroline and again in 1865 after another tragedy, in this case the death of his 5-year-old son Gerald by his second wife, Sarah Carpenter. In 1870, he abandoned the literary world completely and became a hotelier in the south-coast resort of Worthing in West Sussex. Rymer died in London on 11 August 1884 aged 70, and was buried in the grave of his son in Kensal Green Cemetery. His legacy was to fire the public imagination for the first time as to the violent and sexual possibilities of the vampire figure. Unlike John Polidori, Rymer lived to see how the crude sexuality of the Varney saga would, in less than a quarter of a century, be refined by another British writer into one of the finest and most far-reaching of undead tales that, over 140 years after its first appearance, still retains its atmospheric and sensual power.

Joseph Sheridan Le Fanu, a contemporary of Rymer, Edward Bulwer Lytton, Charles Dickens and Wilkie Collins, and who was also the great-nephew of playwright Richard Brinsley Sheridan, was born in Dublin on 28 August 1814. The son of a Protestant clergyman, Le Fanu read classics and law at Trinity College but despite being called to the Irish Bar in 1839, he quickly abandoned a legal career and gravitated into newspaper publishing, becoming the owner of two Protestant editions, *The Warder* and the *Protestant Guardian*, as well as owning shares in three other titles including the *Dublin Evening Mail*. Le Fanu's own talent for writing, and particularly the supernatural tales for which he is highly revered today, had become apparent while he was still a student and many of these stories first saw publication in the *Dublin University Magazine*, an independent cultural journal that had first appeared in 1833. They include 'The Ghost and the Bone-Setter' (1838), the sinister masterpiece 'Schalken the Painter', first published in 1839 and much later given a memorable television adaptation as part of the BBC's 'Ghost Story for Christmas' season in 1979, 'An Account of Some Strange Disturbances in Aungier Street' (1853), and the mystery novels *The House by the Churchyard* (1863) and an early serialised version of *Uncle Silas* (1864); he eventually bought the title of the *Dublin* in 1861 and acted as its editor for several years. Like Rymer, Le Fanu also suffered the debilitating tragedy of losing a wife (in April 1858), his spouse of fourteen years, Susanna Bennett who, between 1845 and 1854, gave birth to their four children, and it was not until after the death of his own mother three years later that he felt able to write fiction again.

Ghost stories were an integral part of the Irishman's output throughout his entire literary life, but it was in this period of maudlin creativity that Le Fanu penned many of his most important and impressive contributions to the genre, of which the compendium of tales entitled *In a Glass Darkly* is perhaps the finest. First published individually in *The Dark Blue* magazine in the winter of 1871 and then as a complete book the following year, this collection of stories with its title a variation on the famous Biblical passage from the thirteenth chapter of the First Epistle to the Corinthians, purports to be a set of case notes of the German physician Dr Martin Hesselius, an imaginative 'portmanteau' plot device that was used with great effect by the British film company Amicus Productions in a number of their multi-episode horror flicks from the mid-1960s onwards. Hesselius has been seen as the forerunner of several psychic sleuths of twentieth-century supernatural literature including Dr John Silence (Algernon Blackwood), Carnacki the Ghost Finder (William Hope Hodgson), Titus Crowe (Brian Lumley), Mark Sabat (Guy N. Smith) and most famously Bram Stoker's Van Helsing. Though it is the vampire-hunting Baron Vordenburg, 'one of the strangest-looking men I ever beheld … tall, narrow-chested, stooping, with high shoulders, and dressed in black' from the volume's famous final 'case' 'Carmilla', who in this instance fulfils the character role that would be first elevated to international fame by Count Dracula a quarter of a century later. As well as the subject of vampirism, Le Fanu also presents a fine study in psychological horror involving a clergyman haunted by the apparition of a spectral monkey ('Green Tea'), as well as accounts of premature burial ('The Room in the Dragon Volant'), a Cock Lane-style haunting ('Mr Justic Harbottle', a revised version of the 'Aungier Street' tale from 1853), and 'The Familiar', another revision of a previous story ('The Watcher', 1851) about a sea captain terrorised by the appearance of a mysterious dwarf. But it is the final story, the novella 'Carmilla' that remains one of the troubled Irishman's most well-known supernatural tales and which most importantly provides the bridge between the Victorian penny blood shockers of Varney the Vampyre and the dark erotic world of Stoker's Dracula and his twentieth-century legions.

Written as a first-person account ten years after the event, Le Fanu sets down the chronicle of a young Austrian woman, Laura, the daughter of a retired English diplomat, and her encounter with a sensual vampire woman, Countess Mircalla Karnstein, known for much of story by the eponymous title of 'Carmilla'. The family, comprising Laura and her unnamed father (a widower), a Swiss governess, Madame Perrodon, and a finishing teacher, Mademoiselle De Lafontaine, live in an isolated castle in a remote forested area of Styria in south-eastern Austria. It is a 'lonely and primitive place' close to the empty and abandoned village of Karnstein, with a ruinous and roofless church 'in the aisle of which are the mouldering tombs of the proud family of Karnstein, now extinct, who once owned the equally desolate château which, in the thick of the forest, overlooks the silent ruins of the town'. In reality the sinister Karnsteins are not as deceased as local history would suppose and soon a carriage accident that occurs close to the entrance of the castle introduces the enigmatic and deadly vampire into the innocent and unsuspecting household.

Offering assistance to two travelling women – a mother and her young daughter – who are stunned when their post-chaise overturns within sight of the castle drawbridge, Laura and her father invite the mysterious Carmilla into their home for a period of three months while her mother continues her urgent journey alone, unaware that their near neighbour, General Spielsdorf's much loved ward Bertha has already fallen victim to the undead aristocrat's bloodlust. Laura recognises Carmilla as a ghostly apparition which had appeared to her at her bedside, seemingly in a dream, as a child, and as what appears to be a plague-like fever brings about the sudden deaths of the local swineherd's wife and a woodman's daughter, Laura herself gradually falls under the vampire's deadly influence: a vision of a strange cat-like familiar visits her at night and her own health begins to fail. Not until the arrival of the tormented General Spielsdorf and the revelation that the blood-drinking Karnsteins have returned from beyond the grave is Carmilla's true identity finally revealed, although the young woman's likeness to a portrait of the late Countess Karnstein dated 1698, recently restored to the castle, hints at the ultimate horror to come. Eventually Spielsdorf, accompanied by Baron Vordenburg, a modern descendant of a local dynasty who drove the Karnsteins to their graves decades before, finally run to earth the grave of the undead Carmilla and bring about her final and ultimate destruction:

> The next day the formal proceedings took place in the chapel of Karnstein. The grave of the Countess Mircalla was opened; and the general and my father recognised each his perfidious and beautiful guest in the face now disclosed to view. The features, though a hundred and fifty years had passed since her funeral, were tinted with the warmth of life…The limbs were perfectly flexible, the flesh elastic; and the leaden coffin floated with blood, in which, to a depth of seven inches, the body lay immersed. Here, then, were all the admitted signs and proofs of vampirism. The body, therefore, in accordance with the ancient practice, was raised, and a sharp stake driven through the heart of the vampire, who uttered a piercing shriek at the moment, in all respects such as might escape from a living person in the last agony. Then the head was struck off, and a torrent of blood flowed from the severed neck. The body and head were next placed on a pile of wood, and reduced to ashes, which were thrown upon the river and borne away, and that territory has never since been plagued by the visits of a vampire.

Sheridan Le Fanu survived his most famous creation by only a year, dying in Dublin on 7 February 1873 at the age of 58. For posterity he left behind an acknowledged masterpiece of the genre whose success derives from its operation on a number of carefully contrived levels. The bloody violence of Carmilla's inescapable fate provides a suitable shocking finale, but the Irishman weaves a haunting atmosphere into his tale far more effective than simple gratuitous bloodletting, sustaining it with great skill during the course of the novella's gradual unfoldment, and providing several macabre and masterly moments that remain disturbingly in the reader's memory: the mysterious vision of a 'hideous black woman' gazing out from the carriage window 'with gleaming eyes and large white eye-balls' and 'teeth set as if in fury'; the deceptive and sensuous languor of her undead lover together with the eerie possibility of her potential return to life. Added to this is Laura's final recollections of her hellish experience and the fancy of hearing 'the light step of Carmilla at the drawing-room door' again. However, by eschewing the Byronic male lead and reversing the sexual polarity through Carmilla's romantic advances towards the ambiguous Laura – whose simultaneous fascination and repulsion comes close to a basic understanding of the workings of the vampire myth in both literature and reality – Le Fanu refines the core of morbid sexuality inherent in the undead theme and, as we will see, provided the all-important stepping stone for greater horrors to come.

2

The Beast of Croglin Grange and Other Strange Happenings

(1100s–Present)

Leaving the literary world of the Victorian vampire, we now cross the threshold into real time and space and spend some time examining several interesting examples of alleged vampirism recorded from in and around the British Isles that bookend a somewhat expansive frame of reference spanning from the twelfth century through to the present day. The geographical distribution of vampire stories across the world is an interesting study in itself, as all countries and cultures have their traditions of vampire-like demons and similar supernatural creatures stretching back into the beginnings of recorded history. Many of these particular vampires fall into the category of, or at least have their origins in, the 'revenant' – a generic term for an unquiet soul of a deceased person, often given physical form as a reanimated corpse or body that exhibits a form of post-mortem behaviour that we would now classify as being vampiric, most noticeably the emergence from the grave or tomb at night, accompanied by some type of blood-drinking activity. The 'vampire' that we recognise today, as London University graduate Dr Tina Rath has commented ('Leaves of Blood', BBC Television, 2009), is essentially a modern phenomenon that has its centre of gravity in the waves of vampire hysteria that swept across Europe in the sixteenth and seventeenth centuries. In broad terms, this vampiric folklore demonstrates the age-old human fascination with both the mysteries of blood and the uncharted realms beyond the grave.

In Mexico, the ancient Mayans feared Camazotz, the bat-like god of the underworld who haunted caves and similar remote locations, and whose activities gave rise to the growth and harvest of agricultural crops; while amongst the many sinister deities present in the mythology of the Aztecs, the Cihuateteo, the corrupted souls of women who died in childbirth, effected an undead existence with several of the traits familiar in other cultures associated with vampiric activity, namely roaming abroad at night in search of unfortunate victims – in this instance unwary children – and a tendency to gather at crossroads, where food offerings would be placed in an attempt to lower the supernatural-affected child mortality rate. Vampire-like spirits and blood-drinking witches, particularly the Lamia, were a contemporary part of the legends of Ancient Greece even before the establishment of the Greek Orthodox Church brought about the idea that the excommunicated dead would become vrykolakas (a long-standing Greek term for a benign revenant-type being particularly associated with the brutal and dangerous modern concept of vampirism). The apparent incorruptibility of buried corpses, perhaps the most powerful catalyst for the development of the vampire myth, played a part in the establishment of the Greek vampire tradition. This was particularly evident on the island of Santorini where writer Anthony Masters (*The Natural History of the Vampire*, 1974) reports the existence of a ghoulish flesh-eating vampire variant, the vrykolatios. Australian aborigines told tales of a tree-dwelling blood-drinker, the dwarf-like Yara-ma-yha-who, which preyed on children and travellers sheltering from the sun; the Filipino Aswang was an attractive female witch that transformed into a blood-sucking bird at night; while in Tibet, Yama, the skull-festooned Nepalese god of death, carried a sword and a cup from which he drank the blood of sleeping people.

Evocatively described by the novelist and historian Peter Ackroyd as 'a land engulfed by mist and twilight', the British Isles are today most associated with accounts of ghosts and hauntings rather than tales of vampires and the undead. Where accounts of apparent vampirism do exist, they are, in the main, ghost stories that have some vampire-like similarity or exhibit phenomena that has been interpreted as having its origins in a vampiric 'entity' or some similar spectral creature. A number of buildings and churches have particular connections with vampire stories and legends, some stretching back over the course of many years, while others, such as Highgate Cemetery in North London, have garnered their associations within a relatively recent time span.

The earliest tales of vampires in Britain date to the twelfth century and the recording of two medieval writers, Walter Map and William of Newburgh. Map, later to become Archdeacon of Oxford, was born in 1140 of apparent Welsh descent. In his early twenties he studied at the University of Paris and subsequently became a courtier of Henry II. By the early 1180s, Map was drawing a stipend from the Diocese of Lincoln; he held offices at Lincoln Cathedral and later made two unsuccessful attempts for a bishopric, one at Hereford and another at St David's in Wales. Map lived a remarkably long life for such difficult times, dying in his late fifties sometime between May 1208 and September 1210. His written legacy is a Latin text known as *De Nugis Curialium* or the 'Trifles of Courtiers', a miscellany of historical accounts and personal insights into his times divided up into five chapters, a number of which contain a selection of ghostly stories that have some form of vampire-like quality. The only surviving manuscript dates from at least 200 years after the work was compiled (between 1181 and 1193), and it has been subsequently edited and republished on two subsequent occasions, the first in 1850 by Thomas Wright of the Camden Society, and later in 1914 by the English ghost story master Montague (M.R.) James.

One of Walter Map's vampire anecdotes reads like an embellished tale of premature burial and concerns an unnamed knight from Brittany, whose wife was laid to rest after having died in an undisclosed manner. Soon after, she is said to have returned to life, having been brought back from beyond the grave by a band of dancing fairies. Rescued from their clutches, the woman went on to bear a large number of children who became known as the 'Sons of the dead' or 'Sons of the dead woman'. Between 1164 and 1179, Roger, son of Robert Fitzroy, 1st Earl of Gloucester, held the office of Bishop of Worcester. During this period, Map records an account of a revenant, dressed in a hair-shirt, seen haunting an orchard after dark. The figure was identified as being that of a local man who died an atheist and who appeared to several people on three separate nights, all of whom recognised the deceased person. Little if any actual blood drinking activity seems to have taken place and if anything paranormal was indeed involved, the incident is more likely to have been some form of apparition. However, word was sent to the Bishop of Worcester, who instructed that the unquiet soul should be laid to rest by erecting a large cross over its grave site. This was duly carried out but appears to have had the opposite effect: Donald Glut (*True Vampires of History*, 1971) describes the figure as leaping back in alarm at the sight of the cross and running away. 'Then the people, acting on wise advice, removed the cross, and the demon rushed into the grave covering himself with earth, and immediately after the cross was raised upon it again so that he was lain there without causing any disturbance.' Nothing, it seems, was heard of this particular vampire again.

The most gruesome of the accounts given in the *De Nugis Curialium* is that of a sinister shapeshifting vampire woman, masquerading as a children's matron in the household of an unnamed knight, who was responsible for the slaughter of three infant babies. Unmasked by a visiting traveller who brands the creature's forehead with the door key from a nearby church, the vampire is revealed to be the demonic double of a virtuous and clean-hearted woman, whose many good deeds and noble actions had aroused the wrath of Hell, whose devils then created a facsimile in her likeness so that her noble reputation would be blighted by its actions. After being exposed – the local woman was still living – the doppelganger makes its escape by climbing through a window and, howling into the night, was never seen again. As with the previous account, no blood drinking is recorded as taking place, the familiar limiting its murderous activity to cutting the throats of the sleeping infants on the mornings following their births.

Another of Map's records concerns a Welsh vampire whose activities were brought to the attention of the Bishop of Hereford, who was at that time Gilbert Foliot (*c.* 1110–87), a Cluniac monk and former Abbot of Gloucester who would later become the Bishop of London. English soldier William Laudun described a wave of sickness and death brought about by the nightly appearance of the apparition of a recently deceased man whose banshee-like calls were causing several of his former lodgers to fall ill and die. The Bishop prescribed a ritual of exorcism that contained a number of elements familiar today through the medium of modern films and literature, namely the exhumation of the vampire's corpse, the cleansing of both the grave and the body with holy water, and the severing of the head from the torso. Despite the ceremony being undertaken as directed, Map notes that the vampire continued to appear in the nights that followed: no explanation is given but it seems likely that some aspect of the ritual was not carried out completely to the letter. Events came to a head when, on three occasions after dark one night, Laudun himself heard his name being called – the signal that soon his life would be drawn away. Taking up his sword, the tormented soldier rushed out and pursued the creature back to its grave, where, with one blow, he struck its head from its body. The brave Laudun succeeded where the other slayers had failed, as the 'demonical wanderer' was heard to call out no more. 'We know that this thing is true,' Glut's English translation of the Latin concludes, 'but the cause of the haunting remains unexplained.'

A contemporary of Walter Map was William of Newburgh, born in Bridlington in the East Riding of Yorkshire around 1136. William, like his southerly counterpart, left a chaptered Latin text, in this instance known as the *Historia rerum Anglicarum*, or History of English Affairs. It is similar in manner to the Trifles of Courtiers, in that it contains a number of paranormal entries now ascribed as being early incidents of vampiric activity. Like Map's vampires, William's tales are notable for their absence of bloodletting or actual instances of the drinking of human blood, with the result that if non-supernatural causes can be discounted, spectres such as the Berwick Vampire are more likely to have been early accounts of crisis ghosts or possibly 'stone tape' apparitions (i.e. echoes or imprints of past events left ingrained into the psychic fabric of a building or atmosphere and subsequently replayed in the presence of a suitably endowed witness or group of people).

One particular haunting was related to William by the monks of Melrose Abbey, a Cistercian Order founded in 1136 in the Scottish borders thirty miles south-west of Edinburgh. Today the picturesque ruin is best known as the burial site of the heart of Robert the Bruce, which was interred there following its return from the crusades in Grenada in 1330. Many years before Robert's death, the abbey became the resting place of a private chaplain who augmented his religious duties in the household of a local noblewoman (herself a patron of the abbey) by hunting with horse and hounds, to such an extent that he became known locally as the 'Dog Priest'. Soon after his death, an apparition bearing his likeness was seen at night attempting to enter the abbey cloisters but was driven away by the power of the monks' prayers. Not long afterwards it began appearing to its former employer, entering her bedchamber at night and uttering such 'loud groans and horrible murmurs' that the woman became distressed and went to the monks of Melrose for help. Soon a deposition from the abbey, comprising two friars and two local villagers, began holding a vigil at the grave of the renegade priest in an attempt to curtail its nightly wanderings. As an already cold night began to grow more bitter, three of the party retired to a nearby house to get warm, leaving one of the monks to keep watch at the graveside. Seizing the opportunity, the vampire attacked but was driven off by the young friar who struck the creature a heavy blow with an axe. The undead man sought refuge in his own grave which, at daybreak, was opened by the monk and the rest of the party, all of whom were presented with a gruesome spectacle: the body of the deceased priest lay uncorrupted in the ground but clearly bore the great wound inflicted the previous night. With shades of the vampire fiction of Le Fanu and the English author E.F. Benson, whose writings we will encounter in more detail in a later chapter, the unquiet grave itself was found to be filled with blood. Wasting no time, the party removed the body and took it to an unfrequented spot outside the walls of the abbey, where it was burnt and the ashes scattered to the wind. 'I have related this story quite simply and in a straightforward manner,' William concluded in his 'History', 'just as it was told to me by the monks themselves.'

Another early British revenant that met its end by fire is one that can be loosely described as the Vampire of Alnwick Castle – a stronghold on the Northumberland coast, thirty miles north of Newcastle. Here, William of Newburgh reports the death and return from the grave of '[a] certain man of depraved and dishonest life' who enjoyed the protection of the lord of the manor but who rejected the Sacrament and expired before making a full confession of his sins. His death was, according to the account given in the *Historia rerum Anglicarum*, the result of a Chaucer-like episode: he died from injuries sustained after falling through a bedroom ceiling while spying on his unfaithful wife who was making love with the son of a neighbouring farmer in the chamber below.

The dead man's likeness was seen walking abroad at night accompanied by the howling of the village dogs, its rotting countenance bringing with it a pestilence that befell nearly every household. In time, Alnwick became a ghost town as the inhabitants either abandoned the area or themselves fell victim to the plague. On Palm Sunday a decision was made to eradicate the plague carrier and a deposition of surviving townsfolk, together with the local priest, made their way to the cemetery where the vampire's grave was duly opened. There the assembled party saw the body that lay within, 'gorged and swollen with a frightful corpulence', its face ruddy and bloated, the clothes it was buried in ripped and soiled where it had been forcing its way up through the ground. When struck a powerful blow with a spade, the corpse spewed forth a welter of fresh blood that left the horrified company in no doubt as to the nature of the danger they were facing. As with the incident at Melrose Abbey, the Alnwick vampire was removed to a spot outside the town and burnt to ashes on a large pyre. Soon the air became clean again and life in Alnwick began to return to normal.

William's writings also contain an account of a similar happening at Berwick, just over twenty-five miles further up the coast from Alnwick, where the plague-carrying apparition of a villainous man was also eradicated in a likewise fashion by being cut up and burnt in a furnace (the close proximity and similarity of the happenings makes it likely that the Berwick Vampire may in fact be the same story retold), while the most far reaching of William's accounts concerns a vampire outbreak in Buckinghamshire where a wife whose husband returned from the grave both by day and by night to plague her was afforded suitable relief by the intervention of Hugh, the Bishop of Lincoln.

Now at such a distance of time, is it possible to explain such strange and macabre happenings as those described in the writings of Walter Map and William of Newburgh? It seems likely that in reality, these early vampire stories were in fact no more than inventions of the Church, put about as a warning to those who were unwilling to confess their sins or who lead atheistic or amoral lives and that the punishment for such ungodly behaviour was to return at night, cursed into wandering the countryside as some kind of zombie-like plague carrier. As has been seen, several of the characters involved, such as the 'Dog Priest' of Melrose Abbey, the Alnwick vampire and the spectre from the orchard in *De Nugis Curialium*, were atheists who died without absolving themselves of their sins; both William and Walter Map describe receiving these accounts from the occupants of religious houses who would either be likely to originate and promote such tales as timely warnings to the masses, or continue to propagate stories from elsewhere that they genuinely believed to be true.

Then, as in later centuries, the ignorance and fear of disease and plague-like illnesses (as Anthony Masters has discussed in *The Natural History of the Vampire*) were a major factor in the creation of the vampire myth from the twelfth century through to the 1600s, involving as it did the mass and sudden deaths of large groups of people, instances of premature burial, and the damage caused by wild animals to unburied or partially interred bodies and human remains, all of which likely gave rise to the belief and fear of supernatural monsters, fears that were all too easily exploited by both the ignorant populace and those in positions of power.

As mentioned above, any true paranormal phenomena that may have taken place at these times is most likely to have been activity that today falls more easily into the remit of the serious psychical researcher, namely the sighting of apparitions or 'crisis' ghosts (visions of living or recently deceased persons that appear to relatives and close friends at or around the moment of death, a phenomenon for which convincing evidence has been collected since the establishment of the Society for Psychical Research (SPR) in the early 1880s, and which would clearly have taken place in earlier times as well as the nineteenth century, when full reports first began to be collated).

In his book *True Vampires of History*, Donald Glut notes the subsidence of vampirism as an English belief for a period of over 600 years from the time of Map and William of Newburgh to the beginning of the early 1800s. Glut was unable to explain the lack of vampire legends in the British Isles at this time and it is true that the great vampire epidemics that swept across mainland Europe, as well as from Greece to the Baltic Sea around the beginning of the eighteenth century, are conspicuous by their absence in Britain at this time, particularly as the great witchcraft purges of sixteenth- and seventeenth-century mainland Europe did make the transfer (the first notable trial for witchcraft together with the first hanging – that of Agnes Waterhouse – took place at Chelmsford in Essex in 1566) and in total around 1,000 people were executed for alleged witch-like activities over a period of around 150 years. Britain was without such Continental classics as the cases of Arnold Paole (or Paul), a former Serbian soldier and the so-called Vampire of Meduegna, one of the most often cited instances of eighteenth-century vampirism, which took place north of Belgrade in the early 1730s; or Peter Plogojowitz, a Serbian peasant who was recorded as killing nine people in the village of Kisiljevo in 1725. Paole's accidental death through a farming accident was the catalyst for a series of purported vampiric attacks on local villagers, as well as sheep and cattle, which only ended with the exhumation and destruction of his blood-gorged and uncorrupted corpse. The young soldier had himself allegedly been the victim of a vampire attack while serving in Turkey, and butchered meat from infected cattle attacked during his return from the grave was thought to have been responsible for a second wave of deaths later the same year, when seventeen bodies were disinterred and destroyed. Similarly, reports of Peter Plogojowitz roaming the countryside in the days following his death eventually led to his grave being opened and the body staked and burnt. An account in a prominent Viennese newspaper stated that fresh blood began to flow from the ears and mouth of the corpse the moment that the sharpened stake was driven through its heart. Vampire epidemics returned to Serbia in 1732 and 1825; the Greek island of Chios experienced an outbreak in 1708, as did Hungary in 1832, while the Polish city of Gdańsk reported vampirism as late as 1855.

Despite a distinct lack of undead hysteria, it is possible to identify some locations around the British Isles that can demonstrate forms of vampire-like association dating from around this particular period. One such legend concerns the twelfth-century parish church of St Andrew's in the Cumbrian village of Dent, formerly in the West Riding of Yorkshire, forty-five miles south-east of Carlisle, where a flagstone adjacent to the church porch is considered to be the final resting place of George Hodgson, known for many years as the Dent Vampire. Hodgson died in 1715 aged 94 and local gossip prescribed his long life as originating in an association with Black Magic and ultimately a pact with the Devil himself. Following his death, Hodgson was buried in the main churchyard, but at some later time his coffin was exhumed and moved to a spot close to the main church doorway, where an iron spike or stake was driven down through the flat memorial stone and seemingly through the body itself. The burial site is still visible today with a circular hole clearly visible in the upper part of the gravestone.

Archaeologists would today classify the treatment meted out to George Hodgson's grave as being a relatively modern example of a 'deviant burial', an Anglo-Saxon ritual rare in Britain, whereby the body of a social outcast or local person suspected of involvement in magical practices was interred in a manner distinct from those normally associated with burials of the period. Characterised by some form of unusual post-mortem activity, including beheading and the impalement of limbs and torsos, one such burial, dating from between 550 and 700 and with its obvious vampiristic connotations, came to light in 1959 in the old minster town of Southwell, Nottinghamshire, when a male skeleton with metal spikes driven through its heart, shoulders and ankles was unearthed during an archaeological survey for Roman remains. A similar 'deviant burial' was unearthed thirty years before in 1921 when the skeleton of a woman, bound with rope and with the thigh bones pierced with iron nails, was discovered in a garden in St Osyth in Cornwall. An account of the incident is given by folklore writer Eric Maple in his book *The Realm of Ghosts* (1964). More recently in County Roscommon in the north-west of Ireland, two eighth-century male skeletons with large stones forcibly inserted into their mouths – most likely to ward off the danger of a potential return from beyond the grave – were recovered from an extensive burial pit containing hundreds of bodies at Kilteasheen on the eastern shore of Lough Key.

In County Waterford on the south-east coast, a long-standing Irish vampire tradition exists surrounding Richard de Clare, 2nd Earl of Pembroke, known as 'Strongbow', and a female vampire creature, the Dearg-due or 'Crimson Bloodsucker', which lures passing travellers to their doom. The exhumation, in 1845, of the coffin of a former steward of Eastbury House in the village of Tarrant Gunville, four miles north-east of Blandford Forum in Dorset, has given rise to the legend of the Tarrant Valley Vampire. Here the body of William Doggett, who committed suicide on 23 June 1786 after defrauding his employer, Lord Melrose, was said to have been unnaturally preserved despite lying in St Mary's churchyard for nearly sixty years. It has been reported that Doggett's ghost – a sinister apparition with a blood-stained face – had haunted Eastbury for several years following his death and that a stake was driven through his heart before the mouldering casket was reburied as part of the rebuilding of the parish church by ecclesiastical architect, Thomas Henry Wyatt.

With a little stretch of the imagination what perhaps could best be described as being our most suitable equivalent of the case of Arnold Paole and the Vampire of Meduegna is what Dan Farson, in his 1977 book *The Beaver Book of Horror*, called the 'The British Vampire', and which is known more universally as the Vampire of Croglin Grange. This well-known story, centred around the small Cumbrian village of Croglin, twelve miles south-east of Carlisle in the very north of England, has, over the years, received a wide press and drawn the attention and comment of an impressive roster of writers and paranormal investigators including, as well as Dan Farson, Charles Harper (1907), Montague Summers (1929), Francis Clive-Ross (1962), D. Scott Rogo (1968), Marc Alexander (1970), Donald Glut (1971), the Revd Lionel Fanthorpe (1997), Richard Whittington-Egan (2005), and most recently Darren W. Ritson and Geoff Holder (both 2012). All these authorities have attempted in various ways, often involving personal visits to the area and much original research, to establish the truth of the vampire story for which the account given by Farson in his *Book of Horror* (and earlier in another popular title, *Vampires, Zombies and Monster Men* from 1975) is a typical rendition and runs as follows.

Three unnamed siblings – a sister and her two brothers – rent an old house known as Croglin Grange, which lies in a remote spot overlooking a churchyard. One night, the young woman is disturbed by the sight of a figure moving across the lawn in the moonlight, and soon a sinister brown skeletal apparition with glowing eyes appears at her bedroom window; petrified and paralysed with fear, she watches as the creature picks away at the lead holding the window pane in place with its long bony fingers. One of the panes falls out and the figure reaches in, opens the window catch and is soon advancing across the room towards her. Finally, as it drags her across the bed and sinks its teeth into her neck, the paralysis is broken and she utters a piercing scream which alerts her brothers to the danger and also seemingly drives the vampire away; the two men find their sister unconscious and bleeding from the throat while the beast of Croglin Grange makes its escape into the night.

The brothers take the young woman on holiday to a Swiss resort to recover from the experience but at her insistence they return to the Grange, where all appears to be normal. Several months later, however, again on a moonlit night, the sinister scratching sounds again at the window, heralding the appearance of the same cadaverous-looking horror; this time the girl is able to scream a warning and her two siblings burst into the room, again driving the apparition away. As it flees across the lawn, one of the brothers aims with a rifle and manages to fire a single shot into one of its legs. The following morning the men follow a trail of fresh blood into the adjacent churchyard that leads them to the mausoleum of a local family. Inside, all of the coffins have been vandalized save one, which contains the brown and mummified creature with a lead slug lodged in its leg – although Farson doesn't mention it in his two accounts, the usual ending to the tale is that the coffin and its contents are burnt to ashes, thus ending the rampage of the Vampire of Croglin Grange.

A barometer of belief and scepticism has swung across the Croglin case for over a hundred years since it was first brought to public attention in 1900 through the published memoirs of English author, Augustus Hare, a prolific travel writer, biographer and raconteur whose books include *Wanderings in Spain* (1873), *Cities of Southern Italy and Sicily* (1883), *Life and Letters of Maria Edgworth* (1894), together with six volumes of autobiography issued in two fascicles under the collective title, *The Story of My Life* (1896 and 1900). Hare's memoirs include references to over a dozen ghost stories, all of which have fallen into obscurity, save for 'The Beast of Croglin Grange' which has survived to take on an unnatural life of its own. Its origins date from 1874 and an episode that bears more than a passing resemblance to the notorious evening at the Villa Diodati over fifty years before, when Hare swapped eerie after-dinner stories with neighbours Captain Edward Fisher-Rowe and Henry Liddell, the 1st Earl of Ravensworth. Fisher-Rowe regaled the company with a family story concerning a gruesome incident at his North Country estate, the particulars of which Hare remembered many years later and set down in the fourth volume of his memoirs, producing the account that we have previously encountered through the pen of Dan Farson. Hare gave no names of the persons involved or dates of the alleged occurrences, but succinctly described Croglin Grange as a single-storey building with 'a terrace from which large grounds sweep away towards the Church in the hollow, and a fine distant view.'

Less than ten years later, Hare's home-grown vampire story had been challenged and for all intents and purposes summarily dismissed: Charles Harper, an early English writer on haunted buildings, examined the case and published (*Haunted Houses*, Cecil Palmer, London, 1907) a number of salient points that cast much doubt on the accuracy of Hare's narrative and the truth of Fisher-Rowe's family yarn: Croglin Grange appeared not to exist, only a building named Croglin Low Hall seemed to be relevant but its geography did not support several essential aspects of the story, being a two-storey building over a mile from the local churchyard where a vault fitting the description of the vampire's resting place was conspicuous by its absence. Another commentator to cast doubt on the story, albeit at a much later date, was D. Scott Rogo, a young American whose productive career in psychical research was to be cut tragically short when he was murdered in his Los Angeles home in 1980 at the age of 40. In an article published in the respected *Fortean Fate* magazine in 1968, Rogo drew attention to the disturbing similarity between the Croglin vampire's method of entry into the young woman's bedchamber and the opening chapters of James Rymer's monumental *Varney the Vampyre*, in which the eponymous bloodsucker of the title menaces Flora, the damsel in distress, by breaking in through her bedroom window and is subsequently driven away by her menfolk in an identical manner to Hare's original account. When the two accounts are read side by side it is difficult not to conclude that either Fisher-Rowe or Augustus Hare had a copy of Rymer's book in their library or at some point in time had at least read its opening pages.

Despite the critical denouement, the Beast of Croglin Grange was nothing if not tenacious in its unwillingness to die. Five years before Rogo had seemingly driven home the final stake, writer Francis Clive-Ross had achieved a partial rehabilitation which had appeared in the *Tomorrow* journal, a spiritual magazine for which the author was both founder and editor. Although he had not discovered the smoking gun evidence for the existence of the undead, Clive-Ross had managed to substantiate or at least support several aspects of Captain Fisher-Rowe's claims: Croglin Low Hall was known as Croglin Grange up until the beginning of the eighteenth century and had at one time been a single-storey house; a church, demolished during the English Civil War, had originally stood adjacent; the vampire story appeared to have been a long-standing tradition in the Fisher-Rowe family and one blocked-up window of the house was identified as being the very point where the 'beast' had made its entrance. Clive-Ross also established that accounts of vampirism were associated with Croglin High Hall, another house in the vicinity, where a human skeleton was discovered concealed behind a wall during alteration work in the 1950s. Soon paranormal writer and novelist Marc Alexander (*Haunted Churches & Abbeys of Britain*, 1978) was able to add more vampires into the mix by relating an account of a former Croglin rector, the Revd Dr Matthew Roberts, who claimed that there was a story of vampire attacks and the sighting of a bat-like creature associated with the grave of another local clergyman, the Revd George Sanderson, who officiated in the village in the late seventeenth century.

In much the same way that the human drama of such cases as Borley Rectory and the 'Amityville Horror' has come under the investigative spotlight in recent years, in 2005 crime historian Richard Whittington-Egan was able to reveal similar aspects of the Croglin case that had previously gone unnoticed. Whittington-Egan established that Captain Fisher-Rowe and his family were in fact tenants of Croglin Low Hall (rather than the owners, as Augustus Hare had been led to believe), having taken on a lease in 1809, and that the vampire story was most likely passed on to them as an attractive local legend, either by the actual owner, a man named Johnson, or by surviving members of the Towry family who may have still been present in the area and who had owned the house from the late 1680s until 1727. Most recently, writer and researcher Geoff Holder (*Paranormal Cumbria*, 2012) has suggested that the vampire story may have its origins in the religious tension engendered by the 1662 Act of Conformity, whereby Puritan ministers installed in country areas by the Commonwealth of England were dismissed by the restored monarchy under Charles II. The Revd George Sanderson, identified by Marc Alexander as a possible source of the Croglin Grange vampire, was a former Puritan clergyman who sided with the Church of England and replaced the current rector at Croglin in 1671. In so doing, Holder suggests he may have stirred up local ill feelings that have survived in later stories of vampires emerging from his grave at night to menace future occupants of Croglin Low Hall. Whether the Beast of Croglin Grange was the aftermath of a religious dispute, a distortion over time of an actual but non-supernatural event (an attack by a starving monkey from a local travelling circus has been suggested), or a genuine paranormal phenomenon will be a mystery that will never be solved for sure.

So far our selected British vampires appear to have their origins in either medieval religious propaganda or unsubstantiated local legends whose origins have become obscured by the passage of time. But is it possible that some facet of the vampire myth, both in this country and elsewhere, has its basis in genuine paranormal phenomena that has been both examined and substantiated through the discipline of organised psychical research? The mention of Borley Rectory above immediately brings to the fore the controversial psychic career of English ghost hunter extraordinaire Harry Price (1881–1948) whose investigation of the famous 'most haunted house in England' during the interwar years continues to draw a wide audience over sixty years after his death. To Price, as for most researchers of his generation, supernatural vampirism belonged to the realm of popular folklore, despite its long-standing origins, rather than to the world of modern paranormal investigation, and as such the subject receives only the most fleeting of mentions in one of his published books and then only in the form of a humorous aside. Nandor Fodor, one of Price's younger contemporaries, wrote in 1934 that supernatural vampirism 'has but vague and elusive points of contact with psychic science' and as such remained for the serious parapsychologist a 'strange traditionary belief'.

Despite the collective dismissal, Harry Price was one twentieth-century paranormal researcher who was to have personal experience of a psychic subject whose extraordinary phenomena seems to have obvious and perhaps far-reaching connections with the shadowy world of the undead. Eleonora (or Eleonore) Zügun, known variously as the 'Poltergeist Girl', the 'Poltergeist Medium' and the 'Devil Girl', was a young Romanian peasant woman who exhibited extraordinary paranormal abilities for a three-year period which ultimately ended as mysteriously as it had begun with the onset of menstruation at the age of 14.

Born in the small village of Talpa, eight miles south-west of Dorohoi in the north of Rumania on 24 May 1913, Eleonora's phenomena appears to have started in early 1925 following a visit to her aged grandmother; a somewhat formidable woman over 100 years old, with a local reputation for second sight and similar witch-like abilities, who lived within walking distance in a village to the north-east of Talpa. On the way to the old woman's house, the young girl found some money on the side of the road; this she spent on sweets in the village, all of which she ate herself. A female cousin complained about her apparent meanness, and the two girls got into a fight which was broken up by the old lady, who warned Eleonora that the money had been discarded on the roadside as a test by the Devil who was now inside her, swallowed down with the sweets.

The grandmother's chiding was seemingly the catalyst that ushered in a wealth of strange and at times frightening psychical phenomena, called by the late Colin Wilson as 'one of the most remarkable poltergeist cases of all time'. The following day, a poltergeist outbreak began in the girl's presence and continued in varying levels of intensity for many months: stones flew up and were dashed against the side of first her grandmother's house and then upon her return to Talpa, the Züguns' own home; windows were broken and objects began moving in her presence; furniture rocked and vibrated as though alive; raps and knocks were heard, while household items were seized as if by an unseen person and thrown at or near to people sitting or standing in the room. Convinced that a *Dracu*, a Romanian word for 'demon', was at work, her family first sent her to a monastery but in April 1925, as the strange and destructive phenomena continued unabated, Eleanora was committed to a lunatic asylum where she would probably have remained had it not been for the intervention of Fritz Grunewald, a German engineer and innovative psychical researcher from Charlottenburg who has been described as the paranormal 'genius of the twentieth century'. Grunewald, who had heard of the happenings after reading reports in a German newspaper, bribed the asylum guards and, in a scene straight out of a melodrama, she was released into his care.

In the few brief months that Eleonora was to spend in the German engineer's company, dozens of inexplicable happenings took place which were duly set down for posterity in the researcher's records: a cooking implement jumped off a hook on the kitchen wall and struck the girl on the arm; a salt cellar flew up from a table when no one was within reach; coins fell about the apartment as if appearing from out of thin air. Within weeks, however, Grunewald was dead from a heart attack at the age of 40 and the young 'devil girl' was back in the monastery at Gorovei, now abandoned totally by her disinterested and superstitious family.

In September 1925, two months after Fritz Grunewald's death, Eleonora was again taken into the care of a sympathetic admirer, another patron of psychical investigation, the Countess Zoë Wassilko-Serecki (1897–1978), a Viennese aristocrat with an interest in paranormal phenomena, who arranged for the young girl to move in with her in her Vienna apartment. Like Grunewald, the Countess witnessed many incidents of convincing poltergeist phenomena in Zügun's presence, accounts of which were later published in a book, *Der Spuk von Talpa* (*The Ghost of Talpa*). It was while the girl was in her care that the most remarkable and disturbing of all Eleonora's phenomena took place. Eerie stigmata-like effects – scratches, weals, lines and vampirish bite marks – began to appear on various parts of Eleonora's young body, including her face, arms and hands, as though she were being physically assaulted by an invisible assailant. The effects appeared in daylight and were both filmed and photographed; despite being kept under close observation by multiple witnesses, the Romanian girl was never caught making the marks, which appeared to be exceedingly painful and lasted for many hours and which caused the victim much upset and distress.

This 'full-scale poltergeist assault' (Alan Gauld, writing in 1979) began in late March 1926. At the end of the following month, Harry Price visited the Countess in Vienna (having been introduced by mutual friends) and experienced the strange happenings for himself. Convinced that some of the poltergeist phenomena was genuine, Price extended an invitation to the Countess and her young ward to visit him in London, where at the beginning of the year he had opened his own National Laboratory of Psychical Research (NLPR) – a rival organisation to the London SPR with which Price enjoyed a frosty relationship for most of his professional psychic career. Price's society occupied a suite of rooms on the top floor of number 16 Queensberry Place, South Kensington, and at the time was the most advanced psychical laboratory in Europe with a purposely equipped séance room, workshop, extensive reference library (much of which was made up of Price's own collection of occult books) and a photographic studio. Eleonora and the Countess arrived in England at the end of September, remaining as Price's guests until 14 October 1926. An account of the young Romanian girl's startling abilities formed the basis of the first official publication of the NLPR, 'A Report on the Telekinetic and Other Phenomena Witnessed Through Eleonore Zügun', which appeared in the society's *Proceedings* in January 1927. In his report, Price reproduced part of a timed protocol taken down by one of his NLPR members, Captain Neil Gow, who experienced one of the poltergeist 'attacks' for himself:

> 3.20. Eleonore cried out. Showed marks on back of left hand like teeth-marks which afterwards developed into deep weals. I got Eleonore to bite her right hand and noted the kind of marks caused by this bite but could trace no similarity between this and the first alleged stigmata.
>
> 3.25. Eleonore gave a soft cry and pointed to her right wrist. She undid the sleeve of her blouse and rolled it up. I saw some freshly-made red marks like scratches. There were several of these, about five inches long. After a few minutes they rose up into heavy white weals.
>
> 4.12. Eleonore was just raising a cup of tea to her lips, but suddenly gave a cry and put the cup down hastily; there was a mark on her right hand similar to those caused by a bite. Both rows of teeth were indicated.
>
> 4.15. Eleonore again raising cup to her lips when she gave a cry. There immediately appeared three long weals extending from the centre of her forehead right down the right cheek. Each was about ten inches long. Eleonore gave every sign of pain. I can state that for several minutes her hands had not been near her head or face.

All of this was 'witnessed' by a competent observer under excellent conditions of control in a modern laboratory in one of the major capital cities of twentieth-century Europe – is it possible that stories of vampires have their basis in such strange and real occurrences?

The English writer and philosopher Colin Wilson, the author of several books on occult and paranormal subjects, was one commentator who made a case for the reality of supernatural vampirism through the medium of poltergeist phenomena. In his essay 'Vampires: Do They Exist?', included as a chapter in the compilation *Unsolved Mysteries: Past and Present* in the early 1990s, Wilson argues that cases such as the famous Vampire of Meduegna and that of Peter Plogojowitz are not as easy to dismiss as would at first be thought. '[I]t seems clear that the vampire is not a physical body that clambers out of its grave – as in *Dracula* – but some sort of ghost or spectral "projection",' he notes. 'What the villagers allege is that the body has been taken *over* [original emphasis] by a demonic entity, which attacks the living and somehow drains their vitality. The corpse that is the home of the demonic entity then flourishes in the grave and even continues to grow new skin and nails.'

Through a retrospective examination of a 1960s poltergeist haunting in a house in East Drive, Pontefract, West Yorkshire, as part of research for his book *Poltergeist!*, first published in 1981, Wilson came to the reluctant conclusion that rather than being the unconscious external manifestations of adolescent children whose dramatic physical effects are created by spontaneous psychokinetic (i.e.. mind over matter) forces, poltergeists were in fact spirits or non-human 'entities' which were attracted to and were able to manipulate the psychic energy produced by pubescent teenagers. Another researcher whose similar conclusions were influential to Wilson's own is Guy Lyon Playfair, a Cambridge graduate and former English teacher and translator whose own experiences of poltergeist phenomena took place in Brazil in the early 1970s, as well as his personal investigation (together with fellow SPR member Maurice Grosse) of the famous Enfield Poltergeist in North London in 1977 – for details of both the Black Monk of Pontefract and the Enfield case, see my book *Extreme Hauntings* (2013). Playfair, as Wilson states in his book *Beyond the Occult* (1988), has likened a typical poltergeist haunting to something akin to a psychic 'football': 'When people get into conditions of tension, they exude a kind of energy – the kind of thing that happens to teenagers at puberty. Along come a couple of spirits, and they do what any group of schoolboys would do – they begin to kick it around, smashing windows and generally creating havoc. Then they get tired and leave it'; the haunting then ceases as rapidly and mysteriously as it began.

Wilson's acceptance of the reality of earthbound spirits (i.e.. those that inhabit a zone of existence close to our physical world or 'Earth plane' and who cannot or are unwilling to accept the fact that they have died and no longer possess physical bodies), has also allowed him to view the subjects of possession – both what is most often and sensationally described as 'diabolical possession' as well as that claimed by mental and physical mediums during spiritualist séances – in a similarly different light. In the latter, suitably gifted persons allow themselves to be used as a conduit or channel for a spirit person to speak or express themselves through the temporary animation of the medium's physical body or senses. The medium is in control of the proceedings, often assisted and protected by a benevolent spirit 'guide' or helper, and can terminate the 'possession' at any given point. While the former scenario, exploited with growing frequency by mainstream cinema over the past forty years, involves the often violent invasion of an unwilling person's body and psyche by an aggressive discarnate personality that may be the earthbound spirit of a deceased individual, or an intelligence that exists outside of this world and has not been present before in human form, i.e. a 'demon'. Wilson has explored the concept of spirit communication and the concept of 'minds without bodies' in books such as *Beyond the Occult* (1988) and *Afterlife* (1985) and has remained consistent in his views on the subject. 'If we can at once concede the possibility of "psychic invasion", as well as the possibility of "spirits", then the notion of vampires suddenly seems less absurd,' Wilson notes (in a version of his essay published in *World Famous True Ghost Stories* in 1994). 'The conclusion would seem to be that the vampire cannot be dismissed as a myth ... There is no fundamental difference between vampires and poltergeists – except that, fortunately, vampire phenomena seem to be far more infrequent.'

For the young Romanian girl, Eleonora Zügun, her invading *Dracu* eventually withdrew when she began her first period at the age of 14 and never troubled her again; Eleonora apparently took up a career as a hairdresser but little if anything is known of her later life.

One controversial poltergeist case from England in the 1930s which contained a mixture of genuine phenomena and deception, and also had a direct reference to vampirism, occurred in Thornton Heath, South London and was investigated by Nandor Fodor, a Hungarian-born researcher and psychoanalyst who wrote about the phenomenon in two books, *The Story of the Poltergeist Down the Centuries* (1953) and *On the Trail of the Poltergeist* (1958). Unlike Harry Price, Fodor's name remains obscure to many in the modern paranormal community although it has been stated that if he had a mind for publicity in the same way as Price exploited his adventures, he could have made some of his investigations as famous as that of Borley Rectory.

A former journalist, Fodor effected a career change in the mid-1920s after meeting Sandor Ferenczi (1873–1933), a follower of Sigmund Freud, and set up his own psychiatric practice in New York; a similar meeting with British-born psychical researcher Hereward Carrington (1880–1958) created a private interest in ghost hunting and Fodor became research officer for the International Institute for Psychical Research, another rival organisation to the SPR and Harry Price's National Laboratory, which was established by the prominent spiritualist writer and thinker, Arthur Findlay.

While in London in the early months of 1938, Fodor was alerted by press reports of strange happenings that were taking place in the house of a married couple and their 17-year-old son. Mrs Fielding, a housewife in her mid-thirties, appeared to be the focus of startling poltergeist phenomena that began on 19 February 1938 with the breaking of drinking glasses and the movement of bedclothes, and which lasted for several weeks (although the exact duration of the case has never been fully established). In his book *On the Trail of the Poltergeist*, Fodor describes a bewildering array of phenomena including the violent movement and projection of household items – crockery, fire coal, vases and furniture – together with the dematerialisation and appearance of objects (termed 'apports' by spiritualists and ghost hunters), strange smells, and the appearance of apparitions, notably a 'double' of Mrs Fielding which was seen entering and leaving the house by her husband when the real Mrs Fielding was several miles away at Fodor's office at the International Institute. What interests us here is that at one point, Mrs Fielding claimed that she had been visited in the night by a vampire who had bitten her in the neck and drawn some of her blood. When Fodor examined her, he found two puncture marks on her throat and she appeared pale and listless, as though her very life blood was being drained away. However, Fodor soon found that Mrs Fielding was faking paranormal effects by concealing items on her body and he witnessed her at one point throwing stones which she later claimed had been projected by a ghost. Although his investigation never reached a satisfactory conclusion, Fodor felt that the housewife was a neurotic who carried out the 'haunting' while in a dissociated state. Although the Thornton Heath vampire may have been an imposter, the case remains an interesting one and it seems likely that some of the reported phenomena were indeed genuine.

The views of informed researchers, such as Colin Wilson, that have been explored above show that a proportion of modern psychical investigators would not necessarily dismiss the possibility of supernatural vampirism out of hand when carrying out a paranormal investigation where vampire-like symptoms or some such phenomena were seemingly being demonstrated. One of the first post-war parapsychologists to take an active interest in vampirism was the late Stephen Kaplan who founded the Vampire Research Centre in New York State in 1974. Kaplan, like Colin Wilson, initially treated the subject as a legitimate branch of paranormal research and set out to establish whether the undead (i.e. spectral entity-like vampire creatures) still existed in the contemporary world. Kaplan's studies brought him into contact with many people who either exhibited a vampire-like lifestyle through their mode of dress or social life, or in some cases (a very small proportion) actually felt the need to consume blood on a daily basis in order to remain youthful or to stay alive. These latter people were what Kaplan eventually felt were 'true vampires' and by the early 1990s numbered in his estimate nearly a thousand people worldwide. Kaplan published aspects of his research in a book *Vampires Are* in 1984 and by the time of his death, at the age of 54 in 1995, had abandoned the concept of vampires as blood-drinking ghosts. Other contemporary investigators, as we will shortly discover, are, however, not so dismissive.

One English researcher with both a long interest in vampirism, as well as the practical experience of investigating a case exhibiting vampire-like phenomena, is Peter Underwood, whose sixty-year career in paranormal enquiry has made him one of the most experienced and respected of British post-war investigators. President of the long-established Ghost Club (whose history can be traced back to the early 1860s) for over thirty years, Underwood, born in Letchworth Garden City in 1923, is the author of over fifty books on paranormal subjects including haunted houses, exorcism, dowsing and reincarnation, as well as several compendium guides to haunted British locations, including the pioneering *A Gazetteer of British Ghosts* from 1971 and most recently *Where the Ghosts Walk* published in 2013. A former invited Honorary Member of the Count Dracula Society, during the course of his career in psychical matters, Underwood has encountered and written about several people who claimed to have had experience of vampirism, both supernatural vampires as well as human 'vampiroids' with a taste for human blood. They include the Revd Christopher Neil-Smith (1920–95), a former North London priest and author of *Exorcist and the Possessed* (1974) who carried out several thousand exorcisms during the course of his Anglican ministry, many of which had allegedly vampiric connections; the explorer Colonel John Blashford-Snell, who described being attacked by a vampire bat during an expedition to Darien Province, Panama, in 1976, during which he lost half a pint of blood and received thirty-two anti-rabies injections in his stomach; Christina Foyle (1911–99), the London-born bookseller who claimed to have been bitten by an unseen 'entity' while spending a night in a haunted room at twelfth-century Beeleigh Abbey on the outskirts of Maldon in Essex; Robert Fordyce Aickman (1914–81), the renowned English ghost story writer who felt he had met a man in Venice who he believed was a living vampire; and the American occultist William Seabrook (1884–1945), who, during a Ghost Club meeting, recounted his experience of meeting a young American woman on a beach who was unable to stop herself from sucking at the fresh blood running from a graze on the writer's naked shoulder: the unnamed woman, who believed she had been bitten by a vampire in her sleep and had become one herself, died the following year of pernicious anaemia according to Seabrook's account.

Perhaps the most interesting of Underwood's correspondents was Dr Devandra P. Varma, a Hindu mystic, editor and for many years Professor of English at Dalhousie University, Halifax, Nova Scotia. Varma, an authority on Gothic literature, rescued over 200 nineteenth-century novels from obscurity and in 1987 lectured to the Ghost Club on his experiences of 'Vigils in Haunted Castles and Fallen Abbeys'. His firm belief in 'the real and actual existence of vampires' was inseparable from the world of Gothic romance to which he dedicated much of his life. 'The vampire is not a ghostly figure appearing like a demon from hell with fangs bared and eyes bloodied,' he confided to Underwood in a letter in 1974, adding:

> He is tall and handsome, his hair dark and well-groomed; despite the waxen pallor of his face and hands, he has flashing dark eyes and a vivid redness in his lips that are curled in a smile. As the undead he casts no shadow and has no reflection [and] he rises from the moist and damp earth in a glowing mist or black fog from the vaults that rest under cobwebs in the faint light of the dim radiance of a rising moon [...] I believe in vampires and I have proofs.

Varma died in New York in 1994, aged 71.

In his book *Exorcism!* (1990), Peter Underwood describes an early British case of haunting which contains a Wilsonesque blend of poltergeist phenomena and vampire-like associations that for the purposes of the present study I am calling the incident of the Yorkshire Vampire. In 1948 (by which time Underwood had already visited the ruins of Borley Rectory and corresponded with Harry Price), inexplicable incidents began to take place in the home of a widowed mother, which in the typical and mysterious ways of the poltergeist seemed to be centred around her 10-year-old son: unusual noises were heard and the child complained of seeing dark shapes in his bedroom at night, while a number of religious items – a Bible, a crucifix and a set of Biblical pictures – began to seemingly move by themselves as though an invisible force or person was somehow upset by their presence. In particular the crucifix would drop or jump to the floor of its own volition and be discovered under the bedstead out of sight, while the boy's Bible seemed to somehow become 'magnetised' and stick to his open hand; when it was placed out of sight this strange effect vanished and the Bible became an ordinary book once more. During these happenings a tapping noise was detected coming from the closed bedroom window and on one occasion the boy reported seeing what appeared to be a pair of red eyes looking in at him, although he at first ascribed the happening as a dream. One night, the boy awoke to find the crucifix, which had been hung on the bed rail above his head, spinning on its chain and when touched, like many poltergeist projected objects, it was warm to the touch. That same night, a 'black smoke' seemed to come into the room through an open fanlight and the next morning the boy appeared pale and listless; the crucifix was found to have been defaced with a diagonal mark which appeared to have been carried out with some form of heavy implement.

After this incident, the boy's mother moved her son to another room where he slept for a week undisturbed. When he was moved back into his bedroom, however, the disturbances began again, after which a local priest and then the family doctor both became involved. On the occasion of his first visit to the house, Peter Underwood (who was asked to meet the boy and his mother at the suggestion of the doctor) discovered that the incidents had begun shortly after the death of the boy's father, who had in fact taken his own life. Having interviewed both members of the family, Underwood was struck from the outset as to the clear suggestiveness as to a case of modern-day vampirism. The widowed woman arranged for the priest to carry out a blessing throughout the entire house, after which nothing out of the ordinary took place. Despite the calm, the case of the Yorkshire Vampire was to in fact reach a dramatic conclusion. '[F]or a few weeks all was quiet,' Underwood recalled many years after the event, 'then I had a frantic call from the mother to come and see what had happened.' On his return to the house, he found the boy seemingly sedated in an upstairs room, his whole demeanour weak and ill while the bedroom in which the incidents took place was a scene of total chaos:

> The window was smashed and glass littered the floor: it had been smashed from the outside. One holy picture was facing the wall, its wire twisted so tightly, where the picture had been turned round and round again and again, that eventually it had to be cut from the wall ... Two other holy pictures lay face down on the floor, their cords and hooks intact. The heavy crucifix lay on its face by the far wall, buckled and bent until it was hardly recognizable, and above it there was a deep indentation where it had struck the wall – it must have been thrown with considerable force. The Bible was underneath the bed, drenched with some abominable matter so that every page had stuck together. And the smell in the room was absolutely foul.

Speaking with the boy's mother, Underwood learnt that the family doctor had prescribed a change of environment and she had made arrangements for them to spend some time with her sister in South Africa. Peter returned one more time, after which the family left the country. 'As far as I know, they never returned to Britain and had no more trouble with vampires. At least they promised to let me know if they did, and I never heard any more from them.' Did a vampire really stalk this unassuming post-war English family, or was it a case of a young boy directing his grief and anger at the sudden loss of his father on the icons and symbols of a faith that suddenly seemed empty and hollow in the wake of such personal tragedy? At one point in the investigation, the vampiresque connotations had made Underwood consult with the Revd Montague Summers, at that time the country's foremost expert on matters connected with the world of the supernatural undead, then living in retirement at his home in South-West London. 'He suggested a complicated idea for catching the vampire,' Underwood recalled, 'with the boy as bait, and then dealing with it in the usual fashion of vampires, but the boy's mother was horrified at the idea and instead obtained holy water and had the room blessed by a priest.' As such, the case of the Yorkshire Vampire still remains unexplained to this day.

The discovery and casting out of vampires and vampire-like 'entities' since the end of the great European epidemics of bloodletting over 250 years ago has traditionally become the province of the religious exorcist and in recent times the most high-profile figure in this aspect in Britain has been Nottinghamshire-born Sean Manchester, an author, musician, lecturer and broadcaster, who over the past three decades has established a reputation as 'the most famous vampire hunter of the twentieth century'. Now most often associated with the case of the Highgate Vampire, Manchester's immersion in the Gothic world and all its associations with the realms of the supernatural undead stems from his claim to be a direct descendant of Lord Byron, and in his writings he has described childhood memories of visiting his grandmother's home in the tree-lined and legend-haunted grounds of Newstead Abbey.

Like Montague Summers, for whose studies and writings he has shown a clear affinity, Manchester, a former portrait photographer, took holy orders and in 1993 was ordained as the Bishop of Glastonbury for the British Old Catholic Church, a branch of Catholicism that has maintained apostolic succession and valid sacraments independent of the Holy See of Rome. The founder of the privately run Vampire Research Society, a sub-group within the equally obscure British Occult Society, whose Presidency he claimed for over twenty years until its dissolution in 1988, Bishop Manchester's assertions to have encountered and destroyed undead vampire creatures during his investigations and ceremonies has brought him both notoriety and criticism in equal measure. Manchester has, however, remained true to his beliefs and claims to extol and practice the ritual of exorcism as a means for unmasking and destroying supernatural evil, the ministry of which he has described to the present author as being the essence of his life's work. 'I absolutely believe in the existence of vampires, there's no question or doubt in my mind,' he noted during an interview in 2004. 'It's part of my theology because if I believe in angels I must believe in fallen angels and these are called demons, and if I believe in the supernatural – and I do – and if I believe in what the Bible teaches – and I do – then to believe in vampires is just a small part of that.'

In his book *The Vampire Hunter's Handbook* published in 1997, Manchester gives an account of his alleged experiences during an investigation held in August 1990 at an isolated spot in Kirklees Park, West Yorkshire, said to be the last resting place of the famous English folk hero, Robin Hood. A Sloane manuscript held in the British Museum dates the site's associations with the notorious outlaw back to the beginning of the fifteenth century and describes Robin's death at the hands of the prioress of Kirklees, most likely Elizabeth de Staynton who, under the pretence of opening a vein to alleviate some unknown malady, bled the unsuspecting Robert of Locksley to death. The body was subsequently buried in unconsecrated ground under a boulder near to the priory, alongside the road from Clifton to the present-day Dumb Steeple monument on Cooper Bridge. Today, the gravesite (on private land owned for many years by the Armytage family) is marked with an inscribed stone, naming the occupant as 'Robert Earl of Huntingtun' and dated 24 December 1247 (8 November in the modern calendar). Surrounded by an iron railing and hemmed in by a thicket of trees, what has the potential to be elevated to the status of a national monument celebrating a world famous folk legend has, as Len Markham has noted in his *Ten Yorkshire Mysteries* from 1995, become 'abandoned to the twilight realm of mysticism and the occult'.

Not surprisingly, ghost stories have grown up around the area, some dating back to the early 1900s. Barbara Green, founder of the Yorkshire Robin Hood Society, interviewed one witness in the late 1980s who claimed to have heard a voice, said to be that of Robin calling out to Maid Marion, coming from the woods surrounding the grave when she visited the area as a child over sixty years before. In October 1963, a local youth, 15-year-old Roger Williams, together with a companion, reported seeing the apparition of a woman dressed in white with flowing black hair and glaring eyes which appeared out of the trees near to the grave site. The figure, which seemed to radiate an aura of intense anger, was visible for a short period before gliding silently out of sight behind nearby foliage. Williams also claimed to have seen the ghost again on a later visit in the autumn of 1972, when showing a musician friend the site of the mysterious grave:

> As I looked up I saw the exact same thing as I had seen that day in 1963. Except this time she stopped not six feet from us. I'll never forget the experience. She wore a long off-white dress kind of squarish around the neck with long sleeves. The dress had some sort of pattern to it. But again it was her eyes I remember most: dark, mad, set in her pale face ... Both times that I saw this apparition things started to happen in my house. Noises, bangings and a feeling like I was being watched.

The vampiric connotations of Robin Hood's death were not lost on Sean Manchester and his Vampire Research Society, and the possibility that the apparition of what appeared to be the long-dead prioress of Kirklees may have been a modern-day vampire, appeared to gather some momentum in the winter of 1987 when, according to Manchester's account, 'finger-width holes' akin to the apertures reported to have been present over the graves of Eastern European vampires in order to allow the undead spectres to escape the confines of the tomb, were observed in the earth in the immediate vicinity of Robin's Hood's grave. Manchester also reports incidents of exorcism being carried out in houses adjacent to the Kirklees Hall Estate at the same time, to remove the haunting presence of seemingly malignant forces. But it was not until the spring of 1990 that the soon-to-be Bishop Manchester described making a clandestine visit to the grave site to carry out a personal investigation. On the night of 22 April 1990, accompanied by two unnamed researchers and an 'armoury of vampire repellents' including holy water, garlic, wooden stakes, crucifixes and communion wafer, Manchester held a vigil among the trees close to the tomb. During the course of the night, all three visitors heard a screaming or wailing noise which seemed to fill the air before fading away, and one of the vampire hunter's companions, while separated from the main group, claimed to have encountered the apparition of a woman clad in dark garments 'who at first appeared serene – then rapidly manifested into a wraith with red eyes, staring and horrible'. A temporary exorcism was carried out by filling the holes in the ground near the tomb with holy water and planting garlic at the site, as well as at the grave of Elizabeth de Staynton, known as the 'Nun's Grave', located in the grounds of the former Kirklees Priory.

Over the next few years sightings of ghostly figures and reports of strange forces and experiences continued to take place in the immediate area, culminating in a visit to the site by the London-based British Psychic and Occult Society (*see* Chapter 10) together with a film crew, who carried out an hour-long ritual, described according to differing sources as either an exorcism or a pagan evocation ceremony. (Whether this latter ritual has succeeded in laying the unquiet ghost of England's famous outlaw or the vampiric spectre of the 'wicked prioress', remains to be seen.)

Blackburn, thirty miles west of Kirklees across the county border into Lancashire, is another northern town with a surprising connection to vampiric myth; in this case the strange and unlucky story of weaver Sarah Ellen Roberts, who in recent times has become known as the Blackburn Vampire, despite being buried over 6,000 miles away in the Peruvian coastal city of Pisco. In June 1993, rumours sweeping across the city reached fever pitch after first a local newspaper, then the national press and Peruvian television reported that an eighty-year-old curse could soon be fulfilled and that the unquiet spirit of Sarah Roberts, an English witch who had been buried alive in a lead-lined coffin for murder and other hideous activities including drinking human blood and devil worship, had sworn she would return from beyond the grave eight decades to the day after her trial and execution.

Refused a Christian burial in her native country, Sarah's husband had allegedly brought his wife's body to Peru where a grave had been bought for the sum of £5, and as the city folk counted down the hours to midnight on 9 June, local shops sold out of improvised vampire hunting kits containing crosses, stakes and garlic, police were forced to hold back crowds of several hundred people keeping vigils at the graveside, while many pregnant women were reported as having left the city in fear that the vampire woman's spirit might live again in one of their unborn children. Despite a crack having appeared across the gravestone several months before, almost as though the undead Sarah – said to be one of the three true 'Brides of Dracula' – was preparing to emerge into the land of the living, the midnight solstice passed without incident and gradually the vampire fever which had gripped Pisco began to die down. The tomb itself, garnered with additional mystique due to its survival undamaged following a devastating earthquake across the region on 15 August 2007 which destroyed 80 per cent of the city, remains a popular tourist site to this day.

The story of how Sarah Roberts became the Blackburn Vampire remains something of a mystery, although the reality of her life in England is known through surviving census records and birth certificates. She was born in Burnley in 1872, the third of four children to William Gargett, a coachman, and his wife, Catherine. At the age of 20, Sarah married John Pryce Roberts, a weaver, in St John's Church, Blackburn, and the couple set up home in Isherwood Street, where they had two children. In 1901, John Robert's younger brother Thomas, a manager at a local weaving mill, emigrated to Lima in Peru where he established a successful cotton mill business. Thomas Roberts and his wife returned to their native Blackburn in July 1907 for a holiday, and they were interviewed by a local newspaper. Much later, in the early winter of 1911, John Roberts went out to South America to visit his brother; late the following year, or early in 1913, he made a return visit, this time taking his wife with him. However, tragedy struck on 9 June 1913, as Sarah Roberts died (possibly in childbirth) and was buried in a municipal cemetery in the fishing port of Pisco, 125 miles south of the capital Lima. Her bereaved husband returned to England and later became a grocer, eventually surviving his wife by a further twelve years. It seems likely that, as Sarah's surviving relatives in England surmised when news of the vampire hysteria broke in 1993, that the strange circumstances of a foreigner arriving in the city from a far off land with a coffin survived in the region as local gossip and fireside tales that, catalysed by a television documentary about vampires in the country earlier in the year, developed into the strange phenomenon that has left an unassuming weaver's wife from the north of England with a perpetual association with the legions of the undead.

For our final case we leave South America and return to England and in particular the potteries of Stoke-on-Trent in Staffordshire for perhaps the most chilling of the entire home-grown vampire stories that have been examined in the present chapter. On 24 November 1972, a young police constable, 22-year-old John Pye, was called to number 3 The Villas, a gloomy boarding house on the south-west side of the town where the landlady and several of her tenants had become concerned about the wellbeing of one of the lodgers, middle-aged Polish pottery worker Demetrious Mykicura (or Myiciura), who had not been seen for several days. Forcing open the door of his tiny first-floor room, PC Pye switched on his torch and found himself stepping into what appeared to be a scene out of a horror film. Mykicura, aged 56, who had lived in England for the previous twenty-five years since the end of the Second World War, was lying dead under the blankets on the small single bed; there appeared to be no obvious cause of death and initially it seemed as though the potter had simply died in his sleep. The Pole had apparently been so frightened of electricity that he had removed the light bulb from the ceiling rose, so PC Pye was forced to carry out his initial examination by torchlight. His landlady, Mrs Rodziewicz, told the policeman that Mykicura had also been terrified of vampires and as PC Pye looked around it became clear that the dead man had turned his cramped bedroom into a veritable fortress against them: crosses and crucifixes had been hung on the walls; salt was scattered around the room and over the bedclothes while two small bags of salt were found in the bed itself, one between Mykicura's legs, the other on the pillow next to his head. Opening the window, PC Pye saw an inverted washing bowl on a flat roof close to the window sill, under which was a bizarre cake of human excrement mixed with garlic, as though the frightened man had been intent on warding off some form of invasion from outside.

An inquest was opened into Mykicura's death and a subsequent post-mortem revealed that death had been due to asphyxiation: what at first appeared to be part of a pickled onion was found lodged in his throat, but John Pye, who had carried out research into vampirism at the local library, told the coroner that salt and garlic were traditional Eastern European repellents against vampire attacks. When the pickled onion was re-examined by the pathologist it was found to be a clove of garlic. Mykicura, who had been born in 1904, had been displaced by the German occupation of Poland and forced to flee the country where his wife and the rest of his family were killed. The verdict of the coroner was that the pottery worker had been genuinely afraid of an attack by vampires and had not been trying to kill himself. 'As a final desperate measure to ward off the vampires, this wretched man had slept with a clove of garlic in his mouth, and the garlic had choked him to death,' Daniel Farson, one of the first commentators on the case wrote in his 1975 book, *Vampires, Zombies and Monster Men*. 'So in a roundabout way, the vampires did get him in the end.' In 2012, the events of Demetrious Mykicura's death were the basis for a feature length Gothic Victorian-era vampire film, *Blood and Bone China*, by film and music video director, Chris Stone. What took place to precipitate the lonely man's solitary fight against the perceived forced of the undead remains a mystery to this day.

3

Bram Stoker: A Benchmark in Blood

(1847-1912)

At some point in the closing decade of the nineteenth century, the exact time and date of which is now lost to human knowledge, a middle-aged ex-civil servant and part-time writer from Clontarf on the north Dublin coast forever changed not only the course of supernatural fiction but at the same time added one of the most recognisable and sinister titles into the mainstream English language. Taking up his pen, Abraham (Bram) Stoker crossed out the name 'Count Wampyr' from one of the numerous pages of manuscript notes he was compiling for a projected – and as yet untitled – novel and wrote down two simple words: 'Count Dracula'. The British vampire would never be the same again and we are still feeling the effects of that simple but momentous decision over 100 years later.

Much has been written in that intervening century about this enigmatic Irishman, his ensuing novel, first published in 1897, the year of Queen Victoria's Diamond Jubilee, and the circumstances which enabled him to create the most famous literary vampire of all time. There have been, to date, four full-length biographies of Stoker himself, numerous papers and periodicals, together with an ever-growing library of articles and essays on this eponymous character and its place within the Victorian Gothic world of its time. Since his death, a raft of writers both famous and obscure, from John Balderston to Stephen King, have adapted, expanded and developed the story of the undead vampire king into a seemingly endless cavalcade of plays, films and contemporary fiction. As a cultural phenomenon, Stoker's character has been used to sell an eclectic plethora of merchandise and consumer products from batteries and board games to potato crisps and ice cream. A Count Dracula Fan Club has been in existence in America since the mid-1960s and its British equivalent, The Dracula Society, established in London in 1973 by actors Bernard Davies and Bruce Wightman, continues to have an active membership four decades on.

The Society organised the first specialist Dracula tour of Romania in the autumn of 1974 and today similar package holidays taking in such locations as Bran Castle in Muntenia and the thirteenth-century Poenari Fortress close to the Wallacian city of Curtea de Argeş, both now woven into the enduring Dracula myth, are a popular mainstay of the Romanian tourist industry. Clearly Bram Stoker's *Dracula* lives up to its formidable reputation as 'the greatest and most influential vampire novel ever written' which, as the writer's great-nephew Daniel Farson noted in his 1975 biography *The Man Who Wrote Dracula*, 'must not be dismissed as a mere shocker'. 'Re-examination,' Farson went on to state, 'proves that it is a classic, more rewarding than any imitation.' A classic, however, that Christopher Frayling, one of the most perceptive of modern Stoker scholars, has aptly described as the 'great enigma' of the writer's life; although he, like so many ordinary readers who have become caught up in the dark, wet and bloody world of Stoker's imagination, unreservedly assigns the book as a masterpiece of supernatural horror fiction.

Bram Stoker, seemingly forever swamped by the shadow of the monster he had unwittingly released, was born in Dublin on 8 November 1847. His father, Abraham Stoker, was for most of his working life a lowly ranked junior clerk in the Irish civil service at Dublin Castle, only rising to the position of Senior Clerk after forty years' employment; Stoker's mother, Charlotte Thornley, was the daughter of Lieutenant Thomas Thornley of the 43rd Regiment of the British Army and originally from Ballyshannon and later Sligo in the north-west. The couple married in 1844 and Bram was the third of nine children, a sickly child who appears to have spent most of the first decade of his life bedridden and was apparently unable to stand upright unaided until the age of 7. Thankfully, Stoker overcame his childhood malady; the recovery was complete and absolute and he grew out of 'the wasted years' into what Dan Farson has coined 'a red-haired giant', a tall strapping youth who would subsequently win several university prizes for running, walking and gymnastics, as well as caps for rugby. Stoker entered Trinity College Dublin at the beginning of November 1864. Despite his sporting excellence he was an average student (Stoker's own claims to have graduated with honours in mathematics are unfounded), eventually leaving with a Bachelor of Arts degree in 1870. Five years later, in 1875, he bought an MA from the university, as was the custom for graduates at that time. During his time at Trinity, Stoker became intensely active on the literary and debating scene and held the premier position in the College Historical Society (as auditor) and also the Presidency of the Philosophical Society. Dan Farson notes that the future writer was proud of his association with the university and as a popular alumnus retained contact with Trinity for many years afterwards.

While at Trinity, Stoker had been laying down the foundations for a career in the Irish civil service and upon graduation went to work, like his father, as a clerk at Dublin Castle. In November 1871, he became an unpaid theatre critic for the *Dublin Evening Mail* and the following year had his first piece of literary fiction, a fantasy story entitled 'The Crystal Cup', published in the *London Society* magazine. After having further stories rejected by London publishers, Stoker turned to the Dublin-based *Shamrock*, a weekly journal that during the spring and early summer of 1875 serialised three lengthy stories in succession: 'The Primrose Path', an account of an Irish carpenter whose dream of working in a London theatre eventually leads to murder and the ruin of his family; a shipwreck story, 'Buried Treasures'; and 'The Chain of Destiny', an early horror tale centred around an ancient family feud in the haunted house of Scarp, where phantom figures materialise eerily from out of the oil paintings. The following year (1876) was to be an important one: Abraham Stoker, who had retired from Dublin Castle ten years before on a full pension, died in Naples at the age of 77 while on a tour of Europe; Stoker travelled to Italy to administer his father's affairs and then returned to Ireland where, in late November of the same year, a landmark event took place in a Dublin hotel.

Born John Henry Brodribb in Somerset in 1838, as Henry Irving he became one of the most lauded actors of his day, noted for his vigorous performances of Shakespeare and the first stage actor to be awarded a knighthood. Stoker had first seen Irving perform in Dublin in 1867 when he played Captain Absolute in a production of Sheridan's *The Rivals* and the experience had been a profound one – so much so that when Irving returned to the Theatre Royal three years later as Digby Grant in James Albery's comedy *Two Roses* it stimulated Stoker's decision to work for the *Mail* for nothing, writing reviews of their productions.

In December 1876, Irving returned to Dublin and gave a performance of *Hamlet* for the students and masters at Trinity College. Stoker's subsequent review of the event – 'Mr Irving's performance was magnificent' – in the *Dublin Evening Mail* pleased the actor to the point that he asked John Harris, the manager of the Theatre Royal, to invite the critic to dinner at his hotel. A few days later the two men met again over supper, during which Irving gave a dramatic reading of Thomas Hood's 1831 poem 'The Dream of Eugene Aram' and presented Stoker with a signed and inscribed photograph. It was a pivotal moment for the 29-year-old Irishman and marked the beginning of what he later described as 'a friendship as profound, as close, as lasting as can be between two men'.

Irving returned to Dublin twice the following year, during which time the pair met socially on several occasions. In June 1878, Stoker visited Irving in London and assisted with the preparation of a production of *The Flying Dutchman* that Irving had commissioned from playwright Percy Fitzgerald (with himself in the title role) following the success of Wagner's opera which had been performed in the capital with much success two years before. The play was staged at The Lyceum, off of the Strand, and occurred at the time that Irving was negotiating to take over the running of the theatre as artistic director, an arrangement that would last for the next twenty years. Stoker's biographer Paul Murray, in his *From the Shadow of Dracula* (2004), notes that the Irishman 'was no passive spectator' to the proceedings: his assistance with editing the text of the play and his appreciation of Irving's larger-than-life performance as the undead sea captain were to plant strange seeds that would begin to bear even stranger fruit just over a decade later. 'Here, surely,' Murray reasons, 'lay part of the genesis of *Dracula*, a terrifying tale of an undead man suspended between life and death.'

During several tumultuous days in early December 1878, Bram Stoker's life changed forever. On 5 December he married Florence Balcombe, a 20-year-old society beauty who for the previous two years had been walking out with Oscar Wilde. Less than a week later, Stoker met Henry Irving in Birmingham. The previous month he had been summoned to Glasgow where the actor had asked him to leave Dublin Castle and take on the role of his personal assistant and acting manager of The Lyceum; Stoker's resignation took official effect on 14 December. His legacy to his former employers was the manuscript of a lengthy treatise, *Duties of Clerks of Petty Sessions in Ireland*, which was published in Dublin the following year and went on to become a standard textbook. Just over twenty years later, the legacy of his new life would also emerge, as *Dracula*.

Stoker's association with Henry Irving lasted for over a quarter of a century right up until the actor's death at the age of 67 on 13 October 1905. As well as taking on the day-to-day running and financial management of The Lyceum, he planned and administered the actor's tour schedules, booked hotel rooms, organised the publicity, advised on the suitability of the many productions, and also accompanied Irving on his trips around the country. On most evenings after a London performance, the two men dined together, most often in a small eatery known somewhat affectionately as 'The Beefsteak Room', close to the rear of the theatre.

There were many successful visits to America, the first of which took place in October 1883 when Irving presented Leopold David Lewis' *The Bells*, which had been an immense success following its premier at The Lyceum on 25 November 1871; Irving almost took the role of Mathias, the burgomaster, with him to the grave, giving his final performance the night before his death. Stoker met and befriended Walt Whitman and Mark Twain, and in England there were associations with many of the literary figures of the day including Arthur Conan Doyle, Jerome K. Jerome and Alfred, Lord Tennyson.

In 1906, Stoker published a two-volume set of *Personal Reminiscences of Henry Irving* in which he gave some insight into Irving's techniques as an actor as well as the political and business life of The Lyceum. Despite his own success as a published writer, the Irishman was to be continually associated in the public eye with his former employer right up until his own death six years later.

In his essay 'The Genesis of Dracula: A Re-Visit', published in 1975, Devendra P. Varma makes the case for some aspects of the Count Dracula character having its origins in the personality and appearance of the Victorian explorer and translator Sir Richard Burton, whom Stoker met for the first time at Westland Row

Station, Dublin, in August 1878; in January the following year they met again in London and six years later, in July 1886, the two men dined together in The Beefsteak Room following a performance of *Faust* at The Lyceum. However, many have seen the larger-than-life Henry Irving as the principal model for the towering and terrifying personality that is Count Dracula and that, forever at the actor's beck and call, Stoker's seemingly slavish devotion, born out of a duality of reverence and fear, resulted in him immortalising his employer in the pages that over the course of seven long years in the twilight days of the 1890s he committed to posterity. Although it cannot be denied that both as an act of worship and revenge, Irving became imprinted in various ways into the story of *Dracula*, the reality is that this famous novel is the sum of many parts, some of which can be demonstrated as going back to the start of the author's early career in writing and journalism. Stoker's genius was to take several disparate strands of both fact and fiction – shipwrecks off the north-east coast, a Scottish castle ruin, the dark stories of a Budapest university lecturer, Le Fanu and Varney, the vampire myths and tales of historical knights of Eastern Europe, as well as his own dark and personal imaginings – and weave them together into one powerfully cohesive structure, the elements of which (quoting Lovecraft again from his 1920s essay 'Supernatural Horror in Literature') 'unite to form a tale now justly assigned a permanent place in English letters'. Almost as remarkable is the fact that through the preservation of Stoker's working notes and papers, today kept as a permanent collection in the Rosenbach Museum in Philadelphia as well as latterly published (in 2008) in facsimile, the entire process of researching and scripting the story can be charted and followed with incredible accuracy.

Today it is common knowledge that the entire epic and bloody story of *Dracula*, 'the terrifying lover who died yet lived', began with a dream, or rather, a nightmare. In the growing aftermath of the novel's publication, Stoker's family tradition put this event down somewhat light-heartedly to a case of indigestion caused by a dish of dressed crab that the author ate one night in Irving's company, during one of their post-performance Beefsteak suppers. Although Stoker himself appears to have been fond of recounting the story, the writer's son Noel, in correspondence with Stoker's first biographer Harry Ludlum in the late 1950s, reiterated that the quip was meant in all honesty to have been a joke. The truth behind the celebrated dream was in fact far from being light-hearted. In March 1890, Stoker seemed unable to get a strange series of images out of his mind and scribbled down the following brief and shaky lines:

> [Y]oung man goes out – sees girl one tries – to kiss him not on the lips but throat. Old Count interferes – rage and fury diabolical. This man belongs to me I want him.

Seven years later, this strange and haunting vision was revealed, transformed into one of the novel's most famous and celebrated passages:

> I suppose I must have fallen asleep; I hope so, but I fear, for all that followed was startlingly real … I was not alone … In the moonlight opposite me were three young women, ladies by their dress and manner. I thought at the time I must be dreaming when I saw them, for, though the moonlight was behind them, they threw no shadow on the floor. They came close to me and looked at me for some time and then whispered together. Two were dark, and had high aquiline noses, like the Count's, and great dark, piercing eyes, that seemed to be almost red when contrasted with the pale yellow moon. The other was fair, as fair as can be, with great, wavy masses of golden hair and eyes like pale sapphires … All three had brilliant white teeth, that shone like pearls against the ruby of their voluptuous lips. There was something about them that made me uneasy, some longing and at the same time some deadly fear … The fair girl went on her knees and bent over me, fairly gloating … Lower and lower went her head as the lips went below the range of my mouth and chin and seemed about to fasten on my throat … I closed my eyes in a languorous ecstasy and waited – waited with beating heart.
>
> But at that instant another sensation swept through me as quick as lightning. I was conscious of the presence of the Count, and of his being as if lapped in a storm of fury. As my eyes opened involuntarily I saw his strong hand grasp the slender neck of the fair woman and with giant's power draw it back … Never did I imagine such wrath and fury, even in the demons of the pit. His eyes were positively blazing. The red light in them was lurid, as if the flames of hell-fire blazed behind them. His face was deathly pale, and the lines of it were hard like drawn wires; the thick eyebrows that met over the nose now seemed like a heaving bar of white-hot metal. With a fierce sweep of his arm, he hurled the woman from him, and then motioned to the others, as though he were beating them back … In a voice which, though low and almost a whisper, seemed to cut through the air and then ring round the room, he exclaimed:-
>
> 'How dare you touch him, any of you? How dare you cast eyes on him when I had forbidden it? Back, I tell you all! This man belongs to me! Beware how you meddle with him, or you'll have to deal with me.'

The narrator of this vivid and erotic tableau is Jonathan Harker, a young newly qualified solicitor, sent on a business trip to Transylvania, 'one of the wildest and least known portions of Europe', to finalise the purchase of property in England by the eccentric but seemingly benign Count Dracula. Dracula was a local nobleman and the last of a line of titled rulers whose ultimate desire is to walk the 'crowded streets of your mighty London, to be in the midst of the whirl and the rush of humanity, to share its life, its change, its death, and all that makes it what it is' in the twilight of his years. The chilling and deadly reality is only apparent to the hapless Englishman once he has become an unwitting prisoner in Dracula's remote and forbidding castle lair: the ageing

Transylvanian knight is in truth the centuries-old vampire King of the Undead, who plans to use his move to England as the stepping stone to unleash a plague of vampiric pestilence across the world, with himself as the fountainhead of its obscene and deadly cult. Using an epistolary structure of diary entries, correspondence and transcribed phonograph recordings (a device most likely inspired by the writings of English novelist Wilkie Collins whose popular books *The Woman in White* (1859) and *The Moonstone* (1868) are written in a similar fashion), Stoker charts an epic battle of good against evil as Harker – who eventually frees himself from the Count's castle stronghold and returns to the West – seeks to destroy the undead menace from the Carpathians and free his attractive fiancé, Mina, from the vampire's sensual and bloody clutches. If, as novelist and critic Kim Newman has suggested, Stoker knew at the time he was writing a definitive novel of supernatural fiction, by the same token it would have been impossible for him, as he drafted out his story, to have any notion that he was in effect creating the blueprint on which the vast twentieth century Dracula industry would ultimately be built, as well as the inexorable influence that his book still has as the literary vampire spreads its membranous bat-wings into and across an entire new millennium.

Despite much copying, transposition, adaptation and exaggeration involving a myriad of books, plays and films dating from the early years of the 1920s (*see* Chapter 7), it is still possible to trace the variations back to the original novel's core set pieces as written down by Stoker during his long journey of the mind back in the first half of the 1890s: Harker's seduction and enslavement by Dracula's vampire brides; the Count's dramatic Dutchman-like arrival in England on a storm-swept schooner; the vampirising and violent destruction of the innocent Lucy; the vampire's shape-shifting physics and his enslavement of a fly-eating lunatic, Renfield; the sexual seduction of Mina, and the Count's final dramatic flight home to Transylvania and elimination at the hands of the vampire-hunting physician Van Helsing (a role originally intended to be divided over three characters but subsequently condensed into one) and his friends.

As revealed through the preservation of his working notes, despite much revision and development over the course of many months, the novel's basic four-part location structure of Eastern Europe, Whitby, London and surrounding area, and then return to Eastern Europe (which as Christopher Frayling has noted probably owes its shape to the author's familiarity with the scenery staging at The Lyceum) was fixed practically from the start, with the dream-inspired encounter with the three vampire women also remaining as a plot mainstay. At first glance, given Stoker's great familiarity with the theatre repertoire of his day, this eerie trio would seem to owe their origins to Shakespeare and the witches from *Macbeth*, but there is evidence that this famous scene goes back to the very beginning of Stoker's literary career and is in fact a variation of one of the Irishman's very first supernatural tales, namely the serialised story 'The Chain of Destiny' from 1875 where the elements of three ghostly figures and the intruding presence of a supreme evil are described by the narrator:

> I thought that I awoke suddenly to that peculiar feeling which we sometimes have on starting from sleep, as if some one had been speaking in the room, and the voice is still echoing through it. All was quite silent, and the fire had gone out. I looked out of the window that lay straight opposite the foot of the bed, and observed a light outside, which gradually grew brighter till the room was almost as light as by day ... It seemed as if there were grouped without the window three lovely children, who seemed to float in mid-air. The light seemed to spring from a point far behind them, and by their side was something dark and shadowy, which served to set off their radiance.
>
> The children seemed to be smiling in upon something in the room, and, following their glances, I saw that their eyes rested upon the other bed. There, strange to say, the head which I had lately seen in the picture rested upon the pillow. I looked at the wall, but the frame was empty, the picture was gone. Then I looked at the bed again, and saw the young girl asleep, with the expression of her face constantly changing, as though she were dreaming ... Again turning to the window, my gaze became fixed, for a great and weird change had taken place. The figures were still there, but their features and expressions had become woefully different. Instead of the happy innocent look of childhood was one of malignity. With the change the children had grown old, and now three hags, decrepit and deformed, like typical witches, were before me.
>
> But a thousand times worse than this transformation was the change in the dark mass that was near them. From a cloud, misty and undefined, it became a sort of shadow with a form. This gradually, as I looked, grew darker and fuller, till at length it made me shudder. There stood before me the phantom of the Fiend.

Fifteen years later, the ghostly children become vampires and 'the phantom of the Fiend' is transformed into Count Dracula.

Five months after his celebrated nightmare, Stoker visited the fishing port of Whitby on the North Yorkshire coast and it was here that several of the major plot devices and set pieces of *Dracula* first began to take shape in the Irishman's mind. He studied the dialects of the local townsfolk and fishermen and wandered among the sea-blown gravestones in the clifftop churchyard of St Mary's, copying out names from off the eroded and tumbling monuments. Then, as now, the vast and imposing ruins of the eleventh-century Benedictine Abbey, said to be haunted by shrouded and weeping figures and the inspiration for Sir Walter Scott's epic poem *Marmion* (1808), dominated the skyline and together with its ghosts eventually found their way into his new novel. Stoker also took his own inspiration from old newspaper reports in the local *Whitby Gazette* held in the town library, particularly an account published on 31 October 1885 about the shipwreck of a Russian schooner, the *Demetri*, out of Varna, which ran aground ahead of a force-8 gale in

Whitby harbour with all sails up; Stoker's fertile imagination soon transformed this particular incident into the perfect vehicle on which to introduce his vampire lord onto British shores.

Amongst the books of the Whitby Philosophical Society, Stoker made another discovery which was to ultimately lead to the decision to make the pivotal name change that we have noted before. In a copy of an historical textbook (*An Account of the Principalities of Wallachia and Moldavia*, written by the former British consul in Bucharest, William Wilkinson, and published by Longmans in 1820) he read an account of the fifteenth-century wars between the Romanians and the Turks and the role of two Wallachian knights, father and son, both princes or Voïvodes named Dracula. In a footnote, the author noted: 'Dracula in the Wallachian language means Devil' and went on to state that 'any person who rendered himself conspicuous either by courage, cruel actions, or cunning' was entitled to use it as a surname. Stoker wrote it down, little realising that it was the catalyst that would create a masterpiece.

In the summer of 1893, three years after his nightmare and the experiences in Whitby, Stoker took the first of several holidays in the remote Scottish village of Cruden Bay (formerly known as Port Errol after William Hay, the 18th Earl of Errol), situated just over twenty-five miles north of Aberdeen on the imposing Buchan coast. Just north of the village, the remains of the sixteenth-century Slains Castle, a former tower house later converted into a baronial mansion, like the windswept ruins of Whitby Abbey, garnered a strange fascination and several commentators have suggested that its presence was the principle inspiration for Count Dracula's castle and the opening section of the novel. Stoker stayed at the Kilmarnock Arms and later in the hamlet of Whinneyfold just to the south of the village. The atmosphere and landscape seeped into the Dubliner's blood and it was here that he set his later 1902 romance, *The Mystery of the Sea*.

Back in London, Stoker began consolidating his holiday researches and fleshing out his story with more detailed information. Using Le Fanu's *Carmilla* as his model, his original intention had been to set the foreign sections of the story in Styria but this was to change. Only a month after the recording of his nightmare, in April 1890, Stoker had dined in The Beefsteak Room with the Hungarian historian Arminius Vambéry, the author of a number of books including *Travels in Central Asia* (1864) and *Hungary in Ancient, Medieval and Modern Times* (1886), who was then in England on a lecture tour. Although no details of their meeting or subsequent correspondence has survived, it was speculated for many years that Vambéry was not only the model for the vampire hunting Van Helsing but also the influence for the presence of Transylvania as the Count's homeland. However, this is not supported by the author's working notes: the Styrian setting was present in the novel's development up until 1892 and as mentioned above, the duties of Van Helsing were initially to have been undertaken by three separate characters: a German professor, a detective and a ghost hunter, all of whom were given names in the early stages of development.

However, Vambéry appears to have made at least some impression as in the final text of the book he is mentioned by name by Van Helsing himself as one of the Dutchman's historical advisors. Vambéry wrote two volumes of autobiography and died in 1913 at the age of 81.

In the old circular Reading Room at the British Museum, Stoker spent time researching the Eastern European history and geography that fills much of the opening leaves of Jonathan Harker's journal in the early pages of the book. There, a selection of volumes such as *Round About the Carpathians* by Andrew F. Crosse (1878) and Emily Gerard's two-volume *The Land Beyond the Forest* (1888) made him decide to replace the original Austrian location with that of Transylvania, and further books such as Charles Boner's *Transylvania* (1865) and an article 'Transylvanian Superstitions', also by Gerard and published in the *Nineteenth Century* magazine in July 1885, underpinned the change and provided necessary facts and figures. Stoker also followed up the lead given by his studies in Whitby and immersed himself in the history of the Wallachian warrior knights Vlad Dracul (d. 1447) and his son Vlad Tepes or Vlad the Impaler, born in Transylvania around 1431 and whose nickname came from the brutal practice of skewering the living bodies of captured enemy soldiers on long sharpened wooden poles, effectively creating forests of dead and dying bodies across the battlefield. A famous woodcut shows Vlad eating a hearty meal in the shadow of a row of impaled victims with a dismembered body at his feet. Stoker impregnated his vampire character with aspects of the nobleman's life and history, and may well have based some of the physical characteristics of Dracula on an illustration in a pamphlet published in Bamburg in 1491, held in the museum's collection. Still highly regarded in Romania as a national hero who, through his soldiering, drove out hordes of Muslim Turks during the European campaigns of the Ottoman Wars and who also created the citadel of Bucharest (now the country's capital), Vlad Tepes was a cruel and bloodthirsty tyrant who is said to have nailed turbans to the heads of disrespectful diplomats, boiled the heads of his enemies in a kettle, burnt beggars alive in order to reduce the risk of the spread of plague, and for good measure, fed mothers the flesh of their own infants before their own executions. After much fighting, a defeat by the Turks at Poenari (where his castle fortress, now one of several 'Castle Draculas' visited by enthusiastic tourists, was overrun, forcing Vlad to escape over the Carpathian Mountains into Transylvania), as well as much political intrigue of the time including arrest and imprisonment by the Hungarian King, Matthias Corvinus, between 1462 and 1474, he was killed by an assassin some time during the winter of 1476/77 and his head exhibited in Constantinople. For many years his body was thought to have been buried at the island monastery of Snagov, twenty miles north of Bucharest, where a traditional gravesite was found to be empty following archaeological work carried out in the early 1930s. Today, another monastery at Comana a similar distance to the south of Bucharest, is now the favoured final resting place for one of the most notorious figures in Eastern European history.

Although the presence of Vlad Tepes in the genesis of *Dracula* is well documented there is more ambiguity regarding one particular aspect of the story as written, namely the location of the tomb of the doomed Lucy Westenra, Count Dracula's first British victim and one of the famous set pieces in the central section of the novel. Stoker's friendship with the Manx author Sir Thomas Henry Hall Caine (1853–1931) who under the nom de plume of 'Hommy-Beg' was given the dedication of *Dracula* in 1897, has led to speculation that Highgate Cemetery in North London (*see* Chapter 10) may have been the inspiration for the lonely churchyard near the fictional 'Kingstead' where the vampire hunters converge to stake and decapitate the undead Lucy and restore her to Christian peace.

In 1882, Hall Caine published some *Recollections of Dante Gabriel Rossetti*, the English poet and illustrator whose wife Elizabeth Siddal, the model for Sir John Everett Millais' famous painting *Ophelia*, was buried in Highgate in February 1862 following a fatal overdose of laudanum. Beset with grief, Rossetti gathered together the handwritten originals of several of his poems in memory of his beloved and, entwined amongst the locks of her copper-coloured hair, they were buried along with a small Bible in the coffin with her. Seven years later, in 1869, Rossetti was persuaded by his disreputable agent Charles Howell (a suspected blackmailer who just over a decade later would be found with his throat cut outside a public house in Chelsea) to carry out an exhumation and retrieve the verses so that they could be included together with several modern poems in a new anthology. Despite obtaining Home Office permission, Rossetti was not present on the night of 5 October 1869 when, by the light of a graveside fire, Howell together with a group of workmen lifted off the slab covering the tomb. After digging down to the casket, they prised off the lid and retrieved the grey calf-bound notebook. Despite the book of verse being eaten through in several places by cemetery worms, Howell later reported that the corpse of Elizabeth Siddal, like some incorruptible saint, looked exactly as it had done on the day she had been laid to rest and according to some accounts, her red hair had continued to grow and in the torchlight was seen to fill the entire coffin. The 'resurrection' poems were quickly published but were not popular; Rossetti soon regretted the incident and died on 9 April 1882, a drug-dependant recluse.

The truth of Charles Howell's description of the exhumed Elizabeth Siddal given his roguish reputation is open to debate and although it is most likely he was attempting to sooth Rossetti's troubled conscious with his account, the allegedly uncorrupted or even 'undead' condition of the body and Stoker's friendly relations with Hall Caine has understandably given rise to the belief that the Irishman was influenced by the story to the point that he fashioned the Lucy Westenra episode around it. Bram may well have visited Highgate Cemetery at some point during his time in London but if this was the case then no record appears to have survived.

If the eerie story did influence anything that Bram Stoker wrote then a good candidate is the short story *The Secret of the Growing Gold*, first published in the *Black & White* newspaper in January 1892. It is a Poe-like tale involving a murderer whose crime is betrayed by the golden hair of his victim (in reality his own sister) which continues to grow through the cracks in the flagstones under which he has improvised a makeshift grave. In his book *Haunted Places of Middlesex* (2004), author Mike Hall suggests that given the geographical information in Stoker's book, a prime candidate for the Westenra tomb is the Rundell mausoleum in the churchyard of St Mary's at Hendon. In a similar ghoulish fashion to the exhumation of Elizabeth Siddal, in September 1828 three men were arrested for breaking into a tomb and removing the skull of the occupant, the mother of one of the actual grave robbers, who claimed at his trial he had decapitated the skeleton to pursue his interest in phrenology.

Bram Stoker's *Dracula* was published at the end of May 1897 by Archibald Constable and Company, bound in bright yellow cloth with suitably contrasting and sanguineous red lettering, and priced at a few shillings. Today, copies of the first printing in the original binding sell for anything between £10,000 and £25,000. During the writing of the present book, a re-bound presentation copy inscribed by Stoker to the American newspaper publisher, Frank Munsey, was on offer by a bookseller in Santa Barbara, California, with a price tag of nearly £50,000. Reception for his new novel was at the time generally positive but it was not until the beginning of the 1920s that a wider appreciation began to gather pace; Stoker would never live to see the hallowed status that his book now enjoys.

'It is an eerie and gruesome tale which Mr Stoker tells, but it is much the best book he has written,' noted the *Glasgow Herald* of 10 June 1897, '[A]s strange event follows strange event, the narrative might in less skilful hands become intolerably improbable; but Dracula to the end seems only too reasonably and sanely possible.' A week before, the *Daily Telegraph* reviewer W.L. Courtney felt confident in stating that the public, now tired of romance, was needful of a deeper analysis of social problems and the essence of character that had been for the most part 'temporarily obscured by the extravagances of the New Woman':

> It is odd that, under circumstances like these, one of the most curious and striking of recent productions should be a revival of a mediaeval superstition, the old legend of the 'were-wolf', as illustrated and modernized by Mr Bram Stoker, in the book which he entitles *Dracula*. For there are two things which are remarkable in the novel – the first is the confident reliance on superstition as furnishing the groundwork of a modern story; and the second, more significant still, is the bold adaptation of the legend to such ordinary spheres of latter-day existence as the harbour of Whitby and Hampstead Heath.

The Athenaeum on 26 June noted: 'It reads at times like a mere series of grotesquely incredible events, but there are better moments that show more power, though even these are never productive of the tremor such subjects evoke under the hand of a master,' and summed up by saying, 'An immense amount of energy, a certain degree of imaginative faculty, and many ingenious and gruesome details are there. At times Mr Stoker almost succeeds in creating the sense of possibility in impossibility; at others he merely commands an array of crude statements of incredible actions.' Other reviewers, although more forgiving as to the literary style, were more critical of the fundamental choice of a supernatural theme. It was, according to the *Observer* of 1 August 1897, 'one quite unworthy of his literary capabilities'.

Perhaps though the most farseeing of reviewers who had some inkling of the novel's eventual and lasting power was that for the *Pall Mall Gazette* (1 June 1897) who, only a few days after publication, enthused in the following and now characteristically familiar way:

> Mr Bram Stoker should have labeled his book 'For Strong Men Only,' or words to that effect. Left lying carelessly around, it might get into the hands of your maiden aunt who believes devoutly in the man under the bed, or of the new parlourmaid with unsuspected hysterical tendencies. Dracula to such would be manslaughter. It is for the man with a sound conscience and digestion, who can turn out the gas and go to bed without having to look over his shoulder more than half a dozen times as he goes upstairs, or more than mildly wishing that he had a crucifix and some garlic handy to keep the vampires from getting at him. That is to say, the story deals with the Vampire King, and it is horrid and creepy to the last degree. It is also excellent, and one of the best things in the supernatural line that we have been lucky enough to hit upon.

A glance through these and several other contemporary reviews of the time show that faced with the novelty of the Dubliner's invention, critics and commentators of Stoker's time saw little beyond the character of Count Dracula and as such the 'Vampire King' was viewed as more or less a traditional one-dimensional villain. As we will see, this interpretation remained more or less constant for half a century and it was not until the reinvention of the Gothic horror film in the late 1950s (*see* Chapter 8) that Stoker's character began to be viewed in much greater depth, in particular the tragedy inherent in the vampire's immortality (an aspect favored by actors Christopher Lee and Gary Oldman, who have both made important big-screen interpretations of the role). In a similar way, with the benefit of hindsight and a greater familiarity with the vampire myth as presented through the literary medium, commentators nearer to our own time have become less impressed with the mechanics of Stoker's writing but still remain convinced as to the effectiveness of the drama and the duality of eroticism and violence that, surging below the surface, repeatedly finds the line of weakest resistance and frequently breaks through. 'There is no doubt that much of Stoker's long and involved book is very badly and sloppily written,' Basil Copper noted in his 1973 study *The Vampire in Legend, Fact and Art*, 'yet such is the fascination of its theme and the excellence of its best passages, that it still somehow survives.' Similarly, Brian Frost (in *The Monster With a Thousand Faces*) notes that 'not without its flaws ... there can be no disputing the fact that *Dracula* is a masterpiece in its own field; for like all those classic works of literature which give us a keener understanding of the forces of darkness it becomes part of the reader's experience, leaving an indelible impression upon his mind.'

Bram Stoker died at his London home in St George's Square, Pimlico, on 20 April 1912 at the age of 64, three days before newspaper pages became filled with the dramatic story of the sinking of the RMS *Titanic*. The cause of death was given as 'Locomotor Ataxia' and 'Exhaustion', which in the mid-1970s was interpreted by Dan Farson as showing that his great-uncle died of tertiary syphilis, contracted possibly from a Paris prostitute during periods of womanising caused by his wife's alleged frigidity. Although it is possible to interpret the death certificate in this way, Stoker's most recent (2004) biographer Paul Murray, after consulting with several modern medical authorities, favored uraemia or renal failure due to a chronic inflammation of the kidneys. Murray also notes that 'the balance of probability is that he was also suffering from syphilis but this was not the direct cause of death'. Stoker was cremated at Golders Green Crematorium and today his ashes reside in a small marble urn mixed with those of his only son Noel Thornley Stoker, who died on 16 September 1961.

In the fifteen years between the publication of *Dracula* and his death, Stoker returned to the medium of the supernatural novel on a further three occasions. *The Jewel of Seven Stars* made the move from 'the land beyond the forest' to contemporary Egypt and described the attempt by a group of archaeologists to resurrect the mummy of an ancient Egyptian Queen, Tera. The novel's nihilistic closing pages caused reviewers many problems when it was first published in 1903 and in a subsequent edition (issued by Rider & Co. in 1912) Stoker made revisions and grafted on a lighter ending. In 1909, Heinemann issued the evocatively titled *The Lady of the Shroud*, a pseudo-vampiric novel again laid out in an epistolary format and featuring another castle setting, this time located on the Dalmatian coast. The eponymous lady of the title is in fact the daughter of a local governor who pretends to be a vampire after falling into a trance and sleeps by day in a glass-topped coffin in the castle crypt. Stoker's final published novel, *The Lair of the White Worm*, a horror yarn involving an ancient evil living in a subterranean pit beneath a family estate in the Derbyshire hills, was published in November 1911 and later in an abridged version in 1925. Despite a strange and outlandishly complicated plot – likened by Dan Farson to an unintentionally funny Gothic acid trip – it remains the Irishman's most successful novel after *Dracula* and was still being reprinted as late as the early 1960s. However, it is with the vampire lord of the undead that Bram Stoker will be forever associated: arguably the most important moment in the history of supernatural horror fiction to which, as to world literature as a whole, it remains a veritable benchmark in blood.

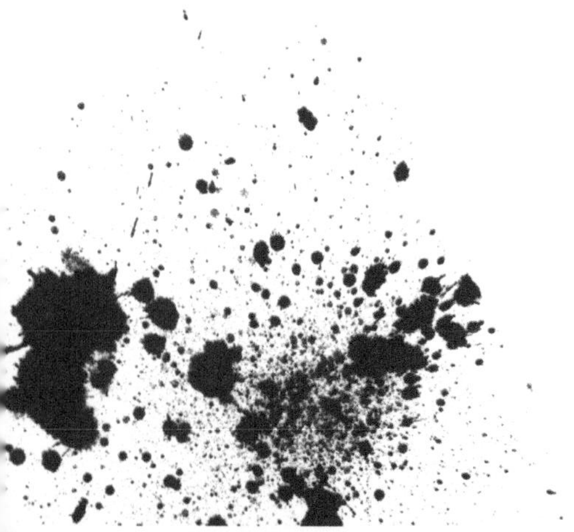

4

The Undead in Britain: Vampire Fiction Before and After the First World War

(1890s-1940)

In 1960, well over half a century after the publication of Stoker's *Dracula*, the English novelist Simon Raven (1927–2001), famously described in a *Guardian* review as having 'the mind of a cad and the pen of an angel', published *Doctors Wear Scarlet*, a contemporary vampire tale with a background of Oxbridge academia set mainly in modern-day Greece. One of the first of several revisionary post-war vampire novels of which the American writer Theodore Sturgeon's *Some of Your Blood* from 1961 is both chronologically and stylistically similar, Raven excised the supernatural elements of the vampire myth from his story (although some of its associated symbolism, such as the bodily staking of dead corpses, remains), and recast the undead legend as a psycho-sexual phenomenon in which the victim, in this case the gifted academic Richard Fountain, uses the physical drinking of human blood as a substitute for normal sexual intercourse. While on a visit to the ancient Greek city of Corinth, Fountain falls foul of the sinister 'vampiress' Chriseis, the leader of a perverted cult of sociopaths who indulge in blood-drinking orgies and similar rituals to which the young Englishman initially submits himself as a cure for his own physical and emotional problems. The root of Fountain's infertility lies in his troubled relationship with Dr Walter Goodrich, Provost of Lancaster College, Cambridge, to whose daughter Penelope he is unofficially engaged. Despite being rescued from the cult's mountain lair and returned to England, Fountain is unable to escape the mental influence of the Greek woman's bloodlust and after killing Penelope with a bite to the throat, the young Cambridge don is secretly poisoned to death by a fellow academic, to protect the reputation of the College.

No less controversial than Sturgeon's novel – again about an individual, in this case a soldier, with a psychological compulsion to drink blood – Raven showed that it was possible to breathe new life into an old format by grounding the horror in contemporary reality without recourse to traditional settings or paranormal clichés. Having said this, it should be mentioned that *Doctors Wear Scarlet* was not in fact the first work of fiction to describe vampirism as a psychologically inspired sexual perversion: the German writer and actor, Hanns Heinz Ewers (1871–1943), whose posthumous reputation has suffered somewhat in literary circles due to his Nazi sympathies, covered similar ground in his 1922 novel *Vampire*, in which a young writer rejuvenates himself by drawing off quantities of his girlfriend's blood during the course of their lovemaking. Reinvention, however, has been the hallmark of much of twentieth-century horror fiction, keen to discard the trappings of a previous age, and in this chapter we will examine a selection of British vampire fiction that both compliments and expands the ground rules that were laid down by Bram Stoker.

In 1894, three years before the emergence of *Dracula*, science-fiction author H.G. Wells neatly transferred the theme across to the plant kingdom in his *The Flowering of the Strange Orchid*, a cautionary tale of vampiric botany involving a blood-drinking flower imported from the remote Anderman Islands into an English greenhouse, where the story's eccentric protagonist, an orchid-collector named Wedderburn, almost falls foul of its sinister attributes. In September 1899, *The Strand Magazine* published another tale of vampire plants, in this instance *The Purple Terror* by London-born Frederick Merrick White (1859–1935), who describes an account of explorers in the jungles of Cuba who are attacked by a forest of sentient blood-drinking vines. Both these stories owe much to an earlier tale, *The Man-eating Tree* by Philip (Phil) Stewart Robinson (1847–1902), published in the collection *Under the Punkah* in 1881 and which describes a monstrous plant-like growth that devours unwary visitors venturing into a glade in a remote area of central Africa. Another Robinson story features a vampire in name only: *Last of the Vampires* (1893) describes a mysterious man-like skeleton washed up on the shore of an Amazon river which proves to be the bones of an explorer mixed with those of a once living pterodactyl.

In 1897, Florence Marryat, a prolific novelist and spiritualist author whose books *There is No Death* (1891) and *The Spirit World* (1894) are highly regarded for their documentation of late Victorian séance room phenomena and mediumship, published *The Blood of the Vampire*, which, despite the title, is again another subtle variation on a familiar theme. In this instance, it is an account of 'psychic vampirism' involving a young woman from Jamaica who subconsciously drains the life force of those around her who become caught up in her charms. A theme used much later by Colin Wilson in his 1976 novel *The Space Vampires* (*see* Chapter 13), who as we have seen has placed much credence to the phenomenon in respect of understanding and validating the vampire myth, the concept of psychic attack was one taken seriously by mystics and occultists in the first half of the twentieth century, particularly by the Welsh writer and practitioner Violet Firth (1890–1946), better known by her alter ego of Dion Fortune, who included practical instructions for the repulsion of such forces in her 1930 book, *Psychic Self-Defence*. Firth's own supernatural novel, *The Demon Lover* (1927), features a rebellious occultist who draws the life force from a young assistant in order to emerge from his own self-imposed exile on the astral plane and return to Earth in physical form. Despite its originality, the publication of *Dracula* in the same year as *The Blood of the Vampire* quickly consigned it to the backwaters of supernatural fiction, a situation compounded by the death of the author from a diabetes-related illness at the age of 62, two years later. After decades of obscurity, a modern critical edition edited by Dr Greta Depledge was issued in 2010.

Here it is worth mentioning an unusual but strangely successful combination of psychic vampirism and vampiric plant life which takes place in Algernon Blackwood's 1911 short story *The Transfer*. The human element of the drama is provided by an unusual character called Mr Frene who unconsciously draws the life and vitality from those around him and absorbs it like 'a great human sponge'. When in company, Frene, a giant of a man with hard black eyes and an enormous face, flourishes, but when isolated and alone he is overcome with lifelessness and languor and droops like an un-watered plant. Drawn to a strangely barren area of an otherwise lushly growing garden known as the 'Forbidden Corner', Frene becomes overpowered by a strange hypnotic force. Soon, the 'Forbidden Corner' has completed its parasitic activity and where once there was lifeless soil, now it is 'full of great, luscious, driving weeds and creepers, very strong, full-fed, and bursting thick with life'; in contrast, Frene is a drained shell and his vampiristic days are over. Blackwood, born in Shooter's Hill, Kent, in 1869, is highly regarded for his collections of supernatural and ghostly stories of which *The Willows* (1907) is often cited as one of the best examples of his ability to create a genuine sense of unease through the use of landscape and atmosphere. A member of the famous Ghost Club, he has been described by someone who knew him as 'a charming raconteur with a commanding presence, an unforgettable face and an enormous knowledge of the occult'. *The Transfer*, which the author considered to be what he termed a 'nature story', first appeared in the magazine *Country Life* and was subsequently published the following year in a compendium entitled *Pan's Garden*. His only other fictional work to include a vampire subject, *The Singular Death of Morton*, a traditional presentation of the myth involving two travelling friends who encounter a mysterious young girl in a tumble-down châlet in Switzerland, languished unread for nearly eighty years after it first appeared in *The Tramp* journal in December 1910, until republication in a compendium of lost vampire stories edited by Richard Dalby in 1987 titled *Dracula's Brood*. Blackwood died at his home in Kent on 10 December 1951, aged 82, and his ashes were later scattered in the Saanemnöser Pass in the Swiss Alps.

As well as transformation and adaptation, traditional presentations of the vampire myth had been commonly present both before the *Dracula* watershed (using Le Fanu as a suitable template) and not surprisingly became more frequent in its immediate aftermath. In December 1894, during the time that Bram Stoker was walking the beach at Cruden Bay and wrestling with the historical Dracula in the British Museum, the young English-born aristocrat Count Eric Stenbock, of Swedish descent and heir to large estates of land in Estonia which had been owned by his family since the 1700s, published *Studies of Death*, a collection of short stories of which *The True Story of a Vampire* is now by far the best known.

Turning Le Fanu's *Carmilla* on its head, Stenbock produced a polarized version of the Irishman's tale involving the predatory Count Vardalek, a homosexual vegetarian vampire whose young male victim Gabriel is the brother of the story's narrator, also from Styria and called Carmela who, now an old woman, relates a series of historic events which happened many years before when she was a child. The Hungarian Vardalek, waylaid at a railway station, befriends the narrator's father and quickly insinuates himself into the household where the object of his unnatural desires, a young boy, gradually sickens and dies. Vardalek vanishes as mysteriously as he arrived, leaving Gabriel's father a broken man who himself dies soon after. Stenbock, who like his vampire character preferred the company of men to women, also wrote poetry and today is most remembered for his eccentric behaviour, which included eating meals with a pet toad on his shoulder and travelling with a life-size doll which he addressed as 'The Little Count' and treated like a son. A drug addict and alcoholic, he died at the age of 35 within weeks of *Studies in Death* appearing in print, after falling in a drunken rage into a fireplace. Buried in a cemetery in Brighton, Stenbock's heart was removed prior to interment and sent to Estonia, where it was placed in a jar and sealed into the wall of the family church at Kusal. A crisis apparition of the tragic writer is said to have appeared to his uncle in Estonia at the moment of his death in England.

A good example of an early twentieth-century post-Stoker British vampire story is *The Tomb of Sarah* by Frederick George Loring, a former naval officer and Post Office telegraph official, which was first published in the *Pall Mall* magazine in December 1900. Taking the Bathory legend (*see* Chapter 5) and overlaying it together with the spectacle of the destruction of the undead Lucy onto the setting of an English country church, Loring creates a neat and atmospheric vignette that has subsequently found its way into a number of story collections and anthologies. The vampire of the title is the evil Countess Sarah, the last of the Kenyon family, murdered in the first half of the seventeenth century and whose imposing black marble mausoleum becomes the focus of restoration work inside the church interior. Choosing to ignore a warning incised onto the tomb marble, which states that '[f]or the sake of the dead and the welfare of the living, let this sepulchre remain untouched and its occupant undisturbed', the narrator, an ecclesiastical architect whose Stoker-like diary entries chronicle the strange happenings, opens the grave where the body of the vampire woman is found in a state of suspended animation lying on a bed of earth. For much of the story, Sarah assumes the form of a huge dog which roams the countryside surrounding the church under the cover of an eerie and supernaturally inspired mist (another element borrowed from Stoker, who himself was inspired by the writings of the Revd Sabine Baring-Gould (1834–1924), a folk song collector and antiquarian, principally *The Book of Were-Wolves* which appeared in 1865). Eventually trapped within a circle of garlic flowers, the Countess is destroyed with the customary stake to the heart. In a similar fashion, Sir Rupert Marvyn, the undead protagonist of the Australian-born British novelist Henry Brereton Marriott Watson's novella *The Stone Chamber*, published the previously year and which owes more to Rymer and Varney than it does to Bram Stoker, is likewise trapped and destroyed in his own tomb, in this instance by fire in an inferno started by an overturned candle.

The church setting of Frederick Loring's tale easily brings to mind the fictional writings of one of supernatural literature's most admired figures, Montague Rhodes (M.R.) James, a former Provost of both King's College, Cambridge and Eton, whose collected ghost stories have for many years been considered some of the finest ever written. A medieval scholar, James was able to effectively combine his deep antiquarian knowledge – together with that of architectural history and geography – with a uniquely personal and subtle understanding of the supernatural story tradition. Initially written for personal amusement to be read out at Christmas time to private gatherings of family members or to groups of pupils in the study of the old Provost's Lodge at King's, the author was in his mid-forties when the first collection, *Ghost Stories of an Antiquary*, was published in 1904. This was followed by a sequel, *More Ghost Stories of an Antiquary* (1911), and later a further two volumes completed a quartet: *A Thin Ghost and Others* (1919) and *A Warning to the Curious and Other Ghost Stories* (1925). Over the years, James populated his tales with a wide range of dangerous spectres and sinister revenants that, once disturbed, enact a horrific revenge on the stories' protagonists who most often are unassuming and unsuspecting versions of the author himself. A small proportion of his thirty collected tales are considered by aficionados to have some kind of vampiric connection, although like James' writing as a whole, the references are exceedingly subtle and far removed from a *Dracula*-like scenario, a novel that the writer himself professed not to care for.

In *Wailing Well*, written specifically for the Eton College Boy Scouts and read aloud around their campfire at Worbarrow Bay, Dorset, in August 1927, James describes the unhappy fate of an obstreperous Scout named Stanley Judkins who defies the instructions of his troop leader and pays a daylight visit to the eponymous watering hole of the title, located amongst an unnamed copse in an isolated area of countryside. Unfortunately for Judkins, the well is haunted by a group of four sinister black-clad apparitions, all 'fluttering rags and whity bones', which crawl out of the trees and tall grass to claim him. The boy's body is later recovered hanging from a tree branch completely drained of blood, and the hapless Scout, now transformed into a revenant, joins the ranks of the well's eerie undead guardians himself.

A characteristically Jamesian plot device of a disturbed antiquarian object releasing a deadly revenant or a supernatural force provides the impetus for *An Episode of Cathedral History*, a middle-period work with vampiric elements written in May 1913 that appeared both in the June 1914 issue of the *Cambridge Review* and the subsequent collection, *A Thin Ghost and Others*. When a mysterious altar-tomb is uncovered hidden beneath the pulpit during alteration work to the interior of Southminster Cathedral, a strange plague-like malady soon begins to afflict the cathedral close, accompanied by the appearance of a black, hairy figure with glowing red eyes which emerges at night through a crack in the mausoleum's stonework. Several of the townsfolk are seen to sicken and die unexpectedly until a delegation lead by the Canon and the Dean accompanied by the Verger, Mr Worby, whose son is a witness and a subsequent narrator of the events, carry out an exorcism and seal the sinister tomb with a metal cross.

In both these stories, James' vampirism is fleeting in the extreme and arguably could simply be read as a curious by-product of the ghostly proceedings. However, James did venture further along the path and an earlier tale, *Count Magnus*, written shortly after the turn of the century and first published in the 1904 anthology, *Ghost Stories of an Antiquary*, is regarded as the most that James went in describing an overtly vampiric menace, with a title that immediately conjures up connections with Stoker, whose story at the time of its composition was less than five years old. The sinister revenant of the title is the Swedish Count Magnus de la Gardie, a former lord of the manor of Råbäck (pronounced 'Roebeck') whose 'Black Pilgrimage' to the ancient Eastern city of Chorazin has enabled him to live on beyond the grave, accompanied by a sinister hooded and tentacled familiar. Disturbed by the story's protagonist, a Mr Wraxall who is visiting the area to collect material for a travel book, Count Magnus emerges from his ornate and padlocked sarcophagus to pursue the hapless writer back to England, where he soon joins the unhallowed ranks of the Jamesian dead; in this instance with the flesh sucked from his bones rather than being drained of blood, James' own idiosyncratic take on the established vampire tradition. James himself survived the horrors of his own imagination and died at Eton on 12 June 1936, aged 73.

Another Englishman whose 'spook stories' as they have become known are similarly highly regarded for their atmosphere and invention is Edward Frederick (E.F.) Benson. A prolific writer and novelist, Benson was born at Wellington College, Berkshire, in 1867 where his father, Edward, was headmaster. A contemporary and friend of Montague James, both were members of the Chitchat Society, the Cambridge literary club where new stories and essays were read aloud for pleasure; Benson was in fact present on 28 October 1893 for what history has now assigned to be an auspicious occasion, when James read the very first of his ghost stories, *Canon Alberic's Scrap-book* and *Lost Hearts*, in public for the first time. Another suitably supernatural connection was Benson's friendship with Charles Lindley Wood (1839–1934), 2nd Viscount Halifax whose famous compendium, published posthumously in 1936 with annotations on the contents by his son as Lord Halifax's *Ghost Book*, is one of the first important collections of allegedly true ghost stories. Benson wrote over sixty novels, between 1893's *Dodo: A Detail of the Day* and *Raven's Brood*, published in 1934, including his 'Map and Lucia' collection which chart the social careers of two upper-class ladies in a small seaside town in East Sussex in the 1920s. As well as extended fiction and several collections of short stories, he also compiled over thirty factual books and biographies, including his own autobiography, *Final Edition*, which was delivered to his publisher only days before his death in London on 29 February 1940.

Like his friend M.R. James, Benson wrote several collections of ghost stories, a number of which not only feature the vampire myth but give it far greater prominence than his older contemporary would ever allow. Of the four tales included here, the most free in its use of the subject is *Negotium Perambulans* (1922), set in a lonely district of West Cornwall, where the undead menace, a slug-like monstrosity which translated from the Latin reads as 'the pestilence that walketh in darkness', is like Count Magnus, able to suck the very essence from its victims to leave them 'no more than a rind of skin in loose folds over projecting bones'.

Benson's most explicit vampire story, *Mrs Amworth*, written the following year, is set in the Sussex village of Maxley, where the eponymous lady of the title has recently returned to her ancestral home following the sudden and mysterious death of her husband, a civil servant in the Indian government. It soon becomes apparent that the affable widow is not as benign as she would make out and when the young son of Mrs Amworth's gardener begins to sicken from an unknown malady, one of the Maxley villagers, a retired professor from Cambridge, suspects he is the victim of a vampire. Despite being struck down and killed by a passing car, Mrs Amworth returns from beyond the grave to menace the wife of the local major, and is finally tracked to her grave and staked to death, in this instance with the blade of a pick-axe, but in a fashion which owes much to the lineage of graveside destruction that we have already encountered:

> He grasped the pick in both hands, raised it an inch or two for the taking of his aim, and then with full force brought it down on her breast. A fountain of blood, though she had been dead so long, spouted high in the air, falling with the thud of a heavy splash over the shroud, and simultaneously from those red lips came one long, appalling cry, swelling up like some hooting siren, and dying away again. With that, instantaneous as a lightning flash, came the touch of corruption on her face, the colour of it faded to ash, the plump cheeks fell in, the mouth dropped.

The coffin is quickly reburied and peace at last returns to the picturesque country village. Despite the stock ending, Benson's story contains some effectively atmospheric moments, particularly the image of the undead Mrs Amworth's disembodied head, nodding and smiling as it floats eerily outside the narrator's bedroom window.

Published in 1924, *The Face* is that of Roger Wyburn who appears in the dreams of an attractive married mother and also on the canvas of a painting by Van Dyke exhibited in a Sussex art gallery. Haunted by a recurring nightmare since childhood of a strange clifftop church where the vampire's presence is sinisterly concentrated amongst the fallen and ruinous graves, Benson's doomed heroine eventually encounters the derelict building in real life where years of erosion by the wind and the sea have brought Wyburn's coffin to the surface, allowing the undead marauder to emerge and finally claim his victim. Perfectly paced, the story's closing lines, far removed from the brutality of the demise of Mrs Amworth, demonstrate the author's mastery of the eventual reveal and revelation of the final horror:

> Half an hour later Dick arrived. To his amazement he heard that a man had called for his wife not long before, and that she had gone out with him. He seemed to be a stranger here, for the boy who had taken his message to her had never seen him before, and presently surprise began to deepen into alarm; inquiries were made outside the hotel, and it appeared that a witness or two had seen the lady whom they knew to be staying there walking, hatless, along the top of the beach with a man whose arm was linked in hers...The direction of the search thus became narrowed down, and though with a lantern to supplement the moonlight they came upon footprints which might have been hers, there were no marks of any who walked beside her. But they followed these until they came to an end, a mile away, in a great landslide of sand, which had fallen from the old churchyard on the cliff, and had brought down with it half the tower and a gravestone, with the body that had lain below.
>
> The gravestone was that of Roger Wyburn, and his body lay by it, untouched by corruption or decay, though two hundred years had elapsed since it was interred there. For a week afterwards the work of searching the landslide went on, assisted by the high tides that gradually washed it away. But no further discovery was made.

Benson's cleverly simple style lays bare the erotic corruption inherent in the vampire myth and projects it with ease into the contemporary world. Hester Ward, the young woman entranced and led to her death, is a willing victim and there is a clear and breathless urgency in her rushed night walk along the cliffs, oblivious of the darkness and its dangers. Such is the need of both the vampire and its victim: the former's bloodlust and the latter's desire and inability to break free from the ultimate will.

The template for *The Face* had in fact been set down twelve years before in what is arguably E.F. Benson's most well-known supernatural story, another vampire tale that has appeared in numerous anthologies since its initial publication in a three-story collection in 1912. *The Room in the Tower* uses the prophetic dream scenario to great effect, unfolding and building with a cumulative power created through a carefully crafted combination of both chilling atmosphere and visceral shock horror effects. From a young age, the narrator dreams of visiting a school friend in a large red-brick mansion in the country which is dominated by the presence of the family matriarch, the sinister Julia Stone. In each episode of the dream, Benson describes his hero's arrival at the estate where afternoon tea is laid out on the lawn. The gathering sits unspeaking with a mounting sense 'of dreadful oppression and foreboding' until finally Mrs Stone breaks the silence and delivers the chilling line which becomes a mantra throughout the entire story: 'Jack will show you your room: I have given you the room in the tower.' The building in question is a three-storey structure located some distance away adjacent to a cemetery which appears to be much older in appearance than the main house. At this point, the narrator becomes fearful:

> Jack instantly got up, and I understood that I had to follow him. In silence we passed through the hall, and mounted a great oak staircase with many corners, and arrived at a small landing with two doors set in it. He pushed one of these open for me to enter, and without coming in himself, closed it behind me. Then I knew that my conjecture had been right: there was something awful in the room ...

Thankfully for the dreamer this is the moment where the nightmare ends and the narrator awakes 'in a spasm of terror'. The same vision occurs with subtle variations over a period of fifteen years: family members age and come and go, on occasion the gathering is held inside the house instead of on the lawn (where Benson includes a brief mention of an eerie card game played with sinister-looking black playing cards), and in its final stages Mrs Stone is absent, having died and been buried in the cemetery alongside the tower. However, the woman's presence still dominates the proceedings and her disembodied voice continues to break the silence and initiate the dreaded walk to the haunted room.

Finally, with an uncanny and inevitable sense of déjà vu, the storyteller, now in his early thirties, travels down to Sussex to stay with a friend who has rented a house for the summer. Stepping out of the car, 'with a sudden thrill, partly of fear but chiefly of curiosity, I found myself standing in the doorway of my house of dream', which is reproduced in life down to the smallest detail. A house party is in full swing and the only bedroom available is of course the dreaded room in the tower in which hangs a self-portrait of the evil Julia Stone, 'old and withered and white haired' and which exhibits a malign vitality 'that foamed and frothed with unimaginable evil'. Despite the painting being removed physically from the room, its corruptive influence remains, and here the world of the supernatural undead begins to make entry into real time and space: as the men manhandle the portrait out through the door, their hands come away from its frame smeared with blood. That night, the story reaches its climax in what, even after repeated readings, remains one of supernatural literature's most chilling and powerful moments:

> I sprang out of bed, upsetting the small table that stood by it, and I heard my watch, candle, and matches clatter on to the floor. But for the moment there was no need of light, for a blinding flash leaped out of the clouds, and showed me that by my bed again hung the picture of Mrs Stone. But in that flash I saw another thing also, namely a figure that leaned over the end of my bed, watching me. It was dressed in some close-clinging white garment, spotted and stained with mould, and the face was that of the portrait … 'I knew you would come to the room in the tower,' it said. 'I have been long waiting for you. At last you have come. Tonight I shall feast; before long we will feast together.' At that the terror, which I think had paralysed me for the moment, gave way to the wild instinct of self-preservation. I hit wildly with both arms, kicking out at the same moment, and heard a little animal squeal, and something dropped with a thud beside me. I took a couple of steps forward, nearly tripping up over whatever it was that lay there, and by the merest good luck found the handle of the door. In another second I ran out on the landing, and had banged the door behind me…

Unlike the protagonist in *The Face*, in this instance the hero survives and the story's final reveal shows Benson's subtle blending of both fact and fantasy: Julia Stone is a suicide (victims of which were historically staked through the heart and buried at crossroads to prevent their return into the world of the living) who took her own life in the haunted room years before, and her coffin, when exhumed, is found to be full of blood, a gruesome set piece previously used by Le Fanu in *Carmilla* and which has an historical precedent in the writings of Walter Map and Dom Augustin Calmet (1672–1757), a French Roman Catholic scholar and vampire authority, author of the notable 1746 study *Dissertation on Apparitions*. Benson's only other vampire-themed story is the much later 'And No Bird Sings' from 1928 which, like its predecessor *Negotium Perambulans*, describes a non-human menace, in this instance a giant blood-drinking leech.

Despite the success of *The Lair of the White Worm*, Bram Stoker's most well-known tale after *Dracula* is the closely related *Dracula's Guest*, a short story published posthumously in April 1914 by his widow Florence in a compendium (*Dracula's Guest and Other Weird Stories*) that contains genre pieces such as *The Judge's House*, *The Squaw* and *The Secret of the Growing Gold*. Often considered to be one of the original opening chapters of *Dracula*, subsequently excised from the main text, either at the request of the publisher in an attempt to shorten what still amounts to a very long novel, or by the author himself to avoid comparison with *Carmilla*, which it closely resembles in both style and content, the origins and provenance of *Dracula's Guest* are in fact obscure and the possibility remains that, even with the obvious connections to its parent novel, it may not in fact be by Stoker at all.

Travelling through the Austrian mountains on his way to Castle Dracula, Jonathan Harker ignores the strident advice of both a local hotelier and his own coach driver, and ventures out alone on foot on the eve of Walpurgis Night to explore a ruined village located some distance off the main highway down a little used and locally shunned road. Caught in a snowstorm, Harker takes shelter in a lonely wood where he discovers the imposing mausoleum of the Countess Dolingen of Gratz and witnesses a vision of the dead woman rising from the tomb as the entire monument is struck and destroyed by lightning. Saved from being frozen to death by a huge wolf (by implication Dracula himself in animal form) which stands guard over his prostrate body and warms the Englishman with its fur, Harker is rescued by a company of Austrian cavalrymen who escort him back to Munich where a telegram is waiting from the Count, announcing that his guest is to be protected at all costs; at which point the traveller collapses into the arms of the maître d'hôtel.

A brief but effective piece which makes use of material set down at an early stage by Stoker in his pre-planning phase of his novel, *Dracula's Guest* has become a staple contribution of many vampire-themed collections. Whether Stoker prepared the short story treatment himself from what amounted to an excised chapter of the main book, or it was ghost written after his death, possibly at the behest of his publisher keen to establish a hook to sell the remaining collection of tales, remains a mystery. On 14 September 1927, on the occasion of the 250th London performance of the *Dracula* stage play, each member of the audience at the Prince of Wales Theatre received one of 1,000 specially printed and bound presentation copies of *Dracula's Guest* which, when opened, contained a black paper bat which startled the reader by flying out of the cover on a length of elastic.

Bram Stoker's relationship with Sir Arthur Conan Doyle dated from 1894, when Henry Irving took the role of Corporal Gregory Brewster in the Lyceum's production of *Waterloo*. A master of mystery and thriller writing, justly famous for adventure yarns such as *The Lost World* (1912) and the creation of Sherlock Holmes, a handful of Doyle's short stories feature expressly supernatural subjects: *Lot No. 249* from 1892 describes the account of an Egyptian mummy, brought back to life and sent on a mission of murder; *The Terror of Blue John Gap* (1910) is a vicious carnivorous creature that survives into the modern world in a lonely cave; while grotesque jelly-like monsters populate the stratosphere in the later tale, *The Horror of the Heights* (1913). An early novella, *The Parasite*, published in 1894, features an elderly spinster whose paranormal powers on occasion cross the threshold into the territory of psychic vampirism, but Doyle resisted the post-*Dracula* fashion of several of his British contemporaries and never produced a true full-blooded vampire story. *The Adventure of the Sussex Vampire*, first published in *The Strand Magazine* in January 1924 and later the same year as one of a dozen stories that make up *The Case Book of Sherlock Holmes*, is a vampire in name only in which a stepmother seen to suck blood from her baby son's neck is in fact saving his life by drawing out the poison from a blow dart fired by his jealous stepbrother. The story is now most famous for Holmes' strident trashing of the vampire myth in an early retort to the faithful Dr Watson: 'Rubbish, Watson, rubbish! What have we to do with walking corpses who can only be held in their graves by stakes driven through their hearts? It's pure lunacy.'

One Englishman who did believe in the reality of the paranormal and claimed to have had personal experience of the world of the unseen was Robert Thurston Hopkins (1884–1958), a regional writer and founder of the Society of Sussex Downsmen, who wrote about his own ghost-hunting activities in books such as *Adventures with Phantoms* (1946), *Ghosts Over England* (1953) and *Cavalcade of Ghosts* (1956). As well as having at one time the allegedly haunted skull of the famous Red Barn murderer William Corder as a family heirloom, Thurston Hopkins' most well-known real-life ghost is his claim to have encountered the apparition of a hanged man in an isolated wood near Burwash on two occasions in the early 1930s (*see Extreme Hauntings*, pp.121-130). Thurston Hopkins contributed at least one fictional story to the canon of British vampire literature, *The Vampire of Woolpit Grange*, published in 1938 in which the bloodthirsty seventeenth-century sorceress Beatrix Springett, 'a witch who walked on the left side of the sun', returns from beyond the grave after the new owner of the eponymous house of the title unwittingly kisses her portrait on the lips while in a somnambulistic trance. The tale is notable for featuring the Van Helsing-like psychical researcher, Forbes Nichols, as well as references to contemporary psychic literature, specifically the spiritualist journal, *Light*. In his later *Cavalcade of Ghosts*, a collection of both true and fictional ghost stories, he includes another story with an undead theme, *The Riddle of the Thetford Vampire*, written ostensibly by another contributor, Michael Saltmarsh, which features a psychic detective, Valentine Vaughn, who is called in to investigate a mysterious plague of bats which have descended on the owners of a Norfolk country house. The book contains two other stories by Saltmarsh, *Old Godet's Ghost* and *Haunted Hands*, all of which, including the vampire yarn, are likely to have been written by Thurston Hopkins himself using a pseudonym.

What in many respects was a golden era for British vampire literature was ultimately to be tempered by the outbreak of the First World War. What potential classics to this and other horror genres were obliterated by the slaughter will never be known. William Hope Hodgson, killed at the age of 40 at Ypres in April 1918, was one such fantasy writer who never lived to see the Armistice. Now revered for such towering classics as *The House on the Borderland* (1908), *The Night Land* (1912), and for the creation of Carnacki the Ghost Finder, a psychic Sherlock Holmes, the lamia-like spectres of Hodgson's novel *The Ghost Pirates*, published in 1909 and using his own experiences as a sailor for much of its detail, perhaps comes closest to what could be considered as a traditional undead tale from his particular pen.

As the years advanced away from the 1897 watershed, the initial impetus supplied by the publication of *Dracula* began to lessen and authors either became disinterested or began to represent the vampire myth in other ways. Brian Frost (in *The Monster With a Thousand Faces*) lists several British writers who attempted to expand the vampire in literature through the inter-war years including Alexander Huth, writing under the pseudonym of M.Y. Halidom (*The Woman in Black*, 1906), Reginald Hodder

(*The Vampire*, 1913), William F. Harvey (*Miss Avenal*, 1920), Henry Carew (*The Vampires of the Andes*, 1925), Lady Eleanor Smith (*Satan's Circus*, 1932), Lewis Spence (*The Red Flasket*, 1932), Walter Starkie (*The Old Man's Story*, 1933), and Florence Mayor's *Fifteen Charlotte Street* (1935). Writers from this period attempted to vary or broaden the vampire concept in other directions, often using variations of the 'psychic vampirism' theme from pre-*Dracula* days that we have already encountered. However, as Frost notes in his monumental study, the lack of a pulp-horror medium, which through publications such as *Weird Tales and Astounding Stories*, both reinvented the horror genre and provided the platform for the establishment of modern science fiction by allowing such influential writers as H.P. Lovecraft, August Derleth, Seabury Quinn, Clark Ashton Smith, Robert E. Howard and Robert Bloch to place their manuscripts, denied Britain the burst of fresh creativity and inspiration that was afforded to American literature in the 1920s and '30s.

In England, popular thriller writing during this period occasionally embraced the vampire theme although in the main it did little in the way of reinvention or expansion of ideas. In 1928, Sydney Horler (1888–1954), a London-born journalist turned thriller author published *The Curse of Doone*, an espionage adventure on which was grafted several undead motives such as a plague of vampire bats and a terrible family legend, that of the Varney-inspired 'Vampire of Doone Hall'. Here genuine supernaturalism was missing but two years later, Horler used the instance of the writing of Doone to fashion a short story, *The Believer*, in which a young man is driven to murder by the influence of an evil vampire-like entity. In 1935, Horler drafted a full-length novel which featured Count Ziska, a Satanist vampire from Sovrania, against which he pitted the forces of good as represented by the Van Helsing-inspired slayer, Paul Metternich. *The Vampire*, a mixture of Stokerian clichés and pot boiler action adventure, added Black Magic into the mix most likely as an attempt to ride on the coat tails of Dennis Wheatley's *The Devil Rides Out* that had appeared the previous year and which quickly established itself as a modern classic. A former Mayfair wine merchant, Wheatley, the young lion, later dubbed by *The Times Literary Supplement* as the 'Prince of Thriller Writers', went on to write over sixty books; although, only a handful of these are the occult novels which in the main keep his name alive today. Despite great personal knowledge and erudition in the field of the Black Arts, the only reference to the subject of vampirism in any of his books is a brief note in his non-fiction coffee table guide, *The Devil and All His Works*, published by Hutchinson in 1974, who also issued *The Devil Rides Out* and Horler's *The Vampire.*

Unlike Sydney Horler, whose macho all-English heroes and prejudiced opinions have consigned him with practically little exception to obscurity, our final inter-war author, Frederick Cowles (1900-48) is a little known writer whose supernatural stories have experienced something of a renaissance in recent years and are now considered of particular merit to the genre. An antiquarian and ghost story collector, Cowles issued two anthologies of his own tales during his lifetime:

The Horror of Abbot's Grange (1936) and the later *The Night Wind Howls* from 1938. *The Horror of Abbot's Grange* is in fact the disgraced sixteenth-century Cistercian monk, Lord William Salton, whose human sacrifices and Satanic meddlings have resulted in his survival beyond the grave as one of the undead, released from his family tomb by the estate's new and unsuspecting tenants who ignore a proviso in the lease not to leave the chapel door unlocked after sundown. As well as the literary influences of writers such as E.F. Benson and M.R. James, Cowles also drew on the emerging cinematic medium for inspiration, as clearly demonstrated in *The Vampire of Kaldenstein* from his second anthology whose central character is a barely disguised pastiche of Hungarian actor Bela Lugosi (*see* Chapter 7). Cowles' third and finest vampire tale is *Princess of Darkness* which lay unpublished for nearly fifty years before its inclusion by Richard Dalby in the 1987 compendium of lost vampire stories, *Dracula's Brood.* Set in Budapest before the Second World War, it describes the unhappy fate of English diplomat Harvey Gorton who is sent on a mission by the British Government to investigate the mysterious Princess Besenyei, a Hungarian aristocrat whose appearances in fashionable society leave a trail of dead and blood-drained suitors in her wake. Despite destroying her 400-year-old father, Prince Lorand, with a stake to the heart, Gorton, who has been entranced by the vampiress with a bite on the mouth, is driven mad by his experience and finally succumbs to her deadly attack when an asylum nurse accidentally breaks the chain holding a small crucifix around his neck, his one and only protection.

Forged by the imagination, undead horrors such as the Princess Besenyei, Julia Stone, Count Magnus and Mrs Amworth are easily banished by the flick of a light switch and a turn of the page. For the next part of our survey we cross the threshold and enter the darkest and most disturbing chapter of British vampire history, when in the minds of the disturbed, the deranged and the heartless, the myth becomes a chilling and horrific reality.

5

The Vampire Murderers

(1920s-2012)

On Friday, 2 August 2002, the jury at Mold Crown Court in Flintshire, North Wales, returned a unanimously guilty verdict in the case of Matthew Hardman, a 17-year-old art student from Llanfairpwll, on trial for the brutal murder of an Anglesey pensioner. Nine months before, on 25 November 2001, Mabel Leyshon, a widow aged 90, was found dead by a meals-on-wheels volunteer in her home, an attractive bungalow called Ger-Y-Twr on Lon Pant: the body had been ritualistically mutilated and two household fire pokers placed at the feet in the shape of a cross. Earlier in the year, the case had been featured on the prominent BBC *Crimewatch* television programme during which Alan Jones, a detective superintendant with the North Wales police, described Mabel Leyshon's death as 'the most horrific murder' he had seen in over twenty-five years of police work.

On the day of the killing, Hardman, who over the previous two years had delivered newspapers to the widow's house and also lived with his mother and her partner a short distance away, broke in through a rear door and stabbed the elderly woman to death as she sat watching television; he then moved the body to another chair and cut out the heart, which he then wrapped in newspaper and placed in a saucepan, after which the murderer then drank a quantity of blood that was drained into the same pan from a wound on the victim's leg. Hardman, the 'vampire' killer, as he was quickly dubbed by the press, was arrested in January 2002 after a kitchen knife and a pair of training shoes, both with forensic evidence linking them to the crime scene, were found in his possession.

As the fourteen-day trial progressed, it became clear that the vampire label was not simply a journalistic appellation but part of a chilling reality as a picture began to emerge of the youth's obsessive search for immortality through a fascination with vampirism and the life-extending cult of the undead.

Born in Amlwch on the north Anglesey coast, Hardman had moved to Llanfairpwll in 1998 aged 13. The same year his father, who was separated from the family, died of an asthma attack; the two were close and the teenager was troubled by the loss. At the age of 16, Hardman enrolled on an art and design course at Menai College in Bangor and began working as a part-time kitchen porter in a local hotel. It was at this time that he began cultivating a gruesome interest in blood and weaponry as well as the fascination with vampirism and Black Magic that was gradually to grow into a deadly obsession. In September 2002, Hardman confided in a 17-year-old German exchange student at a party that towns and villages with high proportions of elderly residents were the perfect hunting ground for the undead, as 'the old were easy targets' and their deaths would be put down to natural causes. After a conversation lasting two hours, the youth became violent and, convinced that the girl was also a vampire, pinned her to the bed and begged to be bitten in the neck. Arrested for a breach of the peace, Hardman subsequently blamed the incident on a cannabis habit and was let off with a caution. At his trial, the arresting officer, Sergeant Nicholson, recalled Hardman punching himself in the face and asking the policeman to smell the blood running from his nose. At the time of the murder, Hardman had completed one full term at Bangor, a favourite painter being the Mexican artist Frida Kahlo, although his own portfolio of work reflected a growing preoccupation with grotesque and macabre imagery. His trial for murder lasted fourteen days. Summing up, the judge, Mr Justice Richards, described the killing as a 'planned and carefully calculated attack' and sentenced Hardman to a minimum of twelve years' imprisonment.

The following year, another trial with vampiric overtones took place at the High Court in Edinburgh when unemployed security guard Allan Menzies, aged 22, stood accused of the murder of a childhood friend, Thomas McKendrick, whose decomposed body had been discovered in a shallow grave in woodland at Fauldhouse Moor on 18 January 2003. In 1996, aged 14, Menzies had been committed to a psychiatric unit for assaulting a school friend and a family member with a knife, where he spent three years being treated for a personality disorder. On his release, Menzies re-established contact with McKendrick and the two youths spent time watching films together. After viewing a copy of Australian director Michael Rymer's 2002 adaptation of Anne Rice's novel *The Queen of the Damned* (1988), Menzies became infatuated with the story's central character Akasha, played by American singer and actress Aaliyah Haughton, who had been killed in a plane crash in the Bahamas six months before the film's release; he later admitted watching the film over 100 times and claimed that the vampire queen had visited him on several occasions. Notes on their 'conversations' were written in a copy of Rice's novel and later read out in court: 'I have chosen my fate to become a vampire,' Menzies confided. 'Blood is much too precious to be wasted on humans.' A Renfield-like reference – 'The master will come for me and he has promised to make me immortal' – was the phrase that would ultimately seal the fate of his 21-year-old friend. On 11 December 2002, Menzies attacked Thomas McKendrick with two knives as the visitor stood with his back to him in his kitchen. As he attempted to escape into an upstairs bedroom, Menzies smashed the youth into unconsciousness with a hammer and continued to rein knife blows down on his unprotected face and neck: a pathologist later reported finding forty-two separate wounds as well as nearly a dozen blows to the skull. After McKendrick was dead, the killer turned the body on its side and confessed to drinking two cups of blood from the gashed neck as well as eating a fragment of skull which had fallen onto the carpet in order to gain his immortality. 'I have got his soul,' Menzies admitted to an arresting police officer. 'There was blood everywhere and I buried him up the woods.' He claimed that the spectre of Akasha had been with him throughout the killing and at one point he had examined his own face in a mirror to ensure that his teeth were covered with blood. After an eight-day trial, Menzies was found guilty of murder and given a life sentence.

Both Matthew Hardman and Allan Menzies committed their savage crimes in the hope that the act of drinking their victims' blood would transform them into living Nosferatu. One modern killer who already believed himself to be one of the legion when he carried out a brutal slaying was American James Riva from Marshfield, Massachusetts, who, in October 1981, was given a life sentence for the murder of his disabled grandmother, 74-year-old Carmen Lopez. On 10 April the previous year, Riva, then aged 23 and who had a history of mental illness dating back to the mid-1970s, loaded bullets coated with gold paint into a rifle and shot Lopez four times through the heart as she sat incapacitated in her wheelchair before stabbing the woman multiple times in the chest with a knife. The killer then drank a quantity of blood directly from the wounds before setting the house on fire in an unsuccessful attempt to destroy incriminating evidence. Riva was arrested the following day and claimed he was inhabited by the spirit of a 700-year-old vampire who had demanded the slaughter in order to survive. Carmen Lopez was, so Riva told the Plymouth District Court, also a vampire herself who regularly drained his life blood at night while he lay asleep; the killing was, therefore, only an act of self-defence.

An examination of supernatural and Black Magic-related crimes in Britain in recent years shows that the 'vampire' madness of killers like Matthew Hardman and Allan Menzies, despite occurring almost back-to-back with one another, are in fact rare occurrences – murders with some form of occult connection are normally the result of a depressing catalogue of botched exorcisms, witchcraft crimes, alleged possessions or killings carried out for the superstitious procurement of body parts for magical purposes.

In June 1991, 20-year-old British-born Kousar Bashir was beaten to death during a week-long Islamic exorcism to rid her of what her immigrant Pakistani parents believed to be a possessing jinn or evil spirit. A post-mortem revealed a horrific catalogue of violent physical abuse including cuts and extensive bruising to the young woman's head, arms and legs, slashes between her breasts, a fractured sternum and sixteen broken ribs, one of which had penetrated through into her lung causing a fatal haemorrhage. At Manchester Crown Court in April the following year, the 'exorcist', Imam Muhammad Bashir (no relation), was found guilty of murder and sentenced to life imprisonment; an assistant was given five years for plotting to cause grievous bodily harm.

In 1975, the case of Michael Taylor from Ossett in West Yorkshire, a member of a Christian Fellowship group, made sensational newspaper headlines when the 31-year-old butcher stood trial for the brutal murder of his wife following an all-night exorcism ceremony to cast out the 'forty demons' that were allegedly causing strange and erratic behaviour. The exorcism, which took place at a church in Barnsley on the night of 5/6 October 1974, was carried out by Father Peter Vincent, an Anglican priest, together with a Methodist assistant. Taylor left the church just after dawn and immediately went to the family home, where he attacked and killed Christine Taylor: the 29-year-old housewife choked to death on her own blood after having her eyes gouged and her tongue ripped from her throat. Taylor carried out the murder with his bare hands and was found a short time afterwards walking naked through the streets covered in blood. Acquitted due to insanity, he was committed to Broadmoor and later spent time in a psychiatric unit in Bradford before being released in the early 1980s.

The first decade of the new millennium was also bookended by two high-profile child murders, each with occult and witchcraft connections. In September 2001, the torso of a Nigerian boy, subsequently named 'Adam' by police, was found floating in the River Thames close to Tower Bridge in London. Detectives investigating the crime concluded the child had been trafficked to England where he had been poisoned and then murdered as part of an occult ritual. At the time of writing, the case remains unsolved.

In March 2012, Eric Bikubi, aged 28, and his 29-year-old girlfriend, Magalie Bamu, both originally from the Democratic Republic of Congo, were jailed for life for the sadistic witchcraft murder of Bamu's younger brother, Kristy Bamu, who was found drowned in the bath at the couple's flat in Newham, East London. The 15-year-old youth had been savagely beaten and tortured over the course of a three-day 'ritual' after being accused of bringing evil spirits and misfortune into the family.

Another British victim of a vampire cult murder was 16-year-old Stacey Mitchell, originally from the village of West Moors in Dorset, who emigrated with her family to Perth in Western Australia in 2001. In December 2006, the teenager was staying in a shared house at number 14 Rutland Avenue, Laithlain, with a lesbian couple, unemployed Jessica Stasinowsky, aged 21, and her partner, Valerie Parashumti, two years her junior, both of whom held a sexual obsession for bloodletting and similar vampire-like fantasies. During the course of Sunday 17 December, neighbours in an adjoining block of flats became aware of a loud argument together with high-volume music and laughter coming from the house that carried on for most of the day. However, raucous parties and abusive behaviour from the couple were commonplace and at the time the disturbance was considered to be nothing out of the ordinary.

Soon Stacey's parents, Ian and Sophie Mitchell, became concerned about their daughter's absence – the teenager had effectively run away from home a short while before but had expressed a recent desire to return – and contacted the Perth police. Four days after the Sunday disturbances, officers discovered the teenager's body locked inside a sweltering outbuilding; Stacey had been dumped head first into a rubbish bin and was so badly decomposed the identity was only discovered through dental records.

At Perth Magistrates' Court, both Jessica Stasinowsky and Valerie Parashumti pleaded guilty to murder, having battered the English girl over the head with a concrete slab and strangling her with a metal dog chain after Stasinowsky had become jealous that Mitchell was attempting to steal away her lover's affections. The couple admitted to becoming sexually aroused by the sight of the teenager's bloody and disfigured body and had filmed much of the attack using a mobile phone, while a recording of J.S. Bach's 'St John Passion' was played a high volume on the hi-fi to cover up the sounds of the slaughter. Both women considered themselves to be vampires, Parashumti having experimented with blood-drinking – first her own, then that of others – since the age of 10. For their vampiric thrill killing, both were sentenced to over thirty years in prison.

In January 2012, Australia's most notorious 'vampire' murder case, one that also showcased a lesbian blood-drinking cult, once again made media headlines around the world when 46-year-old Tracey Wigginton was released from jail after serving twenty-two years for the murder of Brisbane council worker Edward Baldock. In 1989, Wigginton and her lover Lisa Ptachinski, together with two other women, lured their victim to an isolated river bank in the suburb of West End with the promise of sexual favours. There, Wigginton attacked the semi-inebriated Baldock with a knife, killing him with nearly thirty powerful blows that left the head almost completely severed. As the other women looked on, Wigginton drank drafts of blood from the dead man's ruptured throat.

Fortunately for the public at large, but not it must be said for their deeply tragic victims, 'vampire' killers such as Wigginton, Parashumti, Menzies and Hardman, were only able to fuel their deadly bloodlust on a single occasion before being apprehended and brought to justice. But the sweeping scourge of vampirism, born as writer Anthony Masters has noted from 'the cold and foetid breath of superstition', with its plague-like connotations both real and imagined, implies a landscape of darkness littered with a trail of multiple victims, so it should be no surprise that when projected into a violent contemporary world, the legend of the vampire has a natural affinity with the thoughts, minds and actions of that most contemporary of criminal stereotypes, the serial killer.

The crimes of many multiple murderers have vampiric associations or have been described as those of modern living vampires. A disturbing glimpse inside the mind of one such killer whose obsession with the world of the undead became a deadly reality is given in the case of Roderick Ferrell from Murray, Kentucky, who killed a middle-aged couple, the parents of a long-time female friend, who were bludgeoned to death with a crowbar in their home on 25 November 1996. Like James Riva, Ferrell claimed in reality to be a centuries-old vampire creature – 'Vesago', the 'ninth crowned Prince of Hell' – and was the semi-official leader of a group of dysfunctional teenage cultists, the 'Vampire Clan', all of whom received imprisonment for their involvement in the crime. Ferrell himself initially received a death sentence, subsequently commuted to life without parole. Ferrell was quite clear as to what it meant to be, in his words, a 'sanguinary vampire'. 'It equates to the life, it equates to power,' he admitted in a recorded interview while on Death Row in Florida's State Prison. 'It equates to the very foundation of existence; it's the Communion, it's the Holy Wafer on the tongue.'

America's most notorious 'vampire' murderer was Richard Trenton Chase, a schizophrenic misfit originally from Santa Clara County, California, who killed six people including a 22-month-old child during the winter of 1977/78 in various suburbs of Sacramento. Chase both drank the blood and ate parts of the bodies of all but one of his victims, believing that his own body would disintegrate unless he replenished it with the organs and blood of others. Originally satisfied with animal mutilation he eventually gravitated to human murder. On 29 December 1977, Chase killed a 51-year-old man in a drive-by shooting in a suburb of East Sacramento. A month later he attacked a young pregnant woman, Teresa Wallin, aged 22, in her home, shooting her dead before mutilating and raping the body. On 27 January 1978, Chase rampaged through the house of 38-year-old housewife Evelyn Miroth, killing her as well as her 6-year-old son Jason and a middle-aged male neighbour; Miroth's body was violently assaulted and mutilated. Chase escaped from the house, taking with him the body of Evelyn Miroth's young nephew David Ferreira who had been murdered in his crib; his headless body was found three months later dumped in a cardboard box in an alleyway next to a church, by which time the killer had been arrested.

On 8 May 1978, Richard Chase was sentenced to death on six counts of first-degree murder, a defence plea of insanity having been rejected by a jury horrified and sickened by accounts of blood drinking and cannibalism. Just over six months later, the 'Vampire of Sacramento' was found dead in his cell in California's San Quentin State Prison having cheated the gas chamber with an overdose of hoarded Sinequan tablets; he was 29 years old.

Over sixty years before 'Vesago' drove Roderick Ferrell to commit his crimes, a German factory worker in his mid-forties had already become one of the twentieth century's most notorious vampire serial killers. On 2 July 1931 at Cologne's Klingelpütz Prison, Peter Kürten was executed for a series of savage sex crimes against children and young women which earned him the various titles 'Monster of Düsseldorf' and 'The Düsseldorf Vampire'. Kürten was convicted of nine murders but admitted to a catalogue of shocking atrocities including bestiality, human rape and physical assault with a hammer, all of which caused a wave of public panic in the city between early 1929 and May 1930, reminiscent of the hysteria that had surrounded the Whitechapel murders of Jack the Ripper in London in 1888. A violent sadist who obtained sexual satisfaction both at the sight of blood and the achievement of killing and humiliating his victims, Kürten claimed to have carried out his first murder while only a schoolboy, drowning two fellow playmates by pushing them off a raft into a river. Later he began attacking and assaulting sheep and cattle, on one occasion decapitating a sleeping swan in order to drink the blood from its severed neck. Kürten strangled a young child to death during the course of a burglary shortly before the beginning of the First World War, but his reign of terror proper began several years later in February 1929, when he attacked and killed a 9-year-old girl and partially burnt her body. In November of the same year, by which time he had committed several more killings, Kürten murdered a 5-year-old girl in the rural district of Papendelle with a pair of scissors and sent a hand-drawn map to a local newspaper identifying the location of her body. This was his last killing, but the hammer attacks and rapes continued into the following year when, in the spring of 1930, the 'Düsseldorf Vampire' was caught by chance. In May 1930, Kürten picked up a woman traveller at the city railway station and took her first to his lodging house and then to the Grafenberger Forest, where he carried out a sexual assault but let his victim go when she promised him that she didn't know the area well enough to identify him or where he had taken her. The woman, Maria Budlick, wrote to a female confidant about the incident but her wrongly addressed letter went undelivered and when eventually opened by Post Office staff, officials realised its significance and took it straight to the Düsseldorf police. Budlick took officers to a house on the Mettmännerstrasse, where they arrested Kürten on the stairs as he was leaving to go to work. The killer and rapist had in fact been leading a double life as his wife Maria, as well as local residents, considered the husband and neighbour to be the mildest of men who attended church services regularly and took part in local trade union activities.

Peter Kürten's life of sadism and horror was recorded by prison psychiatrist Karl Berg, who later published a full-length account of his crimes. In his book *The Natural History of the Vampire*, first published in 1972, Anthony Masters quotes a German court reporter, M.S. Wagner, who covered the Kürten trial for one of the national newspapers: 'The most extraordinary and horrible point about Kürten's nocturnal prowling lay in the association with the vampire and werewolf of ancient tradition. It was his habit, and his principal satisfaction to receive the stream of blood that gushed from his victim's wounds into his mouth.' A vampire to the very end, Peter Kürten went to his death on a guillotine which had seen service during the French Revolution, walking 'heroically' onto the scaffold after having been told by a prison doctor that there was a medical possibility he might achieve what was for him the ultimate desire: of hearing his own blood running into the basket as the heavy blade cut through his neck. Today, as his victims pass into obscurity, 'The Düsseldorf Vampire' has achieved his own form of living death as Kürten's dissected and mummified head, formerly part of the collection of crime historian Arne Coward, survives as a gruesome relic on display at The Wisconsin Dells 'Ripley's Believe It or Not!' museum in America.

A similar wave of public hysteria and outrage took place in London nearly 120 years earlier when John Williams, an Irish labourer in his twenties, committed the notorious Ratcliffe Highway Murders, when two entire East End families totalling seven people were brutally murdered within days of one another in December 1810. Williams was seen walking towards the King's Arms public house in New Gravel Lane where the publican, Mr Williamson, his wife and their maidservant, Bridget Harrington, were soon found hacked and bludgeoned to death, and later returned to his lodgings in the early hours with a bloodstained shirt. Earlier, the Marr family had been discovered a short distance away in their house on Ratcliffe Highway, beaten to death and their throats cut. Williams was interrogated at Shadwell police station but on 28 December he took his own life by hanging himself from a rail in his cell. Three days later his body was paraded on a cart through the streets and subsequently buried in quicklime at a crossroads near present-day Cable Street. Befitting the savagery of his crimes, a wooden stake was driven through his heart, pinning the corpse to the earth before the grave was filled in.

In his *A Criminal History of Mankind* (1984), Colin Wilson discusses the interesting geographical segregation of human murder, noting the French association with crimes of passion, the prevalence of randomness in American spree killings, and the English love of planned and carefully crafted crimes. The German predilection for brutal and sadistic murder, amply demonstrated by the horrors of the Kürten case, is also matched by those of fellow countryman Friedrich H.K. (Fritz) Haarmann, the 'Butcher of Hanover', another serial killer with vampire associations, who murdered at least twenty-four teenage boys and young men between September 1918 and his arrest on 22 June 1923. Haarmann, a homosexual black market meat trader and sometime police informer, prowled Hanover's railway station and gay cafés, befriending young drifters and wartime refugees who would be enticed back to his lodgings in a house on the Neuestrasse. There Haarmann and his accomplice, Hans Grans, a career criminal and male prostitute in his mid-twenties, killed, stripped and cut up the bodies, disposing of the clothes and selling the flesh for human consumption, on one occasion, cooking and eating sausages made from one of his victims in his tiny kitchen with a client. The killer clearly enjoyed the taste of human blood, admitting to biting the men in the neck as they were strangled to death. Amazingly, other residents in the building were oblivious to the murderous activities and over a period of sixteen months, Haarmann and Grans claimed an estimated two victims a week.

In the late spring and early summer of 1924, human skulls and bones comprising parts of over twenty bodies were discovered washed up on the foreshore of the River Leine. On 22 July, a youth went to the Hanover police accusing Haarmann of indecent behaviour and detectives paid him a visit. When the officers searched the small attic apartment they discovered clothing and articles belonging to numerous missing men; the walls of the room were also heavily bloodstained. The 'Butcher' or 'Hanover Vampire' as he became known in the German press, was quickly arrested and confessed to the crimes, implicating Grans in the murders who later stood trial with Haarmann at the Hanover Assizes accused between them of twenty-seven killings. The hearing lasted fourteen days and 130 witnesses were called to give evidence. Grans escaped with his life and was given twelve years' imprisonment; Fritz Haarmann was not so fortunate and went to his death, executed by the sword, on 15 April 1925, aged 45. Like Peter Kürten, his severed head was preserved for posterity and today survives as an exhibit at a medical school in Göttingen, sixty miles south of Hanover.

Writing in his *The Vampire: His Kith and Kin*, published two years after Haarmann's death, Montague Summers, who we will encounter in detail in the next chapter, described the crimes at the time as being 'probably one of the most extraordinary cases of vampirism known'. In the extended sense of the word, 'Fritz Haarmann was a vampire in every particular,' Summers concluded, noting that it was more than coincidence that the mass murderer met his end by decapitation, 'one of the efficacious methods of destroying a vampire'. The reality was that the true death toll in the Neuestrasse killings was most likely much higher; Haarmann himself thought the total was nearer forty.

One 'vampire' serial killer who casts the longest shadow down through the years is the now notorious Erzsébet or Elizabeth Báthory, a sixteenth-century Hungarian/Slovakian noblewoman known today by various titles such as 'The Blood Countess' and the 'female Dracula'. An obscure figure in the West for over 350 years following her death in 1614, Báthory achieved a renaissance and rediscovery in the early 1960s as tales of her vampire-like activities entered popular culture, first through modern biographies by writers including Valentine Penrose and Donald Glut, but most effectively via screen adaptations of varying accuracy, the most successful of which, Hammer's *Countess Dracula* (1970), we will encounter in more detail in a later chapter.

Born in 1560 to privileged parents, at the age of 14, Erzsébet married Count Ferenc Nadasdy, a Hungarian military officer and nobleman, and the couple established their home in Ĉachtice Castle, an imposing clifftop stronghold overlooking the Slovakian village of the same name, built in the thirteenth century to protect the trade route through the mountains from Moravia. While her husband was away fighting in the Ottoman-Hungarian Wars, Countess Nadasdy developed an appetite for sadism and sexual torture: young female serving staff began disappearing at an alarming rate as initially brutal punishments for trivial or minor failures of duty eventually escalated into a covert killing spree lasting several years. In his *The Vampire Book* (1999), J. Gordon Melton suggests that Ferenc Nadasdy both approved and encouraged his wife's sadistic behaviour and that after his death in January 1604, she spent a period of six years – up until her arrest in the late December of 1610 – perpetrating an orgy of bloody and murderous violence that according to some accounts claimed the lives of over 600 young women. In early January 1611, Erzsébet's estate and land were confiscated and the 'Blood Countess' herself was sentenced to life imprisonment, walled up within a chamber inside Ĉachtice Castle with only narrow gaps in the brickwork for ventilation and feeding; accomplices amongst her staff were immediately executed. Erzsébet survived in solitary confinement for three years but was eventually found dead on 21 August 1614.

Much has latterly been written about the Countess' literal bloodbaths and her psychotic addiction for immersion in the blood of her victims in the vain belief that it rejuvenated her fading looks, and although writers including Sean Manchester, Dan Farson, Donald F. Glut, Peter Underwood and Anthony Masters have committed the legend to print in various commentaries, there is no smoking gun evidence to support the claims other than that Erzsébet was a sadistic killer who, through a titled and privileged position, was able to indulge her deadly and perverted fantasies to the full, aided by a series of cohorts who most likely shared a similar penchant for brutality.

Returning to British shores, one English serial killer now most often identified with vampirism is John George Haigh, a 39-year-old petty criminal turned murderer described by a national newspaper during the course of his trial in 1948 as the 'Vampire of London' but known more consistently to both criminologists and the public alike as the 'Acid Bath Murderer'.

Haigh was born in Stamford, Lincolnshire, in 1909 to strict Plymouth Brethren parents. A bright and talented child he won a scholarship to Wakefield Grammar School and later a musical scholarship, singing in the choir at Wakefield Cathedral. Despite this promising start and an affinity for mechanics and engineering, Haigh quickly gravitated to a life of crime that led ultimately to the deaths of six people and for Haigh himself numerous prison sentences and a final appointment with the hangman. In 1930 he was suspected of theft and four years later, despite marrying and fathering a child, was jailed at the age of 25 for fraud. Abandoned by his wife and his own family, Haigh spent a ten-year period practising as a fraudster for financial gain but was invariably caught out and spent lengthy periods in prison. By 1944 he was living (again by illegal means) at the fashionable Onslow Court Hotel in Brompton Road, South Kensington, at the same time renting a basement room, ostensibly as a workshop, in nearby Gloucester Road. However, a chance encounter with the son of a former employer in a Kensington public house was the catalyst that would quickly lead to murder.

On 9 September 1944, Haigh beat Donald McSwann – for whose father he had worked as a chauffeur in the mid-1930s – to death in his Kensington workshop and destroyed his body by hauling it into a 40-gallon steel drum that was filled with sulphuric acid; within forty-eight hours McSwann had been reduced to sludge which Haigh disposed of by pouring down a nearby manhole. The killer quickly forged documents in McSwann's name and began living off his money. Ten months later, in July 1945, the dead man's parents William and Amy McSwann visited Gloucester Road and were killed and disposed of in the same way. Haigh forged more paperwork and transferred the title deeds of various properties owned by the couple in South London and Beckenham in Kent into his name and emptied the McSwanns' bank account.

The proceeds of the double killing carried him for the next two and a half years, but by early 1948, Haigh's gambling and high living had cleared him of funds and it became necessary to murder again. On 12 February, Haigh drove Dr and Mrs Archibald Henderson, who he had met the previous year, to a small rented storeroom in Leopold Road, Crawley in West Sussex, where he shot them with the doctor's own revolver. Like the McSwanns before them, the Hendersons were destroyed in matching acid baths and Haigh sold all their possessions for £8,000. The 'Acid Bath Murderer's' final killing took place a year later when wealthy widow Mrs Olivia Durand-Deacon, a fellow resident at the Onslow Court Hotel, became convinced that Haigh's engineering skills were the key to realising an idea for creating and marketing a range of artificial fingernails. Soon 69-year-old Mrs Durand-Deacon had joined the Hendersons as human sludge tipped out into the yard of the Leopold Road 'factory' and Haigh, now confident that he had created the means to carry out the perfect murder, happily went to Chelsea police station with a fellow hotel guest to report the woman as missing. However, the duty sergeant, Policewoman Lambourne, became suspicious of Haigh's glib manner and his extensive criminal past was quickly revealed. When items connected to Mrs Durand-Deacon – a Persian lamb coat and jewellery – were found to have been in his possession after the date she was reported missing, he was arrested on 28 February 1949 and returned to Chelsea police station. While in custody, Haigh learnt that his Crawley address had been searched and that police officers had recovered a .38 Webley revolver that appeared to have been recently fired. It was then that he made a now famous outburst: 'Mrs Durand-Deacon no longer exists. I've destroyed her with acid,' Haigh told Detective-Inspector Albert Webb with confidence. 'You can't prove murder without a body.' He was wrong and it was a mistake that was to cost him his life.

Keith Simpson of Guy's Hospital, along with Harley Street's Dr Donald Teare and Professor Francis Camps of the London Hospital Medical College, made up a trio of celebrated post-war forensic pathologists known to the medical and police professions of the day as 'The Three Musketeers'. In 1942, Simpson had provided the forensic evidence that had sent wartime fire-watcher and wife murderer Harry Dobkin to the gallows and at Crawley he soon uncovered damning proof of the continued existence of the deceased Olivia Durand-Deacon's physical existence: gallstones, an acrylic denture, ankle bones, along with 28lbs of human body fat were sifted from the mud in the yard at Leopold Road in Crawley and Haigh was charged with murder. Paperwork in Haigh's room at Onslow Court soon connected him to the disappearances of the McSwanns and the Hendersons, but it was for the killing of Mrs Durand-Deacon that he was sent to trial at the Lewes Assizes in mid-July 1949.

Haigh's defence was one of insanity and while on remand in Lewes Prison he drank his own urine and began regaling Harley Street psychiatrist Dr Henry Yellowlees of shocking childhood dreams and real-life claims of human vampirism. His thirst for blood had been with him since his chorister days at Wakefield Cathedral, when a chilling and ultimately recurring nightmare of a forest of blood-spouting trees had first entered his subconscious sleep state:

> I saw a forest of crucifixes which gradually turned into trees. At first I seemed to see dew or rain running from the branches. But when I came nearer I knew it was blood. All of a sudden the whole forest began to twist about and the trees streamed with blood. Blood ran from the trunks. Blood ran from the branches, all red and shiny. I felt weak and seemed to faint. I saw a man going round the trees gathering blood. When the cup he was holding in his hand was full he came up to me and said 'drink'. But I was paralysed. The dream vanished. But I still felt faint and stretched out with all my strength towards the cup.

According to Haigh, this vision was the catalyst that had led him onto the road of murder. 'I woke up in a semi-comatose state. I always kept on seeing those hands holding out a cup to me that I couldn't quite reach, and that terrible thirst, unknown to any other modern man, never left me.' His strict and austere religious upbringing, with its salvation in the 'blood of the lamb', was, according to Yellowlees, at the core of the 'paranoid structure' that Haigh had created for himself. Haigh claimed he had refreshed himself on the blood of each of his victims, making incisions in their necks with a penknife and collecting blood in a glass; he then consumed the blood through a straw. After the 'vampire' had fed, the bodies were consigned to the acid. As well as the Hendersons, Donald McSwann and his family, and Mrs Durand-Deacon, Haigh claimed that his bloodlust had forced him to kill three other people from whom he obtained no financial gain: two women from Eastbourne and Hammersmith and a young man named 'Max'.

Not surprisingly, confessions of blood drinking and acid baths gave the popular press a field day. 'Vampire horror in London, SW7' announced the *Daily Mirror* on its front page for Thursday, 3 March 1949. 'Every available man in Scotland Yard's crime squads was working last night on the case of the Vampire Murderer,' the tabloid announced. 'For the first time in the Yard's century-old history, detectives were following clues leading to a maniac who – like the vampire of Eastern European folk-lore – drank his victim's blood'. The *Mirror*'s frenzied baying for Haigh's own blood eventually resulted in a contempt of court action which saw the newspaper fined £10,000 and its then editor, Silvester Bolam, sent to prison for three months.

The trial proper opened at Lewes Assizes on 18 July 1949 before Mr Justice Humphries; Haigh was defended by Sir David Maxwell Fyfe while Sir Hartley Shawcross appeared for the Crown. At 4.23 p.m. on the second day, the jury retired to consider their verdict – they were absent for less than twenty minutes and Haigh was found guilty of the murder of Mrs Olivia Durand-Deacon. While waiting in the condemned cell at Wandsworth Prison, Haigh wrote his memoirs, donated his suit to Madame Tussauds, and enquired as to the possibility of whether he could have a dummy run on the gallows, apparently concerned that his build and 'springy step' might give the executioner difficulties. The request was refused and the 'Vampire of London' met the real slayers on 6 August 1949 when he was hanged by Albert Pierrepoint and Harry Kirk.

Although Haigh's confessions of blood drinking clearly read like those of a desperate man stressing insanity as a last ditch attempt to avoid the death penalty, there are some who consider his vampiric status to be a true one. Writing in his *The Vampire in Legend, Fact and Art* in the early 1970s, Basil Copper stated in connection with the case: 'It [Haigh's vampirism] is something which cannot be proved through the evidence produced during the trial, for there was no evidence, but … after sifting the masses of statements made at the time, there is no doubt in my own mind that Haigh was speaking the truth.' Haigh was 'a malformed human being; a vampiric predator whose thirst for blood was slaked on at least six occasions post mortem'. 'That he is an horrific figure does not preclude him from being a sad one,' Copper concluded, adding, 'despite his forebears from the mists of the past, such as Gilles de Rais … he remains a figure mercifully unique in the twentieth century so far'. As we have seen, the cases of Richard Chase and James Riva have proved Copper to be chillingly wrong, while those of Allan Menzies and Matthew Hardman show that the British vampire murderer has survived, and in all doubt may continue to flourish well into the coming years of the new millennium.

6

The Mysterious World of Montague Summers

(1880–1948)

By the time of his sudden death, on 10 August 1948, no one was perhaps associated with the night-black world of the vampire more than Augustus Montague Summers, whose writings on the subject had by then been in print for over twenty years. Only Bram Stoker could be said to have a similar connection in the public mind. But Stoker's world was one of literary fiction, whereas Summers dealt in a world of facts, with a scholarly authority to his pen that commanded both attention and belief. When Summers wrote of the vampire, 'He is neither dead nor alive; but living in death. He is an abnormality; the androgyne in the phantom world; a pariah among the fiends', it was difficult not to imagine that indeed there are such things and that Summers, a living Van Helsing, was at the same time both the Nosferatu's greatest champion and most virulent opponent. 'Throughout the whole vast shadowy world of ghosts and demons,' he notes in the benchmark opening of his 1928 study *The Vampire: His Kith and Kin*, 'there is no figure so terrible, no figure so dreaded and abhorred, yet dight with such fearful fascination, as the vampire, who is himself neither ghost nor demon, but yet who partakes the dark natures and possess the mysterious and terrible qualities of both.' Little wonder that he is the reference point for a legion of writers who have trod the same twilight pathways over the past half century, and remains the idol of those who follow in his footsteps to proclaim the reality of the vampire creature in a modern world shorn of superstition outside of the blood-soaked printed page.

Augustus Montague Summers – bibliophile, academic, writer, occultist, editor, theologian, self-styled priest, school teacher, scholar of the English Restoration theatre, friend of Crowley and biographer of de Sade, demonologist and literary vampire hunter – led, in the words of parapsychologist D. Scott Rogo, 'a curious and mysterious life' that was almost the equal of the strange realms with which he is now forever associated.

He was born in the fashionable suburb of Clifton Down, Bristol, on 10 April 1880 to affluent middle-class parents, the youngest of seven children. The family home, Tellisford House, was a haunted building, where ghostly figures seemed to come and go and were seemingly accepted as being an inoffensive part of the genial surroundings. Summers' father, Augustus William, was a respected local dignitary, a Justice of the Peace and shareholder in Clifton Zoo, who made his name and career in banking. The seeds of his son's literary obsessions were sown in Summers senior's well-endowed private library that was a constant source of fascination from a young age. 'It was the remoteness and the sense of aloofness of the Library that always attracted me, and made it my favourite retreat,' Summers recalled over sixty years later: 'One felt shut off, and strangely individual, a kind of bookish eremite, "the world forgetting, by the world forgot."'

Religious orthodoxy, particularly its ceremonial trappings, also played a large part of Summers' life. Raised in an Anglican environment, after local education at Clifton College, he studied theology at Trinity College, Cambridge, but performed poorly, achieving only a fourth-class Bachelor of Arts degree. He had been sidetracked by book studies of an altogether different nature, namely the homoerotic literature that would accompany him and his homosexuality throughout most of his life. From Trinity, Summers went to Lichfield Theological College. On 14 June 1908 he was ordained into the Holy Order of Deacons and was soon working as a curate in Bath and shortly afterwards in the Bristol suburb of Bitton under an elderly vicar, Canon Ellacombe. By this time he had self-published his first book, a collection of risqué poetry entitled *Antinous and Other Poems* dedicated to the subject of male love, and it was while he was employed at Bitton that Summers himself was prosecuted together with another clergyman, most likely Ellacombe, for pederasty. Details of the trial appear to have been lost and although Summers was acquitted, the scandal forced his resignation and the following year he abandoned the Anglican Church and converted to Catholicism.

It was around this time – 1909 – that Summers would later claim to have had personal experience of confronting an undead menace for himself, although his public association with vampires in both fact and fiction was in reality many years away. While discussing the case of the Yorkshire Vampire with Peter Underwood at his (Summers) home in Richmond in 1947, Summers produced a brass medallion that he claimed had magical properties to ward off evil forces, and was in fact particularly effective in repelling supernatural vampires and similar creatures. How the object had come into his possession is unclear, but according to its owner it had been used with great effect on at least two previous occasions, one of these involving Summers himself.

While travelling in Italy at some point in 1909, Summers claimed he had become aware of an outbreak of vampire-like deaths in an area of Southern Transylvania and had made it his mission to carry out a personal investigation. Travelling to the region, and on the pretence of carrying out a study of the local architecture, he eventually gained access to an unnamed castle close to the area where bodies had seemingly been discovered drained of blood, and whose equally anonymous owner, a Dracula-like individual 'cold and silent', was evidently a local landowner of some wealth and power. During the course of their conversation, Summers brought up the subject of the recent vampire outbreak and casually brought the 'talisman' out of his pocket for his mysterious host to see. '[T]he effect was instantaneous,' Underwood stated when publishing the first account of the incident in the mid-1970s. 'The man's eyes blazed for a moment with anger – or fright – he shrank back and then, recovering himself, he fixed his hypnotic eyes on Summers who immediately felt his strength ebbing away.' The Englishman 'summoned all his strength and picking up the medal, he held it at arm's length before his face for protection'. At this point, his sinister assailant covered his eyes and, ringing for a manservant, Summers was shown the door. That night, in true Hollywood style, the castle was surrounded by a torch-wielding village mob and it together with all occupants was burnt to the ground. After relating the tale, Summers blessed the 'talisman' and gave it to the young ghost hunter in whose possession it remained for over sixty years. 'I found [Summers] a tall and stately man with flowing silver hair,' Underwood wrote over twenty-five years after the event. 'A kindly man who did much to awaken my interest in the occult … He believed completely in the supernatural vampire and had no doubt whatever that I would be called upon to use the talisman many times during my lifetime.'

Back in England after his alleged adventures in Transylvania, by 1913, Summers had added the Reverend Alphonsus Joseph-Mary to his title and began assuming the role of a Roman Catholic priest. The true nature of Summers' religious credentials were, then as now, a matter of conjecture and it remains a controversial subject. Summers appears not to have been a member of any particular Catholic order or diocese, but several people who knew him, including Fr Ronald Knox, a former chaplain of Trinity College, later himself a Roman Catholic, and the Revd Claude Williamson, editor of publisher Nicholson and Watson's 1938 essays on 'Great Catholics', were both convinced that he was correctly in orders. In his lecture essay 'Montague Summers' (1984), first published in 1987 in the collection *The Books of the Beast*, Oxford bibliographer and antiquarian Timothy d'Arch Smith notes that there was no doubting that Summers was a 'good theologian'. Despite being endowed with a legacy from his father, Summers still found it financially necessary to seek paid employment and shortly before the outbreak of the First World War became a schoolmaster, 'a tiring and unrewarding task' according to his biographer d'Arch Smith, teaching English and Latin at various private schools including the Central School of Arts and Crafts in Bloomsbury, Hertford Grammar School and Brockley County School. During this period, which lasted until the mid-1920s, Summers was elected a Fellow of the Royal Society of Literature and in 1918 became a founding member of The Phoenix, a London repertory company that specialised in restoring to the stage long-forgotten and neglected English plays and dramas by such dramatists as William Congreve, John Dryden and George Villiers. Actors who trod the boards for Summers and his friends included Sybil Thorndike, Dame Edith Evans and Ernest Thesiger, most familiar to horror film aficionados as mad scientist Dr Pretorius in James Whale's 1935 classic, *Bride of Frankenstein*.

A more sequestered but nonetheless contemporary role for Summers at this time was as an organiser and speaker for the British Society for the Study of Sex Psychology (BSSSP), much later known as the British Sexological Society, an obscure pressure group for homosexual equality that held regular lectures and published papers under its own auspices. Members included playwright Laurence Housman, the poet Edward Carpenter, and the physician Henry Havelock Ellis. Summers gave several lectures to the BSSSP who, in 1920, issued his paper 'The Marquis de Sade: A Study in Algolagnia'. Timothy d'Arch Smith has suggested that it was through his talks that Summers was introduced to Charles Kay Ogden, an eccentric English polymath who, at the time, was an editor for publishers Kegan Paul's *History of Civilisation* series. Ogden commissioned Summers to produce two volumes on the history of witchcraft, a subject that in previous centuries '[a]ll classes were affected and concerned from Pope to peasant, from Queen to cottage girl'. Summers set to work, drawing upon his collection of occult books that had been amassed during his teaching days over the previous fifteen years: the first volume, *The History of Witchcraft and Demonology*, was published in 1926 and a sequel, *The Geography of Witchcraft*, appeared the following year. The introduction to Summers' *History* provided the witch with a similar powerful and quotable dedication that, as we have seen, was afforded to the vampire two years later. To Summers, the modern twentieth-century witch-hunter, his quarry was:

> ... an evil liver: a social pest and parasite: the devotee of a loathly and obscene creed: an adept at poisoning, blackmail, and other creeping crimes: a member of a powerful secret organisation inimical to Church and State: a blasphemer in word and deed, swaying the villagers by terror and superstition: a charlatan and a quack sometimes: a bawd: an abortionist: the dark counsellor of lewd court ladies and adulterous gallants: a minister to vice and inconceivable corruption, battening upon the filth and foulest passions of the age.

To those whom Summers was more than a passing acquaintance would have recognised that this fiery denunciation and similar pulpit-thumping condemnations of the Black Arts and all their works represented, in effect, a forthright volte-face from certain aspects of the private world behind the veneer of Catholic respectability that had been erected before and during his schoolmastering days. Stories of Summers' heavy interest in Satanism had dogged him since his days at Lichfield College and, along with accounts of his similar interests in young boys, are most likely the reasons for his lack of progression to higher orders. One former friend who knew the hypocrisy of both Summers' words and actions was Geoffrey Evans Pickering, a young actor who, under the stage name of Anatole James, had performed in various Restoration plays at The Phoenix in the early 1920s. James, who had met Summers at the end of the First World War, was also his drinking partner and sexual confidant to whom the Reverend admitted the 'inexhaustible pleasure' and arousal provided by the corruption of devout young Catholics.

On 26 December 1918, Summers, James and a young man named Sullivan had held a Black Mass in a house in Eton Road, Hampstead. Their friendship lasted for a further four years before Summers broke off the relationship. Commenting on the about face represented by the publication of *The History of Witchcraft and Demonology*, Summers' biographer Timothy d'Arch Smith felt that this inquisitorial and literary standpoint was not a means of covering up the author's Satanic past or a convenient line to encourage and improve sales. 'My opinion is that from one of his blasphemies, perhaps from their accumulation since 1908, he had learned a terrible lesson. In his shambling amateur way,' he states in *The Books of the Beast*, '... and it must be emphasized that he was not the sort of practical, by which I mean intellectual, magician who will guard himself against the dangers inherent in such practices of some sort of psychic kick-back – he had discovered (and not a moment too soon) that the god he worshipped and the god who warred against that god were professionals'.

Summers followed his two treatises on the history of witches with his now famous *The Vampire: His Kith and Kin* and its sequel, *The Vampire in Europe* (1929). In the former were laid down the origins and generation of the vampire myth (or reality as Summers would have it), the traits and practice of vampirism, an examination of the vampire in Assyria, the East and the ancient lands, as well as a study of vampire literature up to and including Stoker's *Dracula*. Its follow-up examined the evidence for vampirism in ancient Greece, Rome, England, Ireland, Hungary and Czechoslovakia, and concluded with accounts in modern Greece, where Summers had travelled in 1906 and 1907, and Russia, Romania and Bulgaria. As well as witches and vampires, Summers also added a lengthy study of werewolves to Kegan Paul's list, producing *The Werewolf*, which was first issued in 1933.

In 1928, John Rodker published Summers' translation into English of Heinrich Kramer and James Sprenger's *Malleus Maleficarum*, the '*Hammer of Witches*', a fifteenth-century treatise described as 'the most important and most sinister work on demonology ever written'. First issued in 1486, it was republished at least thirteen times up to 1520 and then again in numerous editions between 1574 and 1669, including translations into English, French and Italian. Writing in the late 1950s, the English-born scholar Rossell Hope Robbins (1912–90) described the *Malleus* as crystallizing 'into a fiercely stringent code previous folklore about black magic with church dogma on heresy, and, if any one work could, opened the floodgates of the inquisitorial hysteria'. Its blood-soaked pages sent countless innocent unfortunates to their deaths, but for Montague Summers, the book had eternal relevance: 'a work which must irresistibly capture the attention of all men who think, all who see, or are endeavoring to see, the ultimate reality beyond the accidents of matter, time and space.'

From the mid-1920s onwards, Summers worked as a full-time writer, authoring, editing and translating a large number of volumes. As well as Charles Ogden at Kegan Paul, he worked as an editor for Francis Meynell's Nonesuch Press, and for the Fortune Press, which had been established by Reginald Caton in 1924 and whom Summers first met in February 1927; within two years he had edited and issued ten books for Caton. His total output across several publishers climbed to a total of over fifty books, including *The Complete Works of Thomas Shadwell* (1927), *A Bibliography of the Restoration Drama* (1935), and *The Gothic Quest: A History of the Gothic Novel* (1938), 'monuments as much to his industry as to his learning'. Summers also edited several collections of supernatural fiction including *The Supernatural Omnibus* (1931) and *Victorian Ghost Stories* (1933) but despite his erudition and experience in all things to do with the occult and the paranormal, he only ever attempted a single work of supernatural fiction, a short story entitled *The Grimoire* which appeared in a collection along with tales by Le Fanu and A.S. Pushkin published by the Fortune Press in 1936.

Summers claimed to have had several encounters with ghosts and phantom figures during the course of his life. In his autobiography, *The Galanty Show*, published posthumously in 1980, he describes an incident at Tellisford House around the turn of the century, of observing the apparition of a woman in a black skirt and patterned shawl wearing a Quaker bonnet which had appeared to him one evening in one of the upper galleries. On another occasion, again at Tellisford and while taking tea in the morning room, Summers and a group of his siblings observed the crisis apparition of a female friend, Miss Teviot, who lived at Bath. The following morning the family received a black-edged card to say that the woman had died around the same time that her figure had appeared in the doorway at Clifton Down.

Ghosts, it appears, seemed to follow Summers around down through the years, as though drawn by his decidedly other-worldly qualities. While living in Bath he claimed to have been passed in the hallway by a phantom woman 'powdered and patched, in sacque and hoop', and in a house in St Giles's, Oxford, his long-standing secretary and literary executor, Hector Stuart-Forbes, who died equally as suddenly as his employer two years after Summers' demise, claimed to have encountered the sinister apparition of a hanging man suspended from a hook behind his bedroom door while Summers sat reading in the library.

Despite his other literary endeavours, it is for his occult writings, and particularly those connected with vampirism that Montague Summers is most remembered and quoted today. His view on the nature of the vampire creature, as has been noted by other authors and commentators, differed from those of previous authorities on the subject. '[T]he essential feature of the Vampire proper,' he states in the opening pages of *The Vampire: His Kith and Kin*, 'lies in the fact that he is a dead body re-animated with an awful life, who issues from his tomb to prey upon the living by sucking their blood which lends him new vitality and fresh energies'. Although this is the popular view held by many whose introduction and education in the subject is through either exposure to Hammer Films or via the many and varied works of fiction (all with a common theme), this was not the case with several of the vampire hunters of the past who struggled to understand the concept of the undead within the science and technology of their day. Two of Summers' illustrious predecessors, Dom Augustin Calmet and the Theosophist and occult writer, Dr Franz Hartmann (1838-1912), were both unhappy with the belief that the physical bodies of vampires rose to attack the living, and considered the phenomenon in terms of the astral projection of the undead being, in essence, that the vampire is a blood-sucking ghost which can be destroyed only by the destruction of the physical body. In his essay, 'The Evolution of the Vampire Belief', published as an introduction to Donald F. Glut's *True Vampires of History* (1971), D. Scott Rogo aptly sums up Summers' 'demonist' theory as expounded in his two seminal works:

> Summers was more intrigued by the blood-sucking belief than the scientific considerations of his day [as demonstrated by the experiences of Nandor Fodor we have already encountered] and felt the vampire to be inherently evil and a device of Satan. [He] stated that the actual mechanics of the vampire are unknown but they are not self-animated.

Summers, as noted by Rogo, 'falls back on the ancient belief that vampires are zombies animated by an evil spirit. This spirit is, of course, a direct emissary from Satan.'

Summers' authority has grown in stature in the decades following his death, his scholarly legacy providing a useful shield against his eccentric personality and his outlandish claims. Despite his earnest assurances, for Peter Underwood the vampire protection medallion remained an interesting but nonetheless inactive and unused curio. In his autobiography, *No Common Task*, published in 1983, Underwood adds a footnote to the incident that perhaps should come as no surprise:

> I did reproduce a drawing of the object in my book about vampires [*The Vampire's Bedside Companion* – *see* Chapter 10], and soon after publication I received a letter from a coin-dealer in Hampstead informing me that the medallion was a Shadwell Dock forgery, or 'Billie and Charlie' as they are commonly called. Apparently these concoctions first came to light in 1858 during the excavation for the new Shadwell Dock, and there are numerous varieties depicting daggers, knights, ecclesiastics and triptychs.

Two mud-raking labourers, William Smith and his companion Charles Eaton, were thought to have manufactured a vast number of similar items (estimated as being between 5,000 and 10,000 pieces) in a forging career lasting several years. The artefacts were created with moulds and buried in the mud of the Thames, then subsequently unearthed as real treasure trove and sold on. The hoax was exposed by a London printer, Charles Reed, who bribed a sewer worker to break into the pair's workshop and steal the fakers' moulds, which were later exhibited at the Society of Antiquaries. Charles Eaton died in 1870 aged 35; the fate of his forging partner, William Smith, is unclear. '[T]he legends around the medallions are quite meaningless, Messrs Smith and Eaton being totally illiterate,' Underwood concluded. 'So much for Montague Summers's vampire-protection medallion!' Today the artefact, stripped of any genuine supernatural connection, resides in the vampirological collection of Bishop Sean Manchester.

Another author who has left an interesting pen portrait of Montague Summers is Dennis Wheatley who in the posthumously published *Drink and Ink* (1979), the third volume of his autobiographical series *The Time Has Come*, admitted that the character of Canon Copley Syle, the sinister priest at the centre of his 1953 novel *To the Devil – A Daughter*, had been modelled on Summers who, together with other occultists of the day – namely Aleister Crowley and Rollo Ahmed – he was introduced to by a London friend, Tom Driberg. A shrewd and erudite man, Wheatley clearly saw through the smokescreen that Summers had erected in his retirement years and, given his contacts and various friendships, may well have heard whiffs of the Reverend's mysterious past. Summers was an 'interesting character', Wheatley remembered. 'It was said that he had never been ordained, but he dressed and, with white curls hanging down the sides of his face, looked like a Restoration Bishop.'

One weekend, Wheatley, together with his wife Joan, was invited down to Alresford in Hampshire where at the time Summers had a house. The couple found the building to be filled with spiders, and in the garden Joan Whealtey came across a disturbingly large toad. 'After dinner that evening,' Wheatley recalled, 'he took me into a small room on the ground floor that had nothing in it except a great heap of books piled up higgledy-piggledy on the floor. Picking up a small volume from the pile he held it out to me and said: "Now this is rare; very rare. And I can let you have it for fifty pounds; only fifty pounds."' Wheatley didn't recognise the title and as well as not wanting it, was not in a position to buy it anyway. 'Never have I seen such a complete change of expression. From having been normally benign his face suddenly became positively demoniac. Throwing down the book, he stamped furiously out of the room.' The following morning, Wheatley surreptitiously sent a telegram to his children's nanny, requesting that she send one of her own saying that their son had been taken ill. The telegram duly arrived after lunch. 'We packed hastily and departed, never to see the, perhaps not so reverend, gentleman again'.

Charles Richard Cammell, one time associate editor of *The Connoisseur* magazine and member of the famous Scottish shipbuilding family, knew Summers when the two men both lived in Richmond, Surrey, in the late 1930s, and had an altogether better opinion. Cammell felt that to describe the man as extraordinary was no exaggeration. 'He was in every respect singular: in appearance, in manner, in his way of life, his interests, his attainments,' he wrote in his book *Aleister Crowley*, first published in 1951. 'Moreover, an atmosphere of mystery surrounded him: he wore this atmosphere, as he wore his clerical garb, his broad black hat … his black, corded monkish robe.' He recalled Summers' 'small, dark house' in Dynevor Road, with its study piled from floor to ceiling with thousands of rare books, and the first-floor chapel where Catholic Mass was celebrated. Cammell also witnessed first-hand the relationship between the mysterious priest and the equally enigmatic Edward Alexander Crowley, better known as Aleister Crowley, the self-styled 'Great Beast' and one of the most notorious men in England. The two met on several occasions, one of the last being in Cammell's presence when they discussed their many shared interests with 'sparkling wit and good-fellowship'. Summers, who described the 'Beast' as 'one of the few original and really interesting men of our age', was an avid collector of Crowleyana, including many of his published books together with a portfolio of press-cuttings and magazine articles about him and his work. Crowley's writings included the prose poem 'The Book of the Law', a channelled text that he believed was a new gospel for mankind, containing as it does the notorious mantra 'Do what thou wilt shall be the whole of the law', and he himself claimed that on one occasion he had fought off the attack of a psychic vampire, sent by occultist Samuel MacGregor Mathers to destroy him during their battle for control of the Order of the Golden Dawn in the early years of the twentieth century. Crowley would often introduce himself to unsuspecting female admirers by delivering what he described as the 'Serpent's kiss', a vampire-like bite that drew blood from their hands, having two teeth filed into sharp points specifically for the purpose.

Montague Summers died at the age of 68 and is buried in East Sheen and Richmond Cemetery, sharing the grave with his secretary Hector Stuart-Forbes. Unrecognised for many years, a simple marker was erected shortly after the fortieth anniversary of his death in November 1988. Discussing the subject of witches and vampires in his autobiography, Summers gave a final insight into the world about which he is still inextricably associated. 'There is room, there always will be, for studies of witchcraft, of hauntings, of the occult,' he wrote. 'We only ask that these books should be written seriously, and with knowledge … The world invisible is infinite. How many there are whose sight is blindly bounded by their own horizons, the wall they have builded of the bricks of gross materialism and denial. If they but guessed what lay beyond that barrier and bourne!' Perhaps then the final word on the mysterious world of Montague Summers should be those that appropriately enough grace his posthumously inscribed gravestone: 'Tell me strange things'.

7

A Silver Scream: The Road to British Vampire Cinema

(1921-1955)

In the introduction to his 1977 book *The Vampire Cinema*, film historian David Pirie states, with intuitive insight, that '[t]here can be few cinematic forms that chart the passage of permissiveness quite as strikingly as the vampire movie'. In previous chapters we have seen how the vampire phenomenon has passed with increasing menace and purpose through the bloodstream of English literature, bringing with it a lurid, sexual reality to the imaginative writings of those authors and dramatists who allowed themselves to fall under its sway. For authors like Bram Stoker, the vampire was a revelation, allowing a deep undercurrent of erotic and sensual exploration, repressed and kept in check by the social conventions of the day, to flow freely through the minds and imaginations of Victorian readers. However, far more than the seemingly boundless possibilities of the printed page, the illusory medium of the cinema film has given the vampire a life and identity, as well as a shocking realism, which would have been practically undreamt of by writers of the nineteenth and early twentieth century.

The world of fantasy and the supernatural was embraced enthusiastically by pioneering filmmakers practically from the very beginning: *The Haunted Castle*, a three-minute short produced by the Frenchman George Méliès in 1896, is considered to be the very first horror film. In the raft of years leading up to the Second World War, the advance of the cinema vampire, including some of its most iconic and enduring images and portrayals, carefully sidestepped Britain and was the province of Continental European and American directors. In England, the vampire was to flourish in an unprecedented explosion of blood and violence during the post-war years, although the inexorable power of Stoker's work meant that the connection to Britain, and particularly fog-shrouded Victorian London, was established from the very beginning.

By 1913, there were an astonishing 600 cinemas in the Greater London area alone, the same year that what purports to be the very first cinematic portrayal of an undead character made its way onto the fledgling silver screen. This was appropriately enough a British short entitled *The Vampire* which, unlike several other one-reel films from the period (despite promising titles including *Vampires of the Coast* (1909) – an American pirate film – and *The Vampire's Tower*, released in early 1914), was the first to unite the vampire name with a purely supernatural subject. Sometimes confused with American director Robert Vignola's 1913 film of the same name, whose title character is a fast-living femme fatale rather than a bloodsucker, *The Vampire*, now sadly a lost film, concerns the exploits of two explorers in India who fall foul of a sinister vampire woman. Shot by one of the adventurers after his companion has been killed, the creature proves immune to bullets and, changing from human form into a snake, the second explorer is attacked and dies.

Interestingly, the mythology and religious landscape of India has a rich tradition of vampire-like creatures that quite befits the subject of this seminal portrayal, regarded as Britain's very first foray into cinematic horror. The pisacha, eerie spectres that haunt lonely roads and deserted crossroads, are said to be the unquiet spirits of deceased criminals, adulterers and liars, who feast ghoulishly on the bones and entrails of hapless travellers. Able to cure illnesses and maladies in humans, the pisacha can be bribed into passing on its medical knowledge with offerings of rice, but if approached in an inappropriate manner or when in a disinterested state, the creature quickly changes its diet to one of human flesh and the unfortunate villager is quickly overpowered. A similar demonic creature, the female jigarkhor, preys on wayward young men and infant babies, eating their livers as well as draining their blood. Perhaps the most bizarre vampiric creature of all, and one that would seem to be more at home in the nightmarish fiction of horror master Clive Barker (*see* Chapter 13) than the lonely byways of India, the penangalan has a detachable head wreathed with writhing intestines and enters the bedchambers of birthing women and gorges itself on the flesh of both mother and unborn child.

From its humble British beginnings, the cinematic vampire had to wait almost a decade before what today is regarded as one of its most iconic interpretations was committed to celluloid. In the summer of 1921, Friedrich Plumpe, better known as Friedrich (F.W.) Murnau, a pioneer of German expressionistic cinema, began work on a free adaptation of Stoker's *Dracula* under the title *Nosferatu*, a vampiric synonym first described by the Scottish-born collector of Transylvanian folklore, Emily Gerard. Sub-titled *eine Symphonie des Grauens* or *A Symphony of Horror*, Murnau's screenplay took liberties with several aspects of the original, due to the fact that his Prana Film company declined to secure the rights to the novel, which at the time were still held by Stoker's widow, Florence Balcombe, who eventually survived her husband by a quarter of a century. Jonathan Harker became Thomas Hutter; the vampire-slaying Van Helsing was reduced to a minor character,

Professor Bulwer; the lunatic Renfield was known as Herr Knock; while for the title character, Murnau transformed Stoker's eponymous anti-hero into a grotesque, skeletal horror, Count Orlok, played by German theatre actor Max Schreck, whose hooked nose, rat-like features and impossibly-long clawed fingers did much to fuel accusations of anti-Semitism on the film-makers' part by later post-war critics, conscious of the analogy between the arrival of the plague-ridden vampire count from far-off Transylvania and the influx of Eastern European Jews in the years that Germany was crippled by political and economic restrictions following the Treaty of Versailles.

Murnau eschewed any connections with Victorian England in his narrative and transposed much of the drama to the fictional German city of Wisborg, although some English language prints that also retain Stoker's original character names replace this with the north-western city of Bremen. Much of the vampire-lore disseminated by Van Helsing in Stoker's *Dracula* is transfered by Murnau's script-writer Henrik Galeen to a fictional narrative, *The Book of the Vampires*, discovered by Hutter at an inn on his journey to Count Orlok's castle, and it is here that one of the most far-reaching changes to the original novel takes place: whereas in Stoker's story, the vampire Count can survive in sunlight, although practically all of his super-natural powers are weakened or limited, for Galeen, the nosferatu was essentially a spectral creature for whom the rays of the morning sun were wholly fatal. When Hutter's wife, Ellen, sacrifices herself to Orlok in order to keep the vampire creature in her bedroom after cock crow, Murnau allows a simple camera dissolve to reduce his sinister undead character to a pile of smoking ashes, thereby imbuing vampire lore with one of its most recognisable, but wholly twentieth-century, elements.

For Friedrich Murnau, *Nosferatu* was to prove to be a 'symphony of horror' in more ways than one. Supported by the Society of Authors, Florence Stoker took out legal proceedings over the plagiarisation of her husband's celebrated work, the court proceedings eventually dragging on for nearly three years. At one point, Murnau declared his Prana Film company bankrupt in order to avoid paying the Stoker estate royalties, but in July 1925, four years after he had begun work on *Nosferatu*, the High Court ruled that all copies of the film should be destroyed, a decision that ultimately was never completely carried out. Several German and English language prints escaped and today, restored and re-scored by a number of contemporary composers including Hammer Film's James Bernard, Murnau's most famous foray into cinematic horror is universally regarded as a seminal masterpiece. The troubled director later emigrated to America where he died in a car crash in March 1931 at the age of 42.

In early 1927, American director Tod Browning, a former variety performer with a penchant for the macabre, drafted an original story treatment titled 'The Hypnotist' as a vehicle for prolific film actor Lon Chaney, the 'Man of a Thousand Faces', whose transformation into *The Phantom of the Opera* in 1925 for Universal had made him a major box office star. Browning took a murder mystery format and, combining aspects of both the Whitechapel crimes of Jack the Ripper with the visual elements of Stoker's *Dracula*, created *London After Midnight* in which Chaney had the dual roles of both Professor Edward Burke, a consulting detective at Scotland Yard in the mould of Conan Doyle, and what at first appears to be the London socialite Roger Balfour, resurrected vampire-like from beyond the grave in the company of a ghostly female assistant. Chaney gave himself a bat-winged costume and grinning mask-like features complete with saw-edged teeth (reminiscent of the fangs given over forty years later to victims of Robert Quarry's Count Yorga) and sinister bulging eyes, an effect created by applying wire monocles to his own face, but despite the clear undead overtones, Chaney's 'vampire' is in fact an ordinary person, Professor Burke in disguise, on an undercover mission to expose and capture a criminal gang. Browning later remade the film in 1935 with Bela Lugosi as *Mark of the Vampire*, by which time Chaney was dead, slain by throat cancer at the age of 47. Perhaps some idea of the power of Chaney's performance on late 1920s British audiences can be judged by the case of Welsh carpenter Robert Williams, who, on 23 October 1928, attacked and killed an Irish housewife named Julia Mangan in Hyde Park with a razor. Williams ineffectively attempted to turn the blade on himself and at his later trial it was alleged in his defence that the 'vampire' make-up from *London After Midnight* had shocked the accused into a temporary insanity: Williams had claimed that prior to the attack he had heard noises in his head and had seen a vision of Chaney dressed as the sinister Burke shouting instructions. The Welshman was sentenced to death but later reprieved.

Today, like the early British *The Vampire*, all copies of *London After Midnight* appear to be lost – a film vault fire in Culver City in the mid-1960s destroyed the last known print – but Chaney's strange and mesmerising performance still survives in several iconic publicity stills and posters.

Despite the success of Browning's cultivation of the albeit pseudo-vampiric subject on British shores, what was to be the cinema's next foray into the twilight world of the undead was again a foreign affair. Inspired by Le Fanu's *In a Glass Darkly*, Carl Dreyer, a Danish director in his early forties, was the first film-maker to see the cinematic potential of the Carmilla character, and together with his French-born financier, the banker Nicolas de Gunzburg, set about adapting the story for the screen. The result was *Vampyr*, a haunting dream-like narrative that ultimately eschewed much of Le Fanu's original ideas; although the concept of a female vampire character was retained and transposed to a village in northern France, where incidents of a mysterious plague are investigated by a visiting researcher, an occult student and savant named Allan Gray, played by De Gunzburg himself under the stage name of Julian West. Only two members of Dreyer's cast were professional players – the Frenchman, Maurice Schutz, and German actress Sybille Schmitz – and the film, shot on location in and around the village of Courtempierre beginning in the summer of 1931, took nearly a year to complete, partly because much of the filming was restricted to the early dawn in order to create a visually strange and almost unearthly atmosphere. Interestingly, the Danish director's depiction of the undead menace is influenced more by the witchcraft purges of fifteenth- and sixteenth-century Europe than by the original *Carmilla* – the vampire is depicted as a sinister old woman rather than as a young and sexually alluring character – although ultimately its destruction is achieved in the traditional manner with a stake through the heart, carried out by the enigmatic Allan Gray (named David Gray in the German release print) accompanied by a village servant. A local doctor, who, it transpires, has been procuring victims for the eerie undead crone, is suffocated by a deluge of flour at a nearby mill. Mostly a silent presentation, but containing some scenes filmed and later dubbed into the then new talkie process, Dreyer's *Vampyr*, sub-titled *The Dream of Allan Grey*, premiered in Berlin on 6 May 1932, but was a financial failure, partly due to the negative reaction by contemporary audiences to the Dane's idiosyncratic cinematography – many scenes were shot through sheets of gauze to create a hazy otherworldly atmosphere – and the screenplay's trance-like depiction of much of the action, but also to the great presence of Universal's first foray into cinematic vampirism, which had burst upon the scene the previous year. Dreyer abandoned filmmaking for over a decade and for many years the haunting *Vampyr* was little known outside of specialist circles. His later output was sporadic and Dreyer, one of the first pioneering directors of the undead, died in Copenhagen of pneumonia in 1968 at the age of 79.

The same year that Lon Chaney was to mesmerise London as the undead Roger Balfour, the stage production of Stoker's *Dracula*, the first officially sanctioned presentation of the story, opened on Broadway. American film actor Edward van Sloan played the vampire-slaying Van Helsing, while Hungarian-born émigré Bela Lugosi took on the title role that in a few brief years was to make him an international star. The play had its origins in a friendship between Florence Balcombe and the Irish actor and stage director Hamilton Deane, who the Stokers had known several years before while living in Dublin. Keen to receive some form of royalties from her late husband's work after the furore over Murnau's *Nosferatu*, Stoker's widow granted Deane the rights to *Dracula* and the production, the complete title of which was *Dracula: The Vampire Play*, premiering in Derby in 1924, toured the provinces for three years before establishing itself in London. Deane opted for the role of Van Helsing, while character actor Raymond Huntley, a later stalwart of many post-war British films including David Lean's *Hobson's Choice* (1954) and the wartime epic *The Dam Busters* (1955), played the vampire count. For its American presentation, Horace Liveright, a former publisher, commissioned an adaptation of Deane's script by the pioneering fantasy screenwriter John Balderston and the production, which opened in October 1927, was a great success, although Liveright ultimately reneged on an agreement with the Stoker estate and died in 1933 at the age of 49 without paying a cent in royalties. Despite the intrigue, Balderston's script was to provide the foundation for the beginnings of the great swell in horror film production in America during the 1930s, a pioneering and now highly-regarded movement that has its origins ultimately in Stoker's benchmark tale of blood and the undead.

Encouraged by the success of Horace Liveright's Broadway production of *Dracula*, Carl Laemmle, a successful German-born former clothing store manager turned film mogul, set about making a big screen adaption for his Universal Picture Corporation. Production problems, including the financial blight of the Wall Street Crash compounded by the death of star Lon Chaney, who as the obvious choice was originally slated to take on the title role, meant that it was not until the autumn of 1930 that filming began on the Universal City lot, the shooting being completed at a rapid pace in just over seven weeks. Director Tod Browning, returning to the genre he had demonstrated a great affinity for with *London After Midnight*, and against initial studio opposition, retained both Bela Lugosi and Edward van Sloan from Liveright's stage version and forged an iconic presentation of the vampire novel, even though Lugosi's portrayal, as David Pirie has noted, reduces the sexual and moral ambiguity of Stoker's written character into a more traditional one-dimensional screen villain.

Lugosi's identification with the vampire role was to cast a long shadow down through the years, in much the same way that British-born Boris Karloff's interpretation of Mary Shelley's *Frankenstein*, which Universal put into production in 1931 following the success of *Dracula*, became the standard depiction of the reanimated creature for thirty years, despite other actors, including Lugosi himself, taking on the part. In 1992, six decades after Tod Browning's film was released, and thirty-six years after Lugosi's own death, Gary Oldman, who played *Bram Stoker's Dracula* for Francis Ford Coppola and Columbia Pictures, identified the most with the Hungarian actor's presentation of the character, following his lilting speech patterns in a number of early scenes, although in reality Oldman's visual and emotional portrayal was worlds apart from Universal's seminal vampire picture.

Even though other actors would take on the role for Universal – Lon Chaney Jr for *Son of Dracula* (1943) and John Carradine in the 1944 and 1945 monster exploitations *House of Frankenstein* and *House of Dracula* – for the film-going public in both Britain and America, Lugosi was Count Dracula for over a quarter of a century. When Columbia set about making a contemporary vampire picture in 1943, and with Universal holding the copyright to the character, Lugosi played Stoker's Dracula in all but name in a drama that reinforced the British roots of the original narrative.

Set during the dark days of the London Blitz, *The Return of the Vampire* cast Lugosi as an eighteenth-century occultist, Armand Tesla, cursed with vampirism after years of historic delving into the infernal world of the undead has finally exposed him to the very source of the evil. When Tesla's body, impaled and immobile it its coffin for 200 years, is unearthed by a Luftwaffe bomb strike on a London cemetery, ignorant workmen remove the stake in the mistaken belief that they are helping a casualty with shrapnel wounds, thereby unleashing a modern vampire plague on the wartime capital. Lugosi's performance, complete with white tie, tails and swirling cloak, follows the blueprint established for Tod Browning twelve years before, although for this later outing, Columbia screenwriter Griffin Jay added a werewolf assistant to the proceedings, clearly inspired by the relative success of Universal's *Frankenstein Meets the Wolfman* the previous year, which had pitched Lugosi's monster against a relatively recent but nevertheless successful addition to the horror film pantheon, the doomed lycanthrope Lawrence Talbot, as played by Lon Chaney Jr in Jack Pierce's original and highly regarded make-up. Eventually, another air raid destroys Tesla's coffin and, forced into the sunlight, the vampire dies in the time-honoured fashion established by Murnau and Henrik Galeen over two decades before.

Although successful as the perpetual man of horror, by the early 1950s, Lugosi's career, together with his health, were both in the doldrums. In 1951, he toured England with a new production of Deane and Balderston's *Dracula* which opened at the Theatre Royal, Brighton, on, appropriately enough, 30 April – Walpurgis Night, the eve of May Day, when witches and dark creatures are traditionally said to gather – and went on to play at a further twenty-one venues across the country including the King's Theatre, Glasgow, Belfast's Grand Opera House, the Shepherd's Bush Empire, and the Alma Theatre, Luton, a purpose-built entertainment venue that sported both a backstage curse and a ghost. Despite over 200 performances, as well as a number of publicity events linked with the Festival of Britain, the play never achieved Lugosi's dream of establishing itself in the West End, and after the final curtain came down at Portsmouth on 13 October, Lugosi and his wife Lillian left for America at the beginning of December. Weakened by years of morphine addiction, Lugosi died of a massive heart attack at his home in Los Angeles on 16 August 1956 at the age of 73, and was buried at the request of his wife and son in his famous Dracula costume. He never lived to see the startling modern rejuvenation of his vampire character, the foundations of which were already being laid on the other side of the Atlantic, his last years filled with poverty only partly alleviated by bit-part appearances in low-budget exploitation pictures, several of which were not completed and screened until after his death.

In all this time, although showing a great affinity for fledgling horror and the world of the macabre, as demonstrated by such contributions such as *Castle Sinister* (1932 – a *Frankenstein* exploitation now lost), *The Ghoul* (1932) starring Boris Karloff, *The Dark Eyes of London* (1939), an adaptation of Edgar Wallace's 1924 novel of the same name with Lugosi as the lead, *The Ghost of Rashmon Hall* (1947) and *Three Cases of Murder* (1955) starring Orson Welles and Alan Badel, the British film industry conspicuously avoided the world of the undead, giving Hollywood a complete monopoly on all aspects of cinema-related vampirism. Even the now highly regarded *Dead of Night*, a portmanteau collection of eerie tales served up by Ealing Studios in 1945 following a wartime glut of home-produced horror titles, the result of a government veto that forced filmmakers to concentrate on boosting national morale rather than draw audiences deeper into a world already filled with shadows, avoided the subject of vampires and blood-letting altogether, and instead concentrated on a mixture of traditional ghost stories, such as E.F. Benson's 1906 short story *The Bus Conductor*, interlaced with more gritty psychological-based horror; while John Gilling's *Old Mother Riley Meets the Vampire*, a British horror comedy starring the then popular vaudeville entertainer Arthur Lucan, made with Lugosi in late 1951 shortly before his return trip to America on the *Queen Elizabeth*, contained no true supernatural content at all: for this outing, Lugosi's character, a mad robot-building scientist named Von Housen, only believes himself to be one of the undead, the result being a sad travesty typical of the actor's final years on screen.

In America, Lugosi's death effectively closed the door on an entire era of horror film production as post-war audiences, now exposed to the real technological horrors of Hiroshima and Nagasaki, became drawn into a film market increasingly driven and dominated by both science-fact and science fiction, one in which the world of vampires and werewolves seemed uncomfortably out of place and perhaps slightly absurd. On the other side of the Atlantic, however, this new atomic age was ultimately to take the world of horror in an entirely different direction, surprisingly back down the dark and fog-shrouded road to its very Gothic roots. And perhaps more surprisingly, this entire process can be traced back to the activities of just one man.

James Henry Kinmel Sangster (b. 1927), named after his birthplace in Rhyl, North Wales, but known more familiarly as Jimmy Sangster, first became associated with the British film industry as a clapper-boy at the tender age of 16, but his fledgling career was interrupted by National Service in the RAF, following which he went to Ealing Studios, working on a handful of post-war dramas as a third assistant director. In 1948, Sangster joined Exclusive Films, a small provincial studio and former distribution company, who, in order to keep production overheads down, were working out of a converted country house called Dial Close on the banks of the Thames at Cookham Dean near Maidenhead. The following year, Exclusive changed its name to Hammer Films and moved to two further temporary studios, nearby Oakley Court, and later Gilston Park, a country club near Harlow in Essex, before finally returning to Berkshire where, in 1951, it established a permanent base at Down Place, renaming it Bray Studios after the village nearby. As Hammer concentrated on 'quota quickie' thrillers and film adaptations of then-popular radio serials such as *PC 49* and *Life With the Lyons*, Sangster found himself moving up the ranks, and although harbouring an ambition to become a screenwriter, the mid-1950s saw him working as a production manager for producer Michael Carreras, by which time an important milestone in Hammer's future development had already been passed.

In July 1953, the BBC broadcast the first episode of a home-grown science-fiction serial scripted by staff screenwriter, Nigel Kneale, which quickly established itself as a television phenomenon. *The Quatermass Experiment*, a modern tale of a sinister alien life-form accidentally brought back to Earth during a government rocket experiment, was a typical atomic thriller of its time, but no one, not least Hammer executive producer Anthony Hinds, who realised the cinematic potential of Neale's story during the first episode's screening, would imagine the direction it would ultimately take his modest provincial company. Hammer had already attempted science fiction with two 1953 films scripted by the Hungarian-born novelist and sometime ghost hunter Paul Tabori: *Four Sided Triangle*, directed by Terence Fisher from William Temple's original novel and with a musical score by the prolific Malcolm Arnold, and *Spaceways*, again helmed by Fisher from an original radio play by David McIlwain, but *The Quatermass Xperiment*, the juxtaposed title emphasising the BBFC's 'X' Certificate for horror classification and with American actor Brian Donlevy in the title role in order to assist distribution across the Atlantic, was a major step forward. Not only did it generate two sequels, both based on original Neale television scripts – *Quatermass II* from 1957 and the eerie *Quatermass and the Pit* (1967), one of the greatest and most successful attempts to merge supernatural horror with science fiction – but its financial success made Hinds and Carreras realise the clear potential in the market and the company quickly set about creating a Quatermass-style picture all of its own.

Hammer's *Xperiment* premiered in London on 26 August 1955 and went on general release three months later, by which time Hammer had already filmed a debut script by Jimmy Sangster, a thirty-minute short entitled *A Man on the Beach*, directed by Josef Losey and starring Donald Wolfit and Michael Medwin. Keen to follow up on the success of *Quatermass*, Tony Hinds encouraged Sangster to develop an original idea using Nigel Neale's character as a blueprint, but with the emphasis more on horror than pure science fiction. Sangster worked quickly and filming for the resulting *X the Unknown* took place in January and February 1956, mostly on freezing night shoots in a gravel pit in Gerrards Cross. American lead Dean Jagger played *Quatermass*-clone Adam Royston, while the sinister monster of the title, a sentient mass of prehistoric mud released by atomic testing from an underground chasm in the Scottish Highlands, was created by Canadian-born technician Les Bowie, who had already destroyed Westminster Abbey the previous year for director Val Guest in the climatic finale of *The Quatermass Xperiment*. A modest success, *X the Unknown* was released in the autumn of 1956 paired with Henri-Georges Clouzot's now highly-regarded psychological thriller *Les Diaboliques*, but for Sangster, it established him as one of Hammer's regular roster of scriptwriters and for who 1956 was to prove itself to be a watershed year.

8

Lord of Misrule: The Rise and Fall of Hammer's *Dracula*

(1956–1974)

The British post-war resurrection of the screen vampire was a mirror-image of America's work in the genre a quarter of a century before. Whereas Universal had brought *Frankenstein* to life through Lugosi's *Dracula*, Hammer was to use Mary Shelley's Gothic nightmare as a doorway to a modern interpretation of Stoker that was as shocking as it was new. During the summer of 1956, Eliot Hyman, a director of the newly founded American film production company Seven Arts, approached Hammer's executive producer James Carreras with a proposal to remake the *Frankenstein* story using a script prepared by two young New York filmmakers, Max Rosenberg and Milton Subotsky. Although Mary Shelley's 1816 novel had long since expired into the public domain, Anthony Hinds, who took charge of the project once Carreras had agreed a British distribution deal, quickly discovered that the American script was a legal time bomb, containing much reused material from the original 1931 Universal presentation that, together with the famous Karloff make-up, was still in copyright and over which the company continued to cast a protective eye. Realising that a Hammer *Frankenstein* would require extensive re-writes in an exceedingly short period of time, Hinds instructed Jimmy Sangster to prepare a new version of the story based on Shelley's original that could be filmed on the constraints of the company's shoe-string budget: a small cast, minimal special effects work and night exterior filming, and all location work restricted to within a thirty-minute travelling distance of Bray. Sangster quickly set to work, unaware that he was writing both himself and Hammer into the pages of British horror history.

Out of necessity, revisions were necessary to Shelley's original story. 'The first major change I made was to make Baron Frankenstein the villain, as opposed to the monster,' Sangster later recalled. 'The Baron … was a well-educated, brilliant, seemingly charming man [who] wanted to create life. Unfortunately everything got screwed up and that's where his true character came out. He became an evil, cold-blooded murderer.' Other changes included removing areas of the novel's sub-plot and reducing the character list to the bare minimum. At this stage, the film was envisaged as a simple black and white presentation with a shooting schedule of three weeks. However, encouraged by the quality of Sangster's new script, Tony Hinds took the decision to devote more time and money to the project, extending filming by an extra week, but most importantly persuading Hammer that *The Curse of Frankenstein* should be shot in colour, a crucial factor that was to reap at the time unimagined rewards. Owed one final film in a three-picture contract, Terence Fisher was brought in as director; while for principal casting, Hinds eschewed an American lead and sought a British television actor as an encouragement to audiences deserting the film theatre for the fireside at home to return once more to the cinema stalls: Peter Cushing, a former repertory player, whose career had taken a quantum leap following a switch to the small screen with successful portrayals as Richard of Bordeaux and Winston Smith in a Nigel Kneale scripted adaptation of Orwell's *Nineteen Eighty-Four*, took on the role of the fanatical Victor Frankenstein; while for the Creature, described as such in order to avoid copyright issues with Universal, Christopher Lee, then a busy but still relatively obscure supporting player, used his impressive height and experience of theatrical mime to great effect, ultimately creating an acting partnership that would dominate cinema horror for the next two decades.

Filmed over the winter of 1956 on a budget of £60,000, *The Curse of Frankenstein* opened to immediate controversy at the London Pavilion on 2 May 1957. A distribution deal with Warner Bros brokered by James and Michael Carreras in America ensured maximum publicity and the film enjoyed excellent business, breaking Warner's then box office records with the largest weekend take recorded up until that time. Although tame by early twenty-first century horror standards, for a late 1950s audience the film was a revelation, brutal in its graphic depiction of Sangster's artificially created man as, under Fisher's defining direction, Len Harris' camera lingered unflinchingly on a gruesome collection of bandaged cadavers, severed hands, dissected eyeballs and rotting skulls. As Howard Maxford has commented in his 1996 study *Hammer, House of Horror*, in its power to shock, *The Curse of Frankenstien* was *The Exorcist* (1973) or *The Silence of the Lambs* (1991) of its time, to which recent genre contributions *The Blair Witch Project* (1999) and *Paranormal Activity* (2007) can now be added.

With the success of their new *Frankenstein*, Hammer had singlehandedly kick-started the post-war revival of Gothic cinema horror, and by the summer of 1957, Tony Hinds and Jimmy Sangster stood on the edge of what was to prove to be the midnight dawn of a new era of screen vampirism, one which was now centred far from Hollywood, amongst the green and pleasant countryside of the Thames at Bray. Although the screen resurrection of Stoker's *Dracula* was the obvious choice, productions which rolled out of the Bray lot following the wrapping of *The Curse of Frankenstein* in early 1957 were to prove an eclectic mixture: they included the studio's final two quota quickie shorts, *Clean Sweep* and *Danger List*, two Second World War dramas, *The Steel Bayonet* produced and directed by Michael Carreras, together with the far grimmer and exceedingly more controversial *The Camp on Blood Island*, an account of Japanese war crimes in Burma, a naval comedy, *Up the Creek*, starring Peter Sellers and Wilfred Hyde White, and a screen version of another Nigel Kneale television play, *The Creature*, which exploited the then contemporary interest in sightings of the mysterious Yeti by climbing teams in the Himalayan mountains: for *The Abominable Snowman*, Kneale supplied his own screenplay and, mindful of his popularity as Victor Frankenstein, Peter Cushing was brought in to play opposite American lead, Forrest Tucker. By this time Hammer had already filmed Kneale's second instalment in his *Quatermass* series, *Quatermass II*, which had preceded *The Curse of Frankenstein* into production and came out on general release the same month.

Although at the box office Hammer were riding on the crest of a wave, as summer began turning into autumn, in the production office, Tony Hinds was finding the establishment of a new Count Dracula less than straightforward. Although their screen portrayal of the Frankenstein character had been influenced by the constraints imposed by the Universal Karloff film, Mary Shelley's actual work had been in the public domain for over a century. To his consternation, Hinds found that under the fifty-year rule, copyright on Stoker's novel would not expire until 1962, and that the rights given by Florence Balcombe in 1930 to Universal Studios were still in place. After a series of protracted negotiations, Universal agreed to transfer ownership to Hammer in exchange for exclusive worldwide distribution of a new *Dracula* film and, with a deal in place, Tony Hinds began marshalling his forces on the tiny backlot at Bray.

Around the same time, Michael Carreras was also experiencing problems with another vampire project of his own, one that if realised at the time may well have changed not only the history of Hammer Films but also the landscape of British horror cinema throughout the 1960s and beyond. Encouraged by the success of *The Curse of Frankenstein* and with the new *Dracula* in pre-production, Carreras had taken the bold step of buying the rights to the late American author Richard Matheson's apocalyptic science-fiction novel *I Am Legend*, published only three years before and now regarded as a modern classic: in 2012, the book was awarded the Vampire Novel of the Century Award by the Horror Writers' Association. Set over a period of three years in 1970s California, it tells the story of Robert Neville, the sole survivor of a global pandemic that has turned the entire population of the world into a race of nightmarish vampire-like creatures. Immune from the effects of the virus, Neville spends the night hours barricaded inside his house, only venturing outside during the day in order to scavenge for supplies and to kill as many of the sleeping swarms of the undead as the daylight hours will allow. At the novel's climax, the vampire hunter, now a prisoner of the creatures himself, commits suicide by poisoning, allowing a new world order of the infected legions to completely take over the world. For his novel, Matheson, born in Allendale, New Jersey in 1926, had been inspired by watching a screening of Lugosi's *Dracula* while in his mid-teens, concluding that 'if one vampire was scary, a world filled with vampires would be really scary', but it would be another ten years before he finally set to work on the story.

For Hammer, Matheson agreed to provide a screenplay based on his original book and was flown to England during the summer of 1957 to carry out the writing. The resultant script, entitled *The Night Creatures*, followed the original closely with some revisions, the principal changes being the relocation of the action from Los Angeles to Canada and the excision of the novel's bleak and nihilistic ending: in his film version, Matheson allowed his hero Neville to survive although the rise of a new ruling vampire society across the world was unchanged. Pleased with the results, Carreras gave the project the green light and went so far as to bring director Val Guest, fresh from his recent outings with *Quatermass*, on board before submitting the screenplay to the British Board of Film Censors, at which point things began to go rapidly wrong. Outraged by its macabre and horrific subject matter, the BBFC flatly refused to consider passing the film and advised Hammer that should production go ahead, the studio would expect an outright ban in Britain; a similar reaction from the Motion Picture Association of America forced Carreras' hand and *The Night Creatures* was promptly abandoned. In mitigation, Hammer sold the screenplay to American producer Robert Lippert who eventually brought a version to the screen (filmed in Rome with a largely Italian cast) in 1964 as *The Last Man on Earth* with horror veteran Vincent Price in the title role, by which time Matheson, unhappy with the result, had distanced himself from the project to the extent of having his name removed from the credits. Matheson's original script for *The Night Creatures* was eventually published in 2006, and today we can only speculate on the effects of its successful production and release back in 1958, but they are likely to have been profound: American film-maker George Romero has acknowledged the debt his 1968 cult classic *Night of the Living Dead*, one of the most influential horror films to emerge from the late 1960s, owes to the novel of *I Am Legend*, discarding as it does the Gothic horror revival spearheaded by Hammer and replacing it with a disturbingly real contemporary setting, something that Tony Hinds and his later successors would be forced to imitate with varying degrees of success, while film historian Dr Peter Hutchings asks a very relevant question in his short paper 'American Vampires in Britain' (published as part of a collection of commentaries on unmade cinema projects in 2008) when he says '[I]s *The Night Creatures* the one that got away, the one that might not just have changed the direction of Hammer horror at the very moment of its formation but also have introduced into horror cinema themes that in actuality were only fully realised later in the 1960s and 1970s?' It seems highly likely, but we will never know for sure.

With their modern vampire epic now abandoned, Hammer directed all of their energies on realising the current project in hand. Filming for *Dracula*, released in America as the *Horror of Dracula* to avoid any confusion with the Lugosi original, began on 11 November 1957 and was completed in twenty-five days, on a budget of just over £80,000. Keen to ensure the continuity of success with their previous foray into Gothic horror, Hinds, together with associate producer Anthony Nelson Keys, employed the same production team that had brought Hammer's *Frankenstein* to the screen the previous year, including direction by Terence Fisher, lighting camerawork courtesy of Jack Asher and with Jimmy Sangster providing a new script based on Stoker's original work. Crucially the lead players from *The Curse of Frankenstein* again took principal parts: Christopher Lee stepping effortlessly into the role of the vampire Count, one he would play intermittently for the next decade and a half and which would return to haunt him for many years beyond, while Peter Cushing's highly personal interpretation of Van Helsing became a similar benchmark that Hammer would employ as an adversary on four more occasions over a similar period of time.

Even though several aspects of Sangster's new script were dictated by commercial and production requirements, Hammer's seminal *Dracula* restores, both to the narrative and the character, much of what was removed from Stoker's drama by previous interpreters: a far-reaching and critical factor for the wholesale resurrection of the vampire film in a Britain teetering on the edge of the social and sexual revolution of the 1960s, where the modern social cult of vampirism in today's society ultimately has its roots. For Sangster, the key to successfully portraying the evil and danger associated with Dracula was to make the character more human rather than overtly fantastic or supernatural. Interviewed many years after the event, the screenwriter summed up his feelings as he set about reinterpreting a benchmark figure in Gothic horror that had gradually lost its power to shock and terrify:

> I just wanted to humanise him a bit more. The more human he became, the less magic or fantasy figure he became, the more threatening he was. We are all frightened – everybody's frightened – of little ghosts and things like that, but it is the real people that are the most threatening.

Lee's interpretation of the character after reading both Stoker's novel and Sangster's script followed this reasoning through with maximum effect, eschewing the lilting accents and exaggerated mannerisms of his predecessor in order to restore the ambiguity of the vampire as written: the Count Dracula that stalked the backlot at Bray during the winter of 1957 was urbane and demonic in equal measure, capable of instant and shocking transformations from the charming cultured host to a spitting and physical personification of supernatural evil, despite a sparing use of screen time and the economic dictates of both production and budget.

This ambiguity and metamorphosis also transferred itself to the vampire's female victims as well as to the fountainhead itself. Dracula's eerie vampire brides, reduced by Sangster to a single mysterious and unnamed woman played by Valerie Gaunt, is, at first, a fragile and deceptively vulnerable figure that, under Fisher's direction, develops sexual allure and life-threatening violence all within the course of a single brief scene. In their book *The Vampire Film*, published nearly twenty years after the Sangster/Hammer *Dracula* first appeared on cinema screens, American historians Alain Silver and James Ursini acknowledge the landmark nature of the film's release within the history of the horror film, not only as the instigator of the cinematic revival of the vampire genre throughout the following decade, but for its explicit exploitation of the underlying factors within the genre itself that Stoker had included so masterfully within the framework of his story:

> Many things left implicit in the naïve manner so endemic to Universal's product or diluted in order to satisfy the needs of censorship surfaced, and the psycho-sexual aspects of the vampire myth were explored to an unprecedented depth. Much of the integrity of the source work was, as a result, restored; and the world of the Hammer vampires was, from the first, one in which psychologists, legend-hunters, and devotees of nineteenth-century literature alive could revel. The male vampire figure became a tall and virile demon … with none of the posturing or ludicrousness which touched some of his predecessors, while the female vampires of his retinue became voluptuous and voracious succubi … The Lucy of the Hammer *Dracula* awaits her deadly leman in bed, breathless and eager. Even the quintessentially Victorian Mina has her repressions dissolved as Dracula bestows kisses and caresses on her before indulging his vampire thirst.

Although it would be twenty years before British audiences would see what still amounts to the most complete and faithful linear presentation of the Bram Stoker original – by this time on the small screen courtesy of the BBC (*see* Chapter 11) – Jimmy Sangster was able to convey all of the factors identified by Silver and Ursini through an adaptation that took many liberties, but at the same time preserved the integrity of the original text, as well as a number of its important set pieces. Gone was Dracula's sea voyage to England and dramatic arrival at Whitby, the entire Renfield sub-plot and the investigation of the Carfax estate; Dracula loses his ability to shape-shift into bats and wolves, Dr Seward is reduced to a bit-part, while Lucy Westenra becomes both Arthur Holmwood's sister and Jonathan Harker's fiancée, with the Mina Murray character assigned as Holmwood's wife. Major revisions were also made to the relationship between Harker and Van Helsing: 'straight lining' the story as much as possible, Sangster makes Harker a vampire hunter from the outset, on a mission to destroy Dracula by posing as a librarian hired to catalogue the Count's vast and rare collection of books. Vampirised by Valerie Gaunt, Harker (played by South African-born actor John Van Eyssen) dies by Van Helsing's hand, staked in a coffin in Dracula's underground mausoleum. While in a dramatic final reel, Sangster followed Murnau's lead of over three decades before as, using an improvised crucifix forged from two crossed candlesticks, the vampire hunter takes his revenge, forcing Dracula into a shaft of morning sunlight following a climatic chase through the halls and passageways of Castle Dracula. Much of the final Cushing/Lee battle was improvised with director Terry Fisher on set while Dracula's spectacular disintegration, created by make-up artist Phil Leaky and effects technician Sydney Pearson, was considered too shocking by the BBFC and ultimately had to wait fifty-five years before being seen in its entirety, salvaged from a Japanese release print and re-mastered for a DVD audience in 2013. Similarly, Lee's seduction and corruption of Melissa Stribling as Mina was another scene that Tony Hinds was forced to re-edit extensively from an alternative viewpoint, but as Alain Silver and James Ursini have pointed out, the underlying eroticism of Stoker's original writing was impossible to ignore in a post-*Curse of Frankenstein* environment. Despite the gruesome brutality of the two on-screen staking sequences and the horror of Lee as the unmasked vampire count, perhaps the film's most disturbing scene is Sangster's re-working of Stoker's 'bloofer lady' sequence, involving the undead Lucy. In this instance, the enticement of her young niece Tania bringing to mind as it does the case of Victorian child killer William Baker, whose murder of 8-year-old Fanny Adams in a field in Alton, Hampshire, in 1867, is near contemporary with Hammer's setting of the original novel.

With the successful release of *Dracula* in May 1958, the modern phenomenon of Hammer Horror was firmly established and Jimmy Sangster soon found his scriptwriting services in high demand, not only by Tony Hinds and Michael Carreras, but also by other studios keen to exploit the same territory. As well as writing *The Trollenberg Terror*, a low-budget science-fiction romp for Tempean Films and a Jack the Ripper exploitation for short-lived Mid Century Film Productions, the remaining months of 1958 and then 1959 saw Sangster produce another three screenplays for Hammer: *The Revenge of Frankenstein*, a direct sequel with Peter Cushing making his second outing as the Baron; *The Man Who Could Cheat Death*, a Dorian Grey pastiche with heavy overtones of Stevenson's 1886 novella *The Strange Case of Dr Jekyll and Mr Hyde*; and *The Mummy*, a re-make that combined elements of a number of Universal's previous Egyptian-themed horror flicks from the early 1940s and which also reunited the duo of Lee and Cushing in lead roles. All three films, together with a new version of Conan Doyle's *The Hound of the Baskervilles* scripted by former exclusive camera operator Peter Bryan, were directed by Terence Fisher, who at the time looked to be single-handedly helming the entire post-war revival of Gothic horror in Britain.

John William Polidori (1795–1821) by Gainsford. His novella The Vampyre, first published in April 1819 and falsely attributed to Lord Byron, created the phenomenon of the aristocratic vampire in English literature. (National Portrait Gallery, London)

The Villa Diodati by moonlight, engraved by Edward Finden in the 1830s and based on an original drawing by William Purser. Its associations with Lord Byron, Mary Shelley and John Polidori have made it one of the most significant locations in the history of horror fiction.

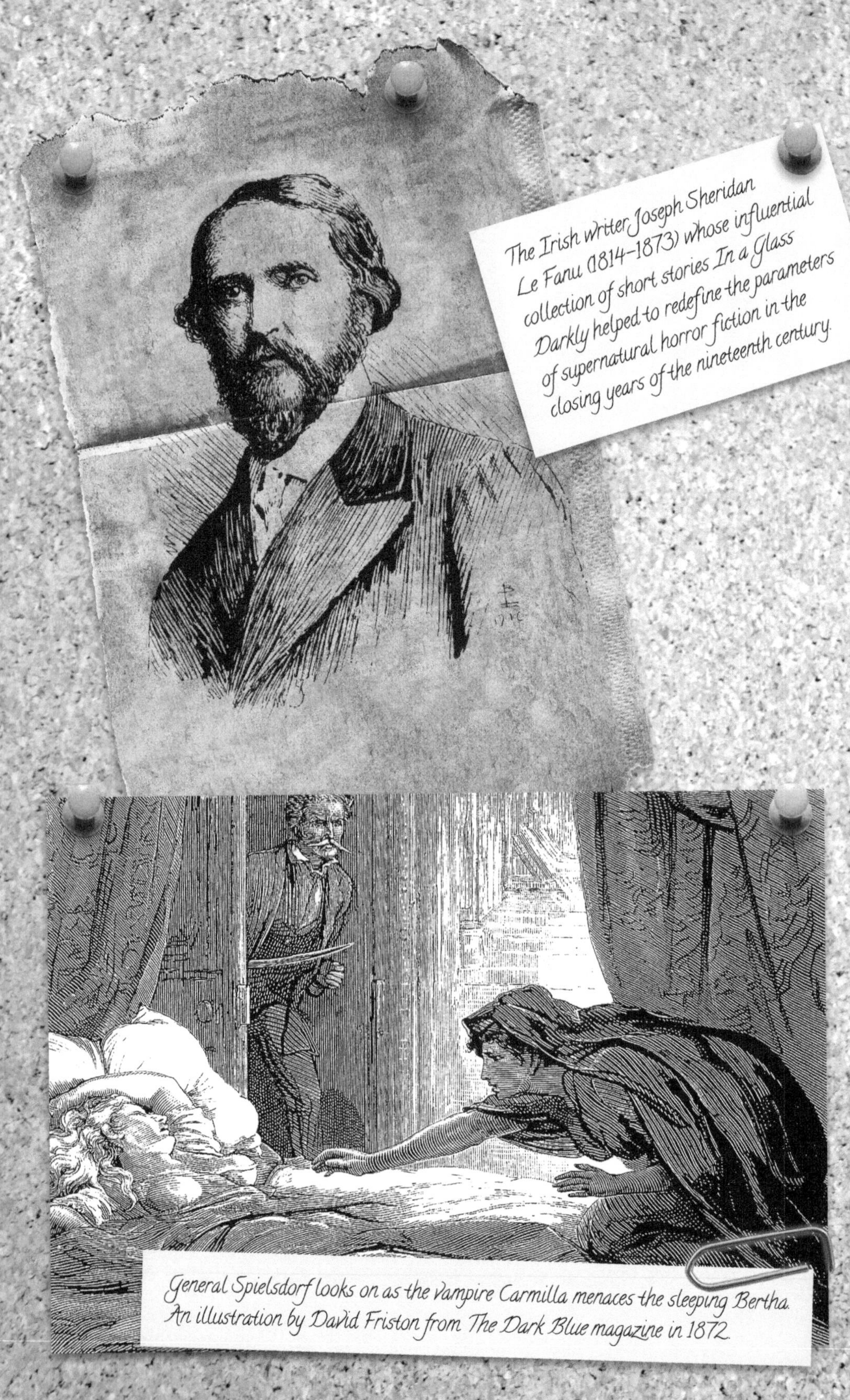

The Irish writer Joseph Sheridan Le Fanu (1814–1873) whose influential collection of short stories *In a Glass Darkly* helped to redefine the parameters of supernatural horror fiction in the closing years of the nineteenth century.

General Spielsdorf looks on as the vampire Carmilla menaces the sleeping Bertha. An illustration by David Friston from *The Dark Blue* magazine in 1872.

A modern view of Croglin Low Hall. The blocked-up window is the traditional entry point for the famous Vampire of Croglin Grange. (Darren W. Ritson)

Mysterious scratches and bite marks appear on the skin of Eleonora Zügun, the 'Poltergeist Medium' or 'Devil Girl'. A photograph taken by ghost hunter Harry Price in London in 1926. (Author's collection)

The famous 'Feast of Blood' front cover of publisher Edward Lloyd's 'penny dreadful' classic, Varney the Vampire, which first appeared in August 1845. Today the series is attributed to the prolific Victorian writer, James Malcolm Rymer.

A portrait of the Irish author Bram Stoker (1847–1912), taken in the 1890s at the time he was planning his new vampire novel, Dracula.

Montague Rhodes (M.R.) James (1862–1936), master of the English ghost story. His highly regarded tales include the vampire classics 'Count Magnus' and 'An Episode of Cathedral History'.

Edward Frederic (E.F.) Benson (1867–1940), the English novelist. His short story 'The Room in the Tower' remains one of the great early twentieth-century vampire tales. (The E.F. Benson Society)

Man of mystery: Montague Summers (1880–1948), pictured in the mid-1920s. He claimed to believe in the literal existence of vampires and the power of the vampire 'talisman'. (Author's collection)

The charmer: Acid Bath murderer John George Haigh, also known as the 'Vampire of London', hanged at Wandsworth Prison on 10 August 1949. (Author's collection)

Jack the Ripper meets Dracula: Lon Chaney returns from the grave in the lost 1927 silent classic, London After Midnight. (MGM Studios Inc)

A publicity shot of Christopher Lee on the Bray Studio back-lot in 1958. With their colour version of Stoker's *Dracula*, Hammer Films continued their landmark series of Gothic horrors that would stretch well into the next decade, despite the studio's budget only stretching to the ground floor of the Count's castle. (Hammer Films)

Jimmy Sangster (1927–2011) directing a film for Hammer in the early 1970s. As a screenwriter in the mid-1950s he reinvented Gothic horror with his ground-breaking scripts for *The Curse of Frankenstein* and *Dracula*. (Hammer Films)

Hammer's most revered director Terence Fisher (1904–1980) prepares Christopher Lee for the blood-drinking episode in the 1965 sequel *Dracula: Prince of Darkness*. (Hammer Films)

Dracula – Prince of Darkness: Lee meets his end under the ice. (Hammer Films)

Ralph Bates dons the ring and cloak as Geoffrey Keen, John Carson and Peter Sallis prepare to Taste the Blood of Dracula in 1969. (Hammer Films)

Lee's final outing as the Count for Hammer in the closing scene from 1973's The Satanic Rites of Dracula. (Hammer Films)

A new decade and a new Hammer vampire: Ingrid Pitt as Carmilla seduces Kate O'Mara in Roy Ward Baker's The Vampire Lovers (1970). (Hammer Films)

The Vampire Lovers: Ingrid Pitt and the gentleman of horror, Peter Cushing. (Hammer Films)

Director Robert Young and members of the cast on location in Black Park for Hammer's 1972 classic, Vampire Circus. (Hammer Films)

Ingrid Pitt courtesy of make-up artist Tom Smith as Peter Sasdy's Countess Dracula (1970). (Hammer Films)

Shapeshifting vampire Emil (Anthony Corlan) claims another victim as the body count mounts in Vampire Circus. (Hammer Films)

The west section of Highgate Cemetery, photographed in the early 1970s during the time of the vampire media phenomenon. (Chris Underwood)

Marianne Morris and Anulka are Vampyres (Essay Films, 1974). (Author's collection)

Sean Manchester, vampire hunter, with the tools of the profession: crucifixes and wooden stakes. A portrait first published in Peter Underwood's *Exorcism!* in 1990. (Photograph copyright Sean Manchester)

The Highgate Vampire case: David Farrant, psychic investigator, in action in 1970, inspecting a vandalised coffin in the terrace catacombs. (David Farrant)

Denholm Elliott and Susan George among the rats in Thames Television's 1968 teleplay of Dracula. (Thames Television)

Montage of press coverage on the Highgate Vampire case. (Photograph copyright Sean Manchester)

Birmingham musicians Black Sabbath, regarded as the architects of heavy metal, whose doom-laden style removed the last vestiges of humour from the horror genre in popular music. (Vertigo Records)

The English extreme metal band Cradle of Filth, who have successfully incorporated the vampire myth into their music and visual style since forming in 1991. (Vlad Barin)

Author Ronald Chetwynd-Hayes (1919–2001): Vampirism with a touch of humour. (Photograph copyright Seamus Ryan)

Writer and film critic Kim Newman, whose *Anno Dracula* series of alternate history novels began an imaginative reinvention of the undead myth in the early 1990s. (Photograph copyright QueenMab/Shipscook Photographic. Contact simon.ball3@btopenworld.com for commercial reuse)

However, Fisher and Hammer were absent for *Blood of the Vampire*, a Sangster script for director Henry Cass' *Artistes Alliance*, that had been rushed into production in the autumn of 1957 following the success of *The Curse of Frankenstein*, but which on release at the end of August 1958 ultimately became sidelined by Hammer's second major horror instalment, which had burst onto cinema screens across the country three months before. Shrewdly for Cass, Sangster produced a screenplay that borrowed heavily from his initial *Frankenstein* script for Tony Hinds, but which also contained elements designed to court attention from future viewers of his then recently completed adaptation of Stoker, which had only just passed from his typewriter onto the back-lot at Bray. Despite the intended similarities, *Blood of the Vampire* is a vampire film in name only as, clearly mindful of charges of plagiarism from Hammer, the undead creature of the title is in fact a human scientist rather than a true nosferatu, resurrected from beyond the grave by an impromptu heart transplant and subsequently kept alive by frequent and gory Eastman Color blood transfusions courtesy of the inmates of a local insane asylum. In the absence of both Peter Cushing and Christopher Lee, noted Shakespearian stage actor Donald Wolfit played the pseudo-vampiric Doctor Callistratus, but despite successfully casting Hammer actress Barbara Shelley as a female lead and proclaiming both a script by Jimmy '*Frankenstein*' Sangster and the tag line 'He begins where Dracula left off!' on his cinema posters, Tony Hinds ultimately had the last laugh nearly twenty years later as, under his firmly established screenwriting pseudonym of John Elder, he recycled much of the basic plot of Cass' film for Hammer as *Frankenstein and the Monster From Hell* in 1974.

Despite the competition, the next two entries in the hierarchy of British vampire cinema were to be wholly Hammer affairs. Filmed over a period of eight weeks beginning at the end of January 1960, *The Brides of Dracula* returned Peter Cushing to the role of Van Helsing in order to provide the continuity in what is now a highly regarded but ultimately loose sequel to the studio's original of two years before. The brides of the title are the vampirised female students of a high-class Transylvanian finishing school, consigned to the ranks of the undead by the release from captivity of a handsome but decadent aristocrat, Baron Meinster, whose former licentious lifestyle has ultimately brought about his corruption and subsequent imprisonment in the family home by an ineffectual but tormented mother, the Baroness, played by Argentinean-born repertory actress Martitia Hunt. David Peel, in his one starring role, donned the cloak and fangs to play the sadistic Baron whose foul bloodlust falls upon both male as well as female victims: at one point, Cushing himself receives the vampire's bite but before its effects fully take over, manages to burn the 'seal of Dracula' from his throat with a white-hot iron and sterilise the wound with holy water. In a set piece finale, Van Helsing rescues the heroine, French schoolmistress Marianne Danielle (Yvonne Monlaur) from the Baron's clutches and in a scene reminiscent of the climax of *Dracula*, uses his flask of holy water to great effect, keeping the vampire at bay while manipulating the sails of a burning windmill to form the deadly shadow of a cross on the body of his stricken opponent.

For this, the studio's first detour away from Stoker's original narrative, Tony Hinds initially turned to the safe hands of Jimmy Sangster to provide a new storyline, and while Terry Fisher was busily filming *The Mummy* on the Bray lot, the architect of Hammer's Gothic horror revival duly completed a full treatment, initially entitled *The Disciple of Dracula*, which established Meinster as the vampire menace from the very beginning and also introduced one of the genre's now forgotten vampire hunters, a mysterious occultist known as Latour. Chronologically, *Disciple* was in fact Sangster's second attempt at a sequel: an initial screenplay, *Revenge of Dracula*, commissioned soon after the release of the original, was passed over, eventually seeing the light of day nine years and several re-writes later as *Dracula: Prince of Darkness* in 1966.

Back in the autumn of 1959, Sangster's new vampire script subsequently underwent several periods of revision, by an un-credited Tony Hinds as well as Peter Bryan and former Conservative MP turned playwright Edward Percy Smith, which brought about a number of changes, most notably the replacement of Dr Latour by Van Helsing and the omission of a late appearance of the spirit of Count Dracula, summoned by Black Magic forces to destroy the evil Baron Meinster in a bloodbath ending that Hinds no doubt realised would never stand up to the scrutiny of the BBFC censor. Although derided by Jimmy Sangster, who in later years became critical of the alterations to his original screenplay, the final version of *The Brides of Dracula* contains several memorable scenes including the final tortured moments of the Baroness Meinster, herself reduced to a vampire creature following an incestuous attack by her own son, as well as the eerie vigil at the locked coffin of the undead student Gina, where one by one the padlocks fall to the floor in a scene clearly inspired by James' unlocking of the coffin at the climax of *Count Magnus*.

The character of Baron Meinster as portrayed by David Peel is a further development of a theme first explored in brief in Fisher's *Dracula* and one which runs through this and several later instalments of Hammer's *Dracula* and related vampire sagas, the concept of the 'cult' of vampirism and its associated moral and physical dangers: the Manson and Koresh-like entrapment and corruption of its followers, the drug-dependency addiction of blood, and as Silver and Ursini describe it, the 'aberrant but essentially natural phenomenon' of the evolvement of the undead creature, a physical as well as spiritual disease-like process initiated once one has reached the nadir of a profligate and licentiate lifestyle. The vampire cult's similarities with those of Black Magic and Satanism was the logical progression that Hammer were to reach in the final entry in the series, 1973's *The Satanic Rites of Dracula*, while the aristocratic decadence of the Baron Meinster in the Sangster/Bryan/Smith/Hinds script reflects in some ways the real life activities of individuals such as Francis Dashwood, instigator of the 'Monks of Medmenham' and the creator of the notorious Hell Fire Caves beneath the church of St Lawrence at West Wycombe in Buckinghamshire.

It would be over two years before Hammer would return to the twilight world of the undead. *Kiss of the Vampire* (known in America as *Kiss of Evil*) not only moved the vampire story forward in time to the early years of the twentieth century, but also gave the subject a quantum leap in terms of the cult-like aspects of vampirism that Fisher had been working around in his previous two films. For this third instalment of the series, producer Tony Hinds handed the directorial reins to Don Sharp, a Tasmanian-born filmmaker in his early forties, whose horror cinema credentials also include *Curse of the Fly* (1965), *Rasputin, the Mad Monk* (1966) with Christopher Lee in the title role, and the bizarre cult classic *Psychomania* (1971), an alternative take on the subject of the living dead involving a devil-worshipping gang of motorbikers led by Nicky Henson. Fisher himself was absent in Germany at the time making a loose adaptation of Conan Doyle's Sherlock Holmes adventure *The Valley of Fear*, and may even have been sidelined by Hammer at this point following poor box office returns on his recent and expensive reworking of the Gaston Leroux classic, *The Phantom of the Opera*, filmed at Bray as well as on location at Wimbledon Theatre. Another Hammer regular conspicuously absent from the production team was Jimmy Sangster, for whom Gothic horror had now lost much of its appeal following the release of Hitchcock's *Psycho* two years before. Sangster would not return to the genre for nearly five years, during which time he instigated a distinct change of direction for the studio, penning a series of psychological suspense films such as *Taste of Fear* (1961), *Maniac* (1963), *Nightmare* (1964), and the following year an adaptation of Evelyn Piper's novel *The Nanny*, starring veteran actress Bette Davis.

Tony Hinds, however, had not lost his enthusiasm for the period horror drama that he had been a major force in reviving for the modern generation of cinema-goers, and with Sangster now in the background, he took on the role of writer for the vast majority of Hammer's ongoing series of *Dracula* and *Frankenstein* films throughout the 1960s, as well as a handful of one-off features that included *Captain Clegg* (1962), an adaptation of Russell Thorndike's *Doctor Syn* smuggling adventures, and *The Reptile* (1966), an original tale of a Cornish village plagued by a shape-shifting lizard woman. For *Kiss of the Vampire*, Hinds took Jimmy Sangster's original *Disciple of Dracula* script out of his desk drawer, retained the opening and closing pages and seamlessly grafted on an entirely new story involving an original cast of both characters and actors. Set in Bavaria before the First World War, Edward de Souza and Jennifer Daniel are the honeymooning English couple, Gerald and Marianne Harcourt, snared into the sinister blood cult of Noel Willman's aristocratic Dr Ravna and his vampiric family after being left stranded at an isolated country hotel when their motorcar runs out of petrol. Invited to dinner in Ravna's mountain-top chateau, Marianne becomes entranced by the sensual piano-playing of the mysterious doctor's son Carl and later, during the course of a masked ball made up entirely of members of the vampire coven, is kidnapped and initiated into the cult by Ravna himself. Abandoned at the hotel and unable to make either the proprietors or the local police believe his story, Gerald eventually finds an ally in a fellow guest, the mysterious Professor Zimmer, played by Welsh film and television actor Clifford Evans, whose daughter has previously fallen victim to the vampire menace. Together they set about rescuing Marianne from Ravna's clutches as well as ultimately bringing about the destruction of the coven itself.

As an original non-*Dracula* offering from Hammer, *Kiss of the Vampire* remains one of the highlights of British vampire cinema from the 1960s that both compliments and contrasts with Fisher's earlier films, while Tony Hinds' re-working of Sangster's material shows how promising *The Disciple of Dracula* would have been if produced in its entirety, its original elements providing the film with some of its most powerful moments. In a lengthy pre-credit sequence, Zimmer interrupts the funeral of his own undead daughter to drive a gravedigger's shovel through the exposed coffin lid into the vampire's heart, initiating a blood-curdling scream and a surge of blood through the shattered woodwork, accompanied by the driving rhythm of James Bernard's richly orchestrated score, itself transforming into a Rachmaninoff-like piano solo, the 'Vampire Rhapsody', now highly regarded by Hammer devotees and which Bernard's biographer David Huckvale suggests has its origins in Richard Addinsell's 'Warsaw Concerto' from the 1941 film *Dangerous Moonlight*. As well as the opening scene, the film's tumultuous finale, in which Zimmer uses an occult ceremony to summon a swarm of vampire bats to destroy the evil doctor and his followers, was also lifted from Sangster's original script, but as filmed is less effective, due to the limitations of the brave but ultimately unconvincing effects supplied by Les Bowie; close-up shots of the bats clinging to Ravna's twitching and dying acolytes are, however, surprisingly effective.

As well as the direct and unused sequences, Sharp's film also shares other areas of common ground with both *Dracula* and *The Brides of Dracula*: the creation of a makeshift cross to keep the vampire menace at bay makes a reappearance, this time smeared in blood on Edward de Souza's naked chest, while like Van Helsing before him, Zimmer at one point has to brave the flames to burn a vampire bite from his flesh, in this instance inflicted by the beautiful vampiress Tania, one of the most sensual of Hammer's vampire women, played with ravishing allure by English actress Isobel Black. For Professor Zimmer, Tony Hinds reused aspects of the Latour character from Sangster's original *Disciple* screenplay, in doing so creating one of the most interesting and underrated of screen vampire slayers, an enigmatic but ultimately tragic figure, driven to alcoholism by the corruption and death of his daughter. Although Zimmer's academic background remains obscure, his knowledge of vampirism is easily the equal of Van Helsing, although his embrace and use of Black Magic in order to raise the nightmarish swarm of killer bats is in direct contrast to Cushing's clinical portrayal of the Victorian parapsychologist, whose origins in the founding of the Society for Psychical Research in England in the early 1880s are contemporary with the fictional timeline of Hammer's ongoing series of films. Throughout his *Dracula* screenplays, Hinds also demonstrates a tendency to drip-feed aspects of Stoker's original novel into the storyline, here restoring the vampires' ability to travel abroad during the daytime hours, albeit protected from direct sunlight by the blinds over the windows of their horse-drawn carriage.

Don Sharp's *Kiss of the Vampire* was released in the autumn of 1963, by which time two figures from Hammer's past were preparing to return to the genre with which they had up until then only had both brief associations and success. Milton Subotsky and Max Rosenburg, whose initial script *Frankenstein and the Monster* had been passed over by Tony Hinds back in 1956, had spent the intervening years attempting to break back into the motion picture industry with their own Amicus Films, a small production company based in Slough, Berkshire, formed in the wake of their involvement with Vulcan Production's *The City of the Dead* (1960), a tale of modern New England witchcraft starring Christopher Lee and Venetia Stevenson, filmed at Shepperton and released the same year as Hitchcock's classic *Psycho*, a film with which it surprisingly shares some plot characteristics.

After a brief and forgettable excursion into musical comedy, the two men steered their fledgling company back towards the genre with which they both had the most affinity and, by 1964, had hit upon a production formula that would make them Hinds' and Hammer's main rivals for the remainder of the decade. Using Ealing Studios' seminal *Dead of Night* as their blueprint, Subotsky and Rosenburg crafted a series of portmanteau films, each a collection of macabre short stories and vignettes, linked together by a framing narrative provided over the course of several films by a series of seemingly benign but ultimately sinister and deadly characters, including a fairground barker, an estate agent, an antique dealer and a mental asylum doctor. As well as the advantage of providing variation to the story across the length of a single film, the portmanteau format also had economic advantages in terms of the films' production in that it was possible to cast a roll call of high-profile leading players who in reality would only be required for a few days' filming on each picture. In this way, stars such as Cushing and Lee, as well as other, mostly British screen and stage actors, including Donald Pleasance, Michael Gough, Ingrid Pitt and Geoffrey Bayldon, a number of whom had or would appear in various films for Hammer at the same time, gave Amicus a similar visual look to their larger rival, with the result that the Americans' pictures were often mistaken for Hammer Films in the public eye, something that no doubt pleased Subotsky and Rosenburg no end given their summary dismissal from the scene back in the mid-1950s.

As we will see, a number of Amicus' multiple-story films (five out of a total of eight) were to feature a vampire episode, the first of which, scripted by Subotsky himself, is now regarded by devotees as one of the highlights of the series, and is worth discussing briefly here. For *Dr Terror's House of Horrors*, former cinematographer

Freddie Francis directed Peter Cushing as the eponymous railway traveller of the title, whose Tarot cards spell death and destruction for five fellow passengers, among them Alan Freeman, Roy Castle, Neil McCallum and Christopher Lee, who board a fog-shrouded night train to nowhere, unaware of the sinister fate that ultimately awaits them all. In giving a contemporary feel to what amounts to a collection of now familiar horror clichés – a voodoo curse, a disembodied hand, a werewolf legacy and a man-eating plant – Subotsky made up for the restrictions imposed by an entirely studio-bound production, while composer Elisabeth Lutyens, daughter of the famous English architect, and retained by Francis after recently scoring Jimmy Sangster's *Paranoiac* for Hammer, used her idiosyncratic serialism to great effect in accompanying the protagonists on the journey to their inevitable doom. For 'Vampire', the fifth and final story, a youthful Donald Sutherland plays newly-wed doctor Bob Carroll, whose work at a small town New England medical practice becomes increasingly complicated with the gradual realisation that his attractive French wife Nicolle (Jennifer Jayne) may be behind the sudden anaemia-like illness of a local schoolboy. Fellow physician Max Adrian convinces Carroll that Nicolle is a vampire and after fighting off an attack himself by a murderous bat in a deserted building, fashions a wooden stake and persuades his younger colleague to finish off his bride in traditional fashion. After Sutherland is arrested by the local sheriff for murder, Dr Blake (Adrian) breaks the fourth wall to reveal that he too is a bloodsucker, with the wry comment that, 'This town isn't big enough for two doctors, or two vampires' before promptly turning into a bat! In his script, Subotsky links his modern story with the cinema traditions now firmly established by Sangster and Hammer – at one point Blake makes an improvised crucifix with his crossed arms in order to ward off the attacking nightwing – while the small town American setting anticipates by ten years Stephen King's benchmark reinvention of Stoker's *Dracula* as *Salem's Lot* in 1975. Now garnered with cult status, *Dr Terror's House of Horrors* went on release in early 1965, the same year that saw the return to the genre of a number of its biggest and most influential players.

During the intervening years following his big break with *The Curse of Frankenstein*, Christopher Lee had appeared in a further dozen films for Hammer, but despite being reasonably happy to continue associating with the horror format, had consistently declined to reprise the vampire role with which he was still inextricably linked. Finally, after an absence of nearly eight years, James Carreras finally persuaded Lee to play Dracula again and in the spring of 1965, Jimmy Sangster received a call to bring the Count to life once more. Now well established as a major screenwriter, Sangster was initially reluctant to take on the job, almost as reluctant as Lee had been to return to the role in the first place, feeling that at this point in his career the project was something of a backward step. In his collection of memoirs *Inside Hammer*, published in 2001, Sangster bluntly summed up his feelings at the time, describing it as 'a hangover from a time long gone.'

> I was fed up with Gothic horror movies and felt that my career had moved well past this phase … I'd done half-a-dozen of my psycho-type movies and I'd written and produced what I considered two of my best works, *Taste of Fear* and *The Nanny*. I'd already started to go to Los Angeles on various assignments; I just didn't want to step back to the time when my name once appeared on the billboard as *Jimmy (Frankenstein) Sangster* [original italics].

Eventually relenting, Sangster agreed to revise his pre-*Brides of Dracula* screenplay for the occasion on the understanding that it would go out under a pseudonym. With this, the final obstacle out of the way, *Dracula: Prince of Darkness* by John Samson and John Elder went into production at Bray on 26 April 1965 and was completed in just over five weeks.

For this, the first true sequel to their 1957 classic, producer Anthony Nelson Keys attempted to reassemble as much as possible the team that had successfully brought the now famous original to the screen. As well as set designer Bernard Robinson and editor James Needs, Terence Fisher, now rehabilitated by the studio after helming *The Gorgon* the year before, returned to the director's chair, while James Bernard seamlessly recycled his previous composition into a new score, based as before around the distinctive three-chord leitmotif highlighting the syllables of the title character's name. One notable absentee, however, was Peter Cushing who, due to prior commitments, was unable to reprise his role as originally scripted in the original version of the story. To overcome this, Sangster created a new vampire slaying adversary whose character ultimately hovers somewhat midway between Stoker's Van Helsing and *Kiss of the Vampire*'s Professor Zimmer, the unorthodox rifle-toting Franciscan monk Father Sandor, played with suitable energy and gruff humour by Scottish actor Andrew Keir, while to provide continuity (as well as making up for a shortfall of screen time on the initial edit) Cushing himself was glimpsed briefly in a pre-credit sequence that replayed the climactic battle and sunlight disintegration of the vampire count from the closing reel of the first picture, now wreathed in swirling mist to hide the change to the new film's widescreen ratio.

In its final presentation, *Dracula: Prince of Darkness* is essentially a film of two halves: the first (and most effective in terms of atmosphere and the creation of a growing sense of unease and menace) leads up to the revival of Dracula, after which the story follows the vigorous physicality of much of Fisher's original, as well as including some of the most powerful visual sequences contained in Hammer's entire *Dracula* series. Set ten years on from previous events, two English couples, Charles and Diana Kent (Francis Matthews and Suzan Farmer) and Charles' brother Alan (Charles Tingwell) and his frumpy disapproving wife Helen, played by Barbara Shelley, are on a sightseeing tour of the Carpathian Mountains. At a wayside inn, the tourists encounter the forthright Father Sandor who, unbeknown to them, has recently prevented a local priest and the mourners at a village wake from mutilating the body of a young girl. With Dracula now dead, Sandor deems the post-mortem stake through the heart unnecessary, but is suitably concerned about the proximity of the now abandoned Castle Dracula to warn the travelling Kents to omit it from their itinerary and continue on with the journey to nearby Carlsbad.

The following day, in now well-worn style, the travellers are abandoned at a lonely crossroad by a frightened coach driver unwilling to drive further in the failing light, and in a scene reminiscent of Harker's original arrival at the Borgo Pass, the safety of what appears to be the timely arrival of a mysterious (and driverless) coach quickly fades as its uncontrollable horses transport the couples up along steadily climbing Transylvanian roads (in reality Black Park near Heathrow Airport) and eventually over a frozen moat into the courtyard of the undead count's silent and seemingly empty mountain-top lair.

Once inside, the Kents encounter the sinister Klove, played by London-born television actor Philip Latham, a former manservant whose late master's perpetual orders are to keep Castle Dracula in a state of readiness to assist and accommodate passing travellers. After the couples have dined and retired for the night, Alan Kent follows Klove down to an underground vault where, in one of the film's most graphic and shocking sequences, he is brutally murdered and his freshly spilt blood used to bring Lee back to life. Soon after, Klove lures the unsuspecting Helen down into the crypt where, after confronting the mutilated body of her husband, she is mesmerised and seduced into the vampire cult by the fully restored Dracula. Charles spends the next day searching for the missing couple, but after Klove has tricked Diana in returning to the castle and with the sun now set, first the vampirised Helen and subsequently Dracula himself attack. Saved by Diana's necklace crucifix and another improvised cross, this time fashioned from the lengths of a broken sword, the Kents escape with Klove's horse and trap and are rescued in the forest by the sudden appearance of Father Sandor, who takes them back with him to Carlsbad Monastery. Sanctuary, however, is short lived as Helen and Dracula soon appear at Diana's bedroom window; Diana receives a bite from Helen on the wrist but her terrified screams force the undead couple to flee before they can gain entry. Using the traditions now firmly established in Hammer's previous two films, Fisher allows Sandor to cauterise the deadly bite with the heat from a lamp chimney, and after Helen is captured by a group of monks and taken to a monastery cell, Charles looks on in horror as the Father Superior drives a stake through her heart.

With Helen now dead, Dracula resumes the attack, gaining access to the building by taking over the mind of the Renfield-like Ludwig (Thorley Walters), the monastery calligrapher and Sangster's belated attempt to pacify the Stoker purists who complained over the years about his omission from the first film, who brings the recovering Diana into a liaison with the Count where she is overpowered and abducted. In a fast-moving chase reminiscent of the closing reel of the 1958 original, Sandor and Kent, now on horseback, pursue Klove as he attempts to drive the caskets containing his vampire master and the entranced Diana back to the relative safety of the castle catacombs. With the advantage of being able to cut across country, the vampire hunters waylay the fleeing wagon at a forest crossroads and Klove is shot down. Now out of control, the driverless wagon crashes on its approach to Castle Dracula, spilling the Count's coffin out onto the surface of the frozen moat, where, freed by the failing light, the vampire engages in a desperate struggle with the stake-wielding Charles. With Diana now safe, Sandor unleashes a fusillade of rifle fire that fractures the ice, and as Kent climbs to safety, Lee, assisted by his regular stunt double, Eddie Powell, sinks to his death in the icy mountain water.

Despite helming another four pictures for Hammer – three *Frankenstein* sequels together with the now highly regarded adaptation (by Richard Matheson) of Dennis Wheatley's 1934 Black Magic thriller *The Devil Rides Out* – *Prince of Darkness* would be Terence Fisher's final *Dracula* film and it remains the most focused of the four Gothic period follow-ups that the studio released during the latter part of the 1960s, focused in the sense of retelling the *Dracula* story within the framework of the original film. Later entries in the Hammer canon would attempt to expand the potential of Lee's Dracula, with varying levels of success, but with his true sequel, Fisher succeeded in bringing together a collection of disparate elements that in one film serve as a textbook definition of 1960s Hammer Horror.

Dracula: Prince of Darkness also stands out as the film that did the most in precipitating the flood of blood and sex that would swamp Hammer's later output of British vampire films throughout the early 1970s. Even given what Fisher and the studio had brought to the screen during the previous eight years, Lee's revivification scene, as the Count's ashes coalesce into a humanoid-like mass of tissue and plasma under a torrent of streaming blood from Alan Kent's cut throat, is as much a benchmark of cinema violence as the appearance of Peckinpah's *The Wild Bunch* four years later, and as originally scripted by Sangster and Hinds would have been even more extreme: the image of Klove removing and tossing aside Charles Tingwell's head to allow the life-giving blood to pour from the severed neck stump fell at the screenplay's first submission to the BBFC. Similarly, Fisher's control of the sexual elements of Sangster's script, which although like the gore was reined in by the censor, shows a masterly use of restraint and subtlety that would gradually become lost in later outings, not only for the Count but also for Hammer's other undead screen legions. Barbara Shelly's baptism into the realms of the undead amply demonstrates a façade of Victorian prudery corrupted by the permissiveness of Lee's supernatural onslaught, and her attempted seduction – as the vampirised Helen – of Suzan Farmer's Diana points towards the overt lesbianism of the later Karnstein trilogy; while the Sangster/Hinds inclusion of Stoker's Mina/Dracula blood-drinking episode, as Diana kneels to lick an open wound on Lee's chest, still retains much of its oral suggestiveness, despite cuts by the censor and Fisher's clever handling of the camera. It is also difficult not to read a sexual subtext into the violent and protracted monastery staking sequence of the captured Helen, now one of the film's most widely repeated extracts, whose gang rape and male supremacy connotations leave little to the imagination.

Dracula: Prince of Darkness went on general release in early January 1966 – for Hammer it was a financial success and garnered the studio some of its most favourable reviews up until that time. Despite this, Jimmy Sangster, although acknowledging Fisher's fine handling and presentation of a number of the picture's most powerful sequences, was unhappy with the final result. 'I think the first Dracula was the best,' he later wrote. 'It was all so new back then. Hammer weren't fully aware of what they'd got hold of, so they weren't trying to repeat the formula. They were *creating* [original italics] the formula, and by the time *Prince of Darkness* came out it was getting well-worn.' With hindsight this is not far from the truth, but Hammer were far from finished and over the next decade would unleash an unprecedented legion of vampire creatures on to the cinema-going British public.

On 29 May 1968, a little over two years after Lee had sunk into his watery tomb at the foot of Bernard Robinson's masterly castle set at Bray, Hammer received the Queen Elizabeth Award to Industry in recognition of the £1.5 million worth of American dollars the company had brought into the country each year since 1965. During that time, a production deal with Eliot Hyman's newly created Warner Bros.-Seven Arts had resulted in Hammer leaving their old home of over twenty-five years, and although now based mainly at Elstree in Hertfordshire, the presentation ceremony took place at Pinewood Studios near Iver Heath in Buckinghamshire, where Freddie Francis was supervising the finale of the fifth entry in what was now an ongoing series of undead features. *Dracula Has Risen from the Grave*, with Lee again in the title role, was an entirely Anthony Hinds scripted sequel to Fisher's previous film and which went on to be one of the studio's most profitable films, breaking London box office records in its first two days of screening alone and prompting Hammer to commission a further two Gothic sequels from the Hinds/Elder pen before the decade was out. But ten years on from their first milestone picture, the continued exposure (as Sangster has posthumously stated) was beginning to tell and, as Hinds struggled to sustain the reinvention of Stoker's great anti-hero, a process he had been a major factor in bringing into being, Hammer's Dracula quickly started to become the one-dimensional screen villain that had been the fate of its Universal predecessor a quarter of a century before.

Despite having a free rein in shaping the direction of Lee's third outing as the Count, Hinds chose both to stick to familiar territory and continue the chronological sequence of events. *Dracula Has Risen from the Grave* opens with one of its best scenes, an original flashback episode to pre-*Prince of Darkness* times, as a country priest discovers the body of a young girl, murdered and concealed inside the bell tower of his church, the desecration of which provides the impetus for much of the film's later events. Twelve months on from Dracula's death, a visiting Monsignor,

Ernst Mueller (television *Maigret* actor Rupert Davies) discovers that the church is still shunned by the village congregation, and as part of his castigation of the resident (and unnamed) priest played by Ewan Hooper, carries out an exorcism of Castle Dracula and seals the entrance doors with the church's altar cross. As a thunderstorm rages over the mountainside, Hooper falls from a ledge onto the frozen ice, under which the body of Lee lies frozen in suspended animation: blood from a gash on his head seeps through to the vampire below and Monsignor Mueller innocently returns to the village, unaware that through his actions Dracula has been restored to life and the local priest is now under his spell.

Unable to return to the safety of his mountain lair, Dracula follows the exorcist back to his home town of Keinenberg where, in a coffin exhumed from a local graveyard, he is concealed in the basement vaults below a tavern, one of whose workers, a university student and part-time cook Paul (Barry Andrews) is the current suitor of the Monsignor's niece Maria, played by then up and coming Hammer starlet Veronica Carlson. Paul's atheistic leanings unsurprisingly rankle with the elderly churchman, and while the lovers continue to meet in secret, Dracula takes his fill from the tavern's promiscuous barmaid Zena (Barbara Ewing) before commencing his night-time seduction of the beautiful Maria, whose orgasmic responses to the vampire's bite were the most overt the studio had yet presented on screen. After confronting Dracula during one of his nocturnal attacks, Mueller is struck down and killed by Hooper's dog-like servant, leaving Paul to hunt down and destroy the vampire himself. After failing to kill Dracula with the traditional stake through the heart, Paul follows the Count and the mesmerised Maria back to the castle where, after a struggle on the parapet, Lee falls to his death, impaled on the original church cross which has come to rest upended in a fissure on the mountainside after being ripped from the castle doors. Now free from Dracula's influence, his former servant intones a Latin prayer for the dead and the vampire's body dissolves until only blood and a discarded cloak remain.

Principal photography on *Risen from the Grave* wrapped on 4 June 1968 and the film was released at the beginning of November of the same year. Despite aspects of Hinds' script attempting to expand the traditionally established vampire mythos – at one point Dracula is able to rip what would have previously been a completely lethal stake out of his body due to the hero Paul's lack of religious conviction – the film gave Lee little to do, and its follow up, the gruesomely titled *Taste the Blood of Dracula*, fared little better. One major improvement, however, is the transfer of the entirety of the action – apart from a pre-credit sequence – from rural Transylvania, thereby omitting the now somewhat hackneyed village inn setting with its usual band of close-mouthed superstitious locals, to Victorian England, superbly realised by producer Aida Young and new Hammer director, the Hungarian-born Peter Sasdy, through a combination of location filming and period studio work and costumes, thereby bringing the story more in line with the contemporary setting envisioned by Stoker himself. As well as

St Andrew's Church, Totteridge, and Tykes Water Lake at Aldenham, several scenes were filmed at London's Highgate Cemetery, which as we will see was perhaps the most appropriate spot in the whole of England to film a vampire picture at the time.

As with the screenplay of *Prince of Darkness*, *Taste the Blood of Dracula* is a film of two parts centred on the now obligatory resurrection scene, of which the first is the most interesting in its attempt to bring new life and variety to Hammer's *Dracula* saga. Under the pretence of organising charity work for London's poor, three outwardly respectable middle-class gentlemen, William Hargood (Geoffrey Keen), Jonathan Secker (John Carson) and Samuel Paxton (Peter Sallis), meet on a monthly basis for what amounts to a hedonistic exploration of the capital's Victorian lowlife. In an East End brothel they encounter Lord Courtley, a titled but bankrupt aristocrat with a penchant for Black Magic, played by Ralph Bates (an up and coming young actor who, at the time, Hammer were grooming for stardom as a potential replacement for both Peter Cushing and Christopher Lee). Courtley persuades the men to buy a collection of curios which he claims are all that remains of Count Dracula – a signet ring, a cloak and clasp, and a glass phial of dried blood – which belong to a shady antique dealer and travelling salesman named Weller (Roy Kinnear), on the understanding that they will each receive immortality by performing a Satanic ceremony for which the items are an essential component. Unbeknown to Hargood and his cronies, Weller has in fact witnessed the previous demise of Dracula (courtesy of a recycling of the closing scene from *Risen from the Grave* intercut into the prologue of the film) while travelling in the Carpathian Mountains and eventually agrees to part with the relics for the princely sum of 1,000 guineas. The four men subsequently gather at an abandoned church where Lord Courtley dons the vampire cloak and instructs Hargood, Secker and Paxton to drink drafts of Dracula's blood, which he has reconstituted into goblets with plasma of his own. Appalled, they refuse, whereupon Courtley himself drinks from a chalice and promptly collapses in agony. Sickened and enraged, Hargood rejects the Satanist's cries for help and in a brutal scene all three men beat Courtley to death before fleeing the church, leaving the aristocrat's body to become transformed by the psychic forces unleashed from the bloodshed into the living form of Dracula himself. Now fully restored to life, Lee swears vengeance on the men who have destroyed his acolyte, thereby setting into motion the bloody and violent events which constitute the second part of the film.

Traumatised by the murder of Courtley, Hargood begins to drink heavily and in an intoxicated state makes a drunken and semi-lecherous attack on his daughter Alice (Linda Hayden) who, against his instructions, has attended a party with her suitor, Paxton's son, Paul. Fleeing into the garden, Alice encounters Dracula who puts the young girl under his spell and, as Hargood approaches, commands her to attack her father; Alice picks up a garden spade and strikes Hargood down, killing him, after which she returns to the ruined church with the Count. Soon after, Alice entices Paxton's daughter Lucy, played by Isla Blair, to the church where she is turned into a vampire and is subsequently discovered sleeping in a coffin by Secker and Paxton, who have braved the return to the scene of their crime in order to check on the body of the dead Courtley. Realising that Lucy is a vampire, Secker attempts to destroy her with an improvised stake ripped from a discarded pew, but Sallis' Paxton is appalled at the thought of mutilating his daughter and drawing a revolver shoots Secker in the arm. Alone in the darkening church, Paxton is confronted by the vampire Lucy together with the entranced Alice who, under Dracula's supervision, pin him into a pew and drive the stake into his chest. Back at his house and now weakened from loss of blood, Secker writes instructions for Paul Paxton on how to overcome the undead menace, but before the papers can be delivered he is attacked by his son Jeremy (Martin Jarvis), who has been corrupted by an encounter with his fiancée, the vampiric Lucy, and as Dracula looks on, Secker is stabbed to death. After the notes are passed to Paxton's son by a disinterested police sergeant (played by Hammer stalwart Michael Ripper) who believes that Jeremy Secker killed his father in a fit of jealous rage, Paul gathers together the usual vampire-hunting paraphernalia and sets off to the abandoned church to rescue Alice from Dracula's clutches. Finally, after a confrontation with Paul, who has sealed the doors of the building with a cross, Dracula is overcome by the religious iconography inside the building and after falling from the organ loft onto the altar, now free of its Satanic symbolism, rots away in a series of camera dissolves into the mass of blood-red dust from which he originally came, leaving the couple to walk away accompanied by James Bernard's lushly scored 'Young Lovers' theme, one of the highlights of the entire picture.

A troubled production both before and after the cameras had finished rolling, *Taste the Blood of Dracula* opened at the New Victoria Cinema, London, on 7 May 1970 on a double-bill with *Crescendo*, Jimmy Sangster's final psychological thriller for Hammer. Not only had Lee initially refused to appear in the film (despite James Carreras having already sold it to Warner Bros.-Seven Arts on the understanding that Lee would play the title role), a situation that generated a substantial amount of rewrites as well as additional out-of-hours' work for Aida Young in eventually persuading the actor to relent, but with the film in the can, the studio were soon threatened with a plagiarism suit by director Freddie Francis' son, Kevin, who claimed that parts of a screenplay he had written and submitted for consideration several months before, entitled *Dracula's Feast of Blood*, had been used without his knowledge or permission. Francis, who apparently didn't accuse Tony Hinds directly of stealing his work, later claimed in an interview that Hammer had had to pay him 'a large sum of money' before *Taste the Blood* could be delivered (two months behind schedule), and although the incident was one of the main reasons for Hinds finally quitting the company during the summer of the same year, the two men later enjoyed a brief but productive relationship during the mid-1970s with Hinds scripting two Peter Cushing vehicles for Francis' Hammeresque Tyburn Films, *The Ghoul* and *Legend of the Werewolf*, which both saw releases in 1975. Aside from the political drama, *Taste the Blood* is the closest that Hammer ever came to bringing much of the sub-text of Stoker's novel to the screen – in his *The Vampire Cinema*, David Pirie highlights the connections between Lee's destruction of the Hargood/ Secker/Paxton households and Dracula as the 'anti-father' who 'stands against every Victorian ideal of the family', and, despite its flaws, it remains one film in Hammer's undead canon that deserves to be known better.

For Hammer, vampires and vampirism perfectly book-ended the ten turbulent years of the 1960s: filming for *The Brides of Dracula* commenced in late January 1960, while principal photography on *Taste the Blood of Dracula* wrapped on 5 December 1969. The swell of social revolution and counter-culture that both marked the closing years of the decade and spilled over into the beginnings of its successor was also matched by the studio's increased exploitation of the world of the undead that reached its peak in the opening years of the 1970s: of the fifteen true vampire films made by Hammer between 1957 and 1973 (not counting *Countess Dracula*, Peter Sasdy's 1971 reworking of the legend of fellow Hungarian, Erzsébet Báthory), nine out of the total were made in the last three years of that period, four of which (including the cameo appearance in *The Legend of the 7 Golden Vampires*) feature the vampire king himself.

Christopher Lee's last Gothic Hammer film as the Count, *Scars of Dracula*, was filmed over the course of less than a month in the spring of 1970, exactly the same time that its far superior precursor – with its arresting 'Drink a Pint of Blood a Day' tagline – began showing in cinemas across the country. A stable mate of Jimmy Sangster's *Horror of Frankenstein*, which had wrapped at Elstree at the end of April, both films were an attempt to establish a new Gothic horror franchise for the 1970s by reworking the original storylines that had been so successful nearly fifteen years before. But despite being the origin of a number of now iconic still shots of Lee as the blood-eyed and fanged lord of the vampires, *Scars of Dracula* only succeeds as a sad parody of Fisher's 1958 classic, and although not exactly the worst film that Hammer ever made, remains a low point on the graph and the absolute nadir of Lee's association with the role.

Forsaking the linking continuity of the previous four films as well as the sophistication established by Peter Sasdy in his use of hypocritical Victorian society as a background for what David Pirie has described as Dracula's 'chaotic and dislocating eroticism', Anthony Hinds returned to a traditional but well-worn Transylvanian setting, now made visually unconvincing via painfully studio-bound filming and, at times, unnecessarily farcical by the inclusion of unhelpful comedic moments courtesy of *Benny Hill* actor Bob Todd and the inappropriate appearance of two dim-witted Pythonesque policemen. Some of the film's humour is in fact accidental, particularly that supplied by the Count's vampire bride Tania (New Zealand-born actress Anouska Hempel) whose husky dialogue is at times indistinguishable from that delivered by Fenella Fielding in Peter Rogers' 1966 Hammer send-up *Carry On Screaming*. Despite Hinds providing Lee with more screen time and extended dialogue than any other film in the series, and the inclusion, at the insistence of director Roy Ward Baker, of a wall-crawling sequence straight out of Stoker's book, the result is a pale imitation with little to recommend it: the aftermath of a bat attack on the congregation of a village church is well handled and Dracula's ability to communicate and receive information through the nightwings that gather in and around the forest trees and castle battlements, a rare nod to a particular aspect of the vampire's ability that through the restrictions of budget Hammer rarely acknowledged or exploited, remain the meagre highlights.

For his second solo take on Stoker's classic, Tony Hinds eschewed both Harker and Van Helsing characters, replacing the former with a young licentious portrait photographer, Paul Carlson (played by Christopher Matthews), while as an unnamed priest, former Hammer actor Michael Gwynne, who provided Peter Cushing's second attempt at creating artificial life in the 1958 sequel *The Revenge of Frankenstein*, becomes the token vampire-hunting adversary.

The screenplay itself is lacklustre from the very start. On the run from the local police after seducing the Burgomaster's daughter, Carlson eventually arrives at Castle Dracula where he is received by the icily courteous Count accompanied by his vampire mistress: on this occasion, Lee has been revived at the film's outset when, as part of a pre-credit sequence recycling effects shot from *Taste the Blood of Dracula*, a bat-like familiar vomits blood on his powdered remains which are conveniently laid out on a roof-top slab. The vampire woman, Tania, in a softcore replay of the 1958 John Van Eyssen/Valerie Gaunt encounter, later shares the youth's four-poster bed, but reveals her true nature by attempting to bite his throat, whereupon Ward Baker stages a clumsy re-enactment of Fisher's masterly first reveal of Lee as the demonic Dracula that quickly degenerates into the crude and increasingly sadistic shock effects on which Hammer's Gothic horrors were now reliant: in this instance, Lee stabs his vampire mistress to death with a dagger before letting a manservant (another Klove, this time played by a post-*Doctor Who* Patrick Troughton, wearing somewhat disturbing Charles Manson-like make-up) cut the body into pieces and dissolve the remains in an acid bath; her young lover shares a similarly gruesome fate, subsequently being discovered drained of blood and skewered on a spike. Carlson's disappearance initiates the customary follow-up investigation, this time courtesy of his law student brother Simon (a fresh faced Dennis Waterman) together with love interest Sarah (Jenny Hanley, later a regular presenter on the long running children's television magazine *Magpie*) who face an increasingly banal series of perils before, in a set piece finale on the castle battlements, Lee is struck by lightning and, wreathed in flames, falls to his death over the parapet, an ignominious demise made all the worse by a particularly unconvincing stunt double and atrocious model work. Lee himself described the entire outing as 'truly feeble'.

As they crossed the threshold of a new decade, recently knighted James Carreras found his company, now minus producers Tony Hinds and Anthony Nelson Keys, sailing far more difficult and challenging waters than would have seemed conceivable at the same point ten years before on the cusp of the Swinging Sixties. Many critics and writers on British cinema horror, among them David Pirie, Howard Maxford, Wayne Kinsey, Marcus Hearne and Jonathan Rigby, unite in their agreement that by the beginning of the 1970s, Hammer were making the wrong films at the wrong time, a situation for which Roy Ward Baker's *Scars of Dracula* is perhaps the supreme example, serving up unfashionable Gothic horror pastiche at a time when a spearhead of contemporary films such as Romero's *Night of the Living Dead* and Roman Polanski's *Rosemary's Baby* (both 1968) were paving the way for William Friedkin to craft *The Exorcist*, the film that changed the international horror landscape forever. Hammer's cinematic presentation of the vampire myth continued to cling to what the studio believed to be a tried and tested formula practically to the end. With hindsight, it seems remarkable that with the success of such contemporary based horror-thrillers such as *Taste of Fear* and *The Nanny*, James Carreras and Tony Hinds never considered the potential of a present-day vampire film at all throughout the 1960s. When Hammer did finally go down the route it was ultimately a case of too little too late, but although the writing was on the wall where the survival of the studio was concerned, the final two entries in the *Dracula* series show the potential results that an earlier decision in this direction may well have brought about.

In the summer of 1971, Warner Bros (now minus the Seven-Arts due to an amalgamation with the Kinney National Service Corporation) brought to Michael Carreras' attention a modern-day vampire feature from American International Pictures that had been financially secure to warrant a sequel, which was then in production. *Count Yorga, Vampire*, which at one point started life as a softcore porn flick titled *The Loves of Count Iorga*, successfully brought a Dracula-like character, in this instance the Bulgarian occultist of the title played by Robert Quarry, to contemporary Los Angeles, replacing the usual Transylvanian castle with a Beverley Hills mansion and injecting the whole undead storyline with new life, particularly as the present-day setting made it easier to take advantage of the new trends that were now appearing in the horror genre: at one point the sequel, *The Return of Count Yorga*, features a zombie-like vampire home invasion straight out of Romero's *Night of the Living Dead.*

Suitably impressed, Carreras commissioned French-born writer and director Don Houghton, whose British work up until that time included television scripts for *Emergency Ward 10* and *Doctor Who*, to write a treatment bringing Count Dracula and his adversary Van Helsing to modern London, thereby setting up a new Cushing/Lee encounter in the roles that had made them famous a decade and a half before. The duo had last shared scenes together in Terence Fisher's 1966 science fiction saga for Planet Film Distributors, *Night of the Big Heat*, based on the novel by John Lymington, before being reunited (after brief cameo appearances in

AIP's *Scream and Scream Again* (1969) and Amicus' *The House That Dripped Blood* (1970)) at the beginning of the year in another Amicus production, a re-working of the *Jekyll and Hyde* formula entitled *I, Monster*. Houghton's script received financial backing from Warner Bros in May 1971 and under the shooting title of *Dracula Today*, a six-week filming schedule began at Elstree at the end of September of the same year with Australian director Alan Gibson at the helm, whose previous feature work for Hammer comprised Jimmy Sangster's 1969 *Crescendo*.

For what Michael Carreras and the Hammer board hoped would be the start of another ongoing series, Houghton eschewed any attempt to connect his story with the studio's previous outings and provided the film with its own independent set of Gothic beginnings. Despite this break with the past, the film in fact shares much common ground with elements from Peter Sasdy's *Taste the Blood of Dracula*, particularly as regards to the revival of Dracula himself, although there are no direct connections in terms of storyline. Set in 1872, a pre-credit sequence establishes the film's origins as it depicts the last moments of both the vampire count and his nemesis Lawrence Van Helsing as they fight to the death on top of a runaway coach careering through the precincts of London's Hyde Park. As the coach overturns, Dracula is fatally wounded, impaled on one of the coach wheel's splintered spokes and, as a dying Van Helsing looks on, is quickly reduced to ashes, a portion of which, together with his customary signet ring, are recovered by a disciple. As the vampire hunter is laid to rest, Dracula's ashes are buried nearby and in a well-staged reveal, Gibson uses Van Helsing's tombstone to mark the passage of a hundred years as the film's opening titles transport the audience from the sombre sights and sounds of a Victorian funeral into a modern world cluttered with jet plane noise, tower cranes, motorway flyovers and rush hour traffic.

In Hammer's take on Swinging London, the Van Helsing family have done very well for themselves: Lawrence Van Helsing's grandson, Lorrimer, a London University lecturer in anthropology and European history, lives in a fashionable Chelsea townhouse with his attractive granddaughter Jessica (Stephanie Beacham) who, to the predictable displeasure of her conservative peer, enjoys the raucous company of a group of gate-crashing teenage fun-lovers complete with the best assortment of bells, kaftans and beads that Carnaby Street can provide. At the suggestion of a new group member, the unimaginatively named Johnny Alucard ('Dracula' backwards having first been used by Lon Chaney Jr in Universal's *Son of Dracula*), the group agree to hold a Black Magic ritual for kicks at nearby St Bartolph's, an abandoned church on the Thames Embankment, whose derelict churchyard unbeknown to Jessica and her friends contains both Lawrence Van Helsing's grave and Dracula's buried remains. Like Lord Courtley before him, Alucard (played with suitable mystique by Londoner Christopher Neame) is a Dracula devotee whose family heirlooms include a glass phial of the master's ashes and the familiar silver signet ring, and with his midnight Black Mass underway, follows in Ralph Bates' footsteps by mixing up a cocktail laced with his own blood as an offering to the Devil. Soon events get out of hand and as the terrified teenagers – including Jessica's boyfriend Bob (Philip Miller) – scatter, Laura (former Lamb's Navy Rum model Caroline Munro in her first feature film for Hammer) gets left behind to become the revived Lee's first modern victim. Back at the Cavern coffee bar, a regular meeting place on the King's Road, Johnny persuades the group that Laura has left to visit her parents in Kent, but the others aren't convinced and soon the girl's bloodless corpse is discovered in a shallow grave by children playing on a nearby building site.

For Inspector Murray (Michael Coles) of the Met's Special Branch, all roads lead to Lorrimer Van Helsing and his family. Suspecting a cult murder, Murray visits the Van Helsing home and his descriptions of the body together with his granddaughter's involvement lead the lecturer to suspect a modern-day outbreak of vampirism is taking place. Soon Johnny has lured another member of the group, Gaynor Keating (singer and actress Marsha Hunt, the inspiration for The Rolling Stones' 1971 single 'Brown Sugar') to St Bartolph's, where Dracula takes his fill before vampirising Alucard himself, who embraces his new undead lifestyle with relish by attacking and killing a customer at a local launderette. Another victim is Jessica's boyfriend Bob who subsequently lures her to the Cavern bar, where she is overpowered and taken to the church to be mesmerised by the Count in readiness for enslavement into the new vampire legions. Now convinced that Dracula has returned to exact his revenge on the modern-day descendants of Lawrence Van Helsing, Lorrimer tracks Johnny to his Chelsea flat where, after a violent struggle, the vampire is destroyed, writer Houghton updating the traditional running water peril first used by Hammer in the finale of *Prince of Darkness* by having Alucard fall backwards into a bath, where the torrent from the shower head proves fatal. With the disciple now dead, Van Helsing persuades Inspector Murray to allow him to face his nemesis alone at St Bartolph's, and as the sun sets, both vampire and vampire hunter square up for a brief but well-staged showdown containing much of the same energy and physical action deployed for Terence Fisher at Bray a decade and a half before. After temporarily incapacitating Dracula with a silver-bladed knife, Van Helsing unleashes a deluge of holy water, forcing Dracula to overbalance into a stake-lined pit in the derelict churchyard. As the Count crumbles and with his psychic spell now broken, Van Helsing leads Jessica to safety, but neither are able to help the unfortunate vampire novice Bob, whose bloodless body, previously drained by Dracula, is discovered amongst the overgrown tombs.

Filming for *Dracula Today* concluded in early November 1971 but it would be over ten months before – as the re-titled *Dracula A.D. 1972* – the film went on general release in September of the same year, neatly tying in with the date on the deceased Lawrence Van Helsing's gravestone. The delay, however, was no doubt a contributing factor to its overall lack of success, as despite being something of a cult classic today, Hammer's first foray into contemporary vampirism was not the financial winner that Michael Carreras hoped for, the fading fortunes of hippie youth culture coupled with the oncoming austerity of the first half of the new decade resulting in the picture seeming outdated almost from the very start. Despite this, *Dracula A.D. 1972* has much to recommend it, notwithstanding the strong performances from its principal stars, particularly the return of Cushing after an absence of many years in his two vampire-hunting incarnations, now ably supported by Michael Coles' Inspector Murray, whose relationship would be further developed in the film's follow-up; cinematographer Dick Bush makes the most of the modern settings and extensive location shooting, while Don Mingaye's set designs for the ruined environs of St Bartolph's Church are a vast improvement on Scott MacGregor's previous *Scars of Dracula* inns and castle for whose Gothic environs it provides a suitable and realistic substitute. However, Houghton's confinement of Lee within a Gothic bubble amid the sprawl of urbanised London worked for some and not others: Lee himself, initially sceptical as to the value of bringing the Count into the modern era, later relented and felt it to be a workable compromise, reflecting that the Victorian period was 'arbitrary, the accident of Stoker having lived at that time'. Others, such as David Pirie in *The Vampire Cinema*, felt it showed a failure to successfully relate the vampire figure to contemporary society, leaving *Dracula* disempowered and useless at the expense of highlighting the then highly novel phenomenon of setting a horde of teenage vampires loose in the capital.

Although the disappointing performance of *Dracula A.D. 1972* would cast a long shadow, Hammer's confidence in the potential of their new contemporary undead saga was such that plans for a sequel were put in place almost from the outset. For what would be Christopher Lee's penultimate film for the studio, as well as his last Hammer *Dracula* (but not final screen appearance as the character), much of the production continuity was retained, with Alan Gibson handling directorial duties and Don Houghton providing a new screenplay, as well as taking on the role of joint-producer with former accountant and production supervisor, Roy Skeggs. With the novelty factor of bringing vampires to the modern-day streets of London having quickly expired, the need to find a way of convincingly integrating the undead theme into a contemporary storyline was of crucial importance if another modern *Dracula* was to have any reasonable chance of success.

For his new Hammer script, Houghton stripped away the last vestiges of Gothic horror from the proceedings and, in a bold move, turned to the world of espionage and counterintelligence for inspiration, cleverly grafting the previous film's vampiric elements onto a plotline that on its own would be practically indistinguishable from the writings of Ian Fleming and the Bond spy thrillers prevalent throughout much of the proceeding decade. The result, laced with liberal episodes of Satanism and bloodletting, is surprisingly one of the best entries in Hammer's entire *Dracula* series, and despite some heavy and at times unimaginative direction, shows how effective it can be to make the fantasy element of supernatural horror dangerously real through a combination with ordinary everyday scenes and happenings. Perhaps the most successful element of Houghton's treatment, however, is its full and graphic presentation of the cult-like ensnarement of the vampire myth, an element that runs with increasing development through several of Hammer's previous entries in the series, and which here finds its ultimate representation in the tormented mind of scientist Julian Keeley, convincingly portrayed by character actor Freddie Jones, whose previous work for Hammer involved playing against Peter Cushing in Terence Fisher's masterly *Frankenstein Must Be Destroyed* (1969) three years before.

Houghton's heady mixture of occultism and spy thriller violence is apparent from the very beginning. Following reports of potential security risks involving a group of initially unidentified VIPs, MI5 director Torrence (William Franklyn) and department chief Colonel Matthews (Richard Vernon), initiate a clandestine investigation into the activities of the Psychical Examination and Research Group, an obscure paranormal society operating from an isolated house in London's Home Counties. From microfilm images obtained on a covert camera, Torrence identifies four prominent public figures – an Army Chief of Staff, a Nobel prizewinning scientist, a wealthy London landowner and, most troublingly for him, the Rt Hon John Porter MP, a serving cabinet minister with direct responsibility for his own department – whose association with devil worship and Satanic offerings suggests a front for an espionage network attempting to infiltrate the high echelons of the British Government; a fifth person who, despite being photographed, strangely leaves no image on the negative, remains unidentified. After an undercover agent, Hanson, is killed attempting to escape from the mysterious Pelham House, Matthews launches an independent enquiry headed by Special Branch's Inspector Murray (again played by Michael Coles) who in turn, intrigued by descriptions of cult-like blood sacrifice, turns to Lorrimer Van Helsing for help. Shocked to learn that an old university friend, the bacteriologist Julian Keeley, is one of the men under surveillance, Van Helsing visits him at his London office where Keeley reveals he has been instructed to create a new and deadly strain of bubonic plague 'more virulent than any known specie', which is required to be delivered to Pelham House on the 23rd of the month. Before the vampire hunter can learn more, the men are attacked by one of the afghan-clad motorcycle riders employed to guard the building: Van Helsing, stunned by a glancing shot from a handgun, wakes to find Keeley hanged and the petri dishes containing the new virus missing.

At Pelham House, Murray and Torrence, accompanied by Van Helsing's granddaughter Jessica, now elevated in Houghton's script from teenage groupie to trainee scientist and played by a pre-*New Avengers* Joanna Lumley, meet the mysterious Chin Yang, a Chinese occultist reported by Hanson to be behind bloody human sacrifices carried out on the premises. In the cellar, they find crates containing the bodies of a number of vampire women, as well as Jane, Torrence's secretary, who has been kidnapped and also transformed into one of the undead. Using an improvised stake, Murray kills the unfortunate woman and the three investigators escape from the house, although their freedom is shortlived. Soon, with Torrence dead and Jessica and Inspector Murray held captive, the truth behind the new outbreak of modern vampirism at Pelham House becomes chillingly clear: Count Dracula, resurrected from his grave in St Bartolph's churchyard and now posing as millionaire property developer D.D. Denham, whose office block headquarters have been built on the site of the demolished church, plans the ultimate act of vengeance on the human race by releasing Keeley's deadly plague spores at midnight on the 'Sabbat of the Undead', ending his own nihilistic existence by wiping out the whole of mankind, but not before cursing Jessica with the vampire's bite as final revenge on the house of Van Helsing. Porter becomes the first hideous victim of the plague but before the contagion can spread fire tears through the building, incinerating the infected politician and releasing Van Helsing's granddaughter from the vampire lord's spell. As Pelham House burns, Dracula, the anti-Christ, is ensnared in the branches of a hawthorn tree and, streaming with blood from a gruesome crown of thorns, is dispatched by Cushing for the final time with a fence paling.

Filmed over the winter of 1972/73, principal photography on what was eventually released as *The Satanic Rites of Dracula* wrapped on 3 January. A decade and a half separates this, the most assured of Hammer's two modern takes on the vampire myth, from Fisher's Gothic original, echoes of which are still present despite the passage of the years. At one point, Michael Coles, like Cushing before him, fashions an improvised crucifix while fighting off the vampirised Chin Yang, and the Special Branch policeman remembers enough of Van Helsing's vampire lore from the previous film to demonstrate another interesting interpretation of the running water defence, this time dispatching a cellar-full of undead female slaves by operating the overhead sprinkler system. Houghton's concept of Dracula masquerading as a millionaire businessman is convincing and effective, enabling the Gothic castle setting to be effectively replaced with a concrete and glass office block, in the same way that writers Colin Wilson and Terrance Dicks would later employ a spaceship in the same role when faced with overlaying the vampire myth into another genre, in this case science fiction.

That Hammer never considered expanding their contemporary vampire series with another instalment after Lee decided not to reprieve the character is both unfortunate and also an indication of how important the studio felt the character of Count Dracula to be to a modern interpretation. With hindsight, the Van Helsing/Murray partnership is one area of Houghton's screenplay that showed the possibilities for further development, while the success of ABC television's Richard Matheson-scripted *The Night Stalker*, a modern vampire story set in contemporary Los Angeles which aired in January 1972 and later became the pilot of a series, *Kolchak: The Night Stalker*, starring Darren McGavin as the intrepid newspaper reporter of the title, proved that with imagination there was much potential for updating and transferring Gothic horror into the present day. Hammer had in fact already ventured into television in the late 1960s with *Journey to the Unknown*, a collection of contemporary fantasy and science fiction tales produced by Tony Hinds in partnership with Twentieth Century Fox, and would do so again in the early 1980s with their eponymous *Hammer House of Horror* series for ITC Entertainment.

Given the fact that throughout their history, Hammer never fought shy of exploiting potentially profitable genres or experimenting with already established themes, it should perhaps be no surprise that their final feature presentation involving Stoker's *Dracula* would again take off in a completely different direction in the hope of achieving some degree of financial success.

Hoping to cash in on the great early 1970s surge of Western enthusiasm for martial arts and kung fu, brought about in no small way by the initial success of Bruce Lee classics *Fist of Fury* (1972) and *Enter the Dragon* (1973), Michael Carreras himself took the decision to 'enter the dragon', in this instance a co-production with the Hong Kong-based Shaw Brothers studio for a new Anglo-Chinese horror film, the deal being brokered by Don Houghton's wife Pik Sen, whose father was a personal friend of media mogul, Run Run Shaw. At the time the project seemed to recommend itself, particularly as ABC's *Kung Fu* television series, starring a young David Carradine (son of *Dracula* actor John), was a small screen hit both in Britain and America; a vampire theme also appeared an obvious choice with star Peter Cushing agreeable to return to the Van Helsing role, coupled with Chinese folklore's long association with the subject: the undead chiang-shih, vicious reanimated corpses that, as well as demonstrating many aspects of the traditional Western vampire, also have the ability to transform themselves into terrifying flying demons covered with long white hair – innately cinematic in their own right – have appeared in numerous stories and folktales, including writings by the famous Qing Dynasty writer Pu Songling, best known for his short story collection *Strange Stories From a Chinese Studio*, first published in English in the late 1880s.

Despite its potential, *The Legend of the 7 Golden Vampires* (also known as *The Seven Brothers Meet Dracula*), directed by Hammer regular Roy Ward Baker and filmed entirely on location on Shaw's Hong Kong back-lot in the closing months of 1973, was a long way off hitting the mark. Scripted by Don Houghton, who, as in earlier undead treatments, establishes a new timeframe completely independent from previous entries in the Hammer series – in this case 1904 Chungking – it tells the story of Lawrence Van Helsing's journey into the Chinese hinterland to locate and destroy the eponymous vampire lords of the title, who, together with a horde of zombie-like minions, hold the remote and semi-mythical village of Pin Quay in a grip of murderous fear. Described, perhaps a little unfairly, by vampire historian J. Gordon Melton as 'one of the great disasters in horror film history', its one saving grace is the presence of Peter Cushing in what was to be his final performance in a role he had made very much his own and who, despite the martial arts mayhem and lacklustre material, delivers a solid performance from beginning to end.

For Roy Ward Baker it was a production beset with difficulties, mostly brought about by East meets West clashes in ways of working and on-set protocols, with the result that many aspects of Houghton's script are unconvincing or poorly realised, particularly the horse-riding vampire lords themselves, a concept given a far better cinematic treatment by Spanish director Amando de Ossorio two years before in his seminal zombie classic, *Tombs of the Blind Dead* (1971). The greatest disappointment, however, is the inclusion of Count Dracula, grafted almost as an afterthought into the proceedings and represented throughout most of the film by the devil-worshipping monk, Kah, whose physical body he has taken over. With Christopher Lee now refusing to have any further dealings with Hammer in the part, actor John Forbes-Robertson bravely allowed himself to be bookended into the opening and closing scenes for Dracula's token appearance, now made even more ludicrous by inappropriate lighting and bizarre Widow Twankey-style make-up which, as horror film aficionado Alan Frank wryly notes in his 1976 commentary *Monsters and Vampires*, makes him closer to a pantomime king than the evil lord of the undead. Sadly, Hammer had come full circle, reduced to presenting the one-dimensional screen villain that Terence Fisher had summarily dismissed back in 1958, now also impotent through an unsubtle transfer of all sensual and erotic elements to a subsidiary character, in this case the sexual shenanigans of a travelling heiress played by glamour actress and former Miss Norway, Julie Ege.

With limited distribution in the West due to Warner Bros' general disinterest in the final product, *The Legend of the 7 Golden Vampires*, Hammer's penultimate horror, marked an unworthy final association with a literary character that played such a major part in the studio's reinvention of post-war British horror. The cinematic rehabilitation of Stoker's *Dracula* would be a slow process that would not begin until late in the same decade, but for British cinema-goers, screen vampirism was far from dead in the opening years of the 1970s: the legions had in fact been given a remarkably rich and bloody new lease of life.

9

Sex and Blood: Hammer's Legions and Beyond

(1970–1988)

On 1 July 1970, the British Board of Film Classification made a sweeping revision to the certification of all films shown in British cinemas, the first overhaul of its kind for nearly twenty years. Although the overall structure remained the same, an 'AA' rating was added for persons aged 14 and over, while the 'X' certificate saw its threshold raised to 18, a watershed that now allowed filmmakers greater freedom in testing the censor with the levels and quality of sex and violence possible in new productions. It was a change that had been anticipated across the industry, not least by Hammer Films' Managing Director, Sir James Carreras, who in his Wardour Street office was already planning how his famous company, now facing an uncertain future without an American major studio for both finance and distribution, would respond. With the potential for Hammer and its competitors to serve up increased helpings of blood and sex, the subject of vampires and vampirism was the obvious choice, and Carreras, always the showman, already had just what was needed on his desk.

By 1969, Sheridan Le Fanu's *Carmilla* had already received three cinema treatments, all by foreign studios. As well as Carl Dryer's *Vampyr* that we have already encountered, two later versions, both somewhat more faithful to Le Fanu's original narrative, had surfaced in the first half of the decade. In 1960, the French filmmaker and screenwriter Roger Vadim directed a modern adaptation set in contemporary Italy, entitled *Blood and Roses*, with his then Danish wife, Annette Strøyberg as Carmilla, seemingly possessed by the spirit of her vampire ancestor after the detonation of an unexploded Second World War bomb opens up an ancient family crypt.

Four years later, Christopher Lee took a break from the back-lot at Bray and also travelled to Italy, where he played Count Ludwig Karnstein for director Camillo Mastrocinque in a period version, *La cripta e l'incubo*, known variously in England as both *Terror in the Crypt* and *Crypt of the Vampire*. In both modern versions, the lesbianism inherent in Le Fanu's writing is ever-present but held in check through stylised and artistic direction: Vadim allows Carmilla and her friend Georgia to kiss during a thunderstorm; while in the latter Laura and the vampiric Lyuba enjoy gentle caresses as they stroll hand-in-hand through the grounds of the Karnstein estate. A few brief years later such subtleties would be a thing of the past.

In England during the summer of 1969, film producer Harry Fine, a former stage director, together with his business partner Michael Style, the driving forces behind a fledgling production company entitled Fantale Films, approached East End-born Tudor Gates to prepare a screenplay for a new version of *Carmilla*, one that would exploit the sexuality of Le Fanu's sub-text to the full. Gates, an experienced writer in his late thirties whose previous assignments included BBC dramas and script work for Dino De Laurentiis on the science fiction exploitation *Barbarella* (1968), drafted a synopsis which soon found its way into Hammer's London office. 'I first wrote a 12-page outline,' Gates later recalled to Hammer historian Wayne Kinsey for his book *Hammer Films: The Unsung Heroes* (2010), 'In that, I introduced all the shock elements: the cutting off of heads, the nudity – everything was in those 12 pages. This went to Jimmy Carreras and he gave it to an artist who produced a poster. Jimmy went to [American International Pictures] and, on the basis of the outline and the poster, he sold the picture.' During the autumn and winter of 1969, Gates produced his full script and filming began at Elstree on 9 January 1970. Despite the presence of genre veterans Peter Cushing and Roy Ward Baker, it soon became clear that *The Vampire Lovers* was to be like no other Hammer film before it, one that would also elevate its principal female lead to international stardom in much the same way that *The Curse of Frankenstein* and *Dracula* had springboarded Lee to success back in 1957.

Although sharing scenes with Clint Eastwood and Richard Burton in Brian Hutton's 1968 Second World War classic *Where Eagles Dare* the previous year, it was as the undead Carmilla that the cinema-going public first took notice of Polish-born actress Ingrid Pitt, although only four out of a total of nearly forty screen and television roles are the ones that as the 'Queen of Horror' she is now most often remembered.

A Holocaust survivor, Pitt had relocated to California in the mid-1950s chasing the dream of a Hollywood career; after a handful of minor parts she arrived in London and at an after-premiere dinner to celebrate the release of Clive Donner's period epic *Alfred the Great* (1969) found herself sitting at a table next to Hammer impresario Sir James Carreras, a chance meeting that resulted in her being cast the following day without a screen test in the role of Carmilla Karnstein as well as her mysterious and deadly alter-egos, Marcilla and Mircalla. As the vampire's attractive and willing victims, Roy Ward Baker had already assembled a premier line-up of 'Hammer glamour' – Kate O'Mara, Pippa Steel, Dawn Addams, Kirsten Betts and Madeline Smith – together with a solid supporting cast that included Peter

Cushing as General von Spielsdorf, George Cole, Jon Finch and Ferdy Mayne, who had recently played vampire Count von Krolock in Roman Polanski's undead spoof *The Fearless Vampire Killers* (1967).

For his screenplay, Tudor Gates returned the action to its original setting of late eighteenth-century Styria and the drama follows Le Fanu's story very closely: the ingratiation of the vampire into the Spielsdorf household and the death of the General's niece, the carriage accident that allows Carmilla into the home of Laura (now renamed Emma) and her father, together with the final destruction of the undead menace by the tormented general accompanied by the vampire-hunting Baron Vordenburg (renamed von Hartog by Gates and here played by television *Sherlock Holmes* actor Douglas Wilmer); only the appearance of an unnamed 'man in black' (John Forbes-Robertson) is a somewhat unnecessary intrusion whose presence, almost in the manner of an afterthought, provides the proceedings with a seemingly obligatory Stoker-like character, here entirely unneeded. In character terms, the nude romps and breast biting for which *The Vampire Lovers* is now famous obscures one aspect of the vampire character that Pitt on occasion brings to the surface very well, namely the nosferatu's lonely curse of immortality, consigned to a living death for which all other human loves and relationships must ultimately pass away. For Ingrid Pitt herself, although acknowledging its audience appeal, Gates' 'brazen exploitation' of the sexuality behind Le Fanu's character was of secondary importance. 'I never saw the lesbian story everyone got so excited about after the film's release,' she later commented. 'To me it was a story about a couple of friends, bored to death with their sheltered lives, one of who just happened to be a vampire … We played the nude scenes for fun, two young women horsing around.' As Hammer's Karnstein series progressed, however, such 'playful innocence' would be quickly replaced by more direct and less subtle elements.

Another overlooked aspect of Gates' writing is an interesting addition to the existing canon of cinematic vampire lore, in this case the supposed need for an undead being to wrap itself in its original winding sheet in order to rest in the tomb during the daylight hours, a bizarre phenomenon superbly realised in the film's pre-credit sequence by cinematographer Moray Grant accompanied by composer Harry Robinson's unearthly score. This interesting trait used by Le Fanu in his novella actually stems from the writings of the aforementioned French Benedictine monk, Dom Augustin Calmet, a noted commentator on vampirism, who reported an incident alleged to have taken place in the Moravian village of Liebava, where an unnamed Hugarian vampire hunter was said to have enticed a vampiric creature that had been terrorising the vicinity to its death, by baiting the monster with its stolen shroud from the belfry of a nearby church; Montague Summers reproduces the complete account in his 1928 book *The Vampire, His Kith and Kin* and claimed that the vampire 'talisman' he passed to ghost hunter Peter Underwood had been used during this exact incident. Gates' opening is a carbon copy of Underwood's later account (included in his book, *The Vampire's Bedside Companion* in 1975 – see also the incident of the Highgate Vampire in the next chapter), as related by Summers himself in 1947. Watched by a horrified Baron Hartog, whose mission to destroy the evil Karnstein menace is an act of revenge for the death of his sister, an eerily draped figure twists and gropes amongst the mist-drenched monuments in search of its mouldering sere-cloth; the creature's reveal – as the beautiful vampiress Kirsten Betts – and savage beheading provides one of a number of gory set pieces for genre aficionados, balanced by Cushing's ultimately grand staking and decapitation of the sleeping Carmilla as final retribution for the loss of the tragic Laura; only Le Fanu's gruesome seven inches of blood and fiery funeral pyre are absent.

Although the breakthrough came as Le Fanu's *Carmilla*, it is for her second and final film for Hammer that Ingrid Pitt will be forever identified. *Countess Dracula*, a vampire film in name only, is a fictionalised retelling of the life and death of Hungarian serial killer Erzsébet Báthory, whose bloody crimes we have already briefly encountered, here renamed as the Countess Elizabeth Nadasdy whose ageing looks are supernaturally rejuvenated by full and frequent immersions in the freshly spilt blood of her virgin victims. Unfortunately each transformation is only temporary, being followed by increasingly sudden and gruesome returns to senility, with the result that piles of bloodless corpses soon begin to fill the crypts and wine cellars of Nadasdy Castle, as the Countess, masquerading as her own daughter, plots to marry her young suitor, a dashing Hussar played by Sandor Eles. Disaster, however, ultimately overtakes the wedding party and in a last desperate attempt to retain her unnatural youth and beauty, the crazed Elizabeth launches a murderous attack on her own virgin daughter Ilona before being arrested and sentenced to death. Despite frequent gory set pieces, including the arresting sight of a naked Ingrid Pitt daubing herself with blood with a giant sponge, the film's final scene is the one that lingers most in the mind as the evil Countess, now reduced to a hideous crone-like apparition courtesy of make-up artist Tom Smith, awaits the arrival of her executioner, gazing up through the bars of her dungeon prison to the taunts and curses of a band of village peasants.

Atypical of Hammer's output of the time, due to the efforts of Hungarian producer and director Alexander Paul and Peter Sasdy to craft an historically inspired costume drama, albeit with horror elements, rather than an out and out exploitation, the film benefits from a strong cast including Nigel Green as the Countess' long-time advisor and sometime suitor, Captain Dobi, and Maurice Denham playing the Nostradamus-like scholar and castle librarian, Master Fabio. The paucity of the more traditional Hammer budget is belied by the reuse of standing sets from former Pinewood productions, notably a Spanish village built for the 1966 Cliff Richard film *Finders Keepers* and several impressive castle interiors recently constructed for Charles Jarrot's *Anne of a Thousand Days* (1969) starring Richard Burton as Henry VIII. Despite having her entire dialogue dubbed over in the final release print, the character remained Pitt's favourite and one to which she would return several years later, providing guest narrations for English extreme metal band Cradle of Filth on their 1998 studio album *Cruelty and the Beast* (*see* Chapter 12).

Now a recognised horror name, Pitt returned to a pure vampire role the same year for director Peter Duffell in *The House That Dripped Blood* (1970), the second of Amicus Productions' portmanteau films to feature an undead episode, written by acclaimed *Psycho* author Robert Bloch, who had also provided material for the studio's two previous genre entries, *The Skull* (1965) and *Torture Garden* (1967), another compendium of tales which featured amongst other things a haunted piano and the resurrection of Edgar Allan Poe. Although not as prolific as Hammer, the British-based Americans Milton Subotsky and Max Rosenberg had spent the time since their debut with *Dr Terror's House of Horrors* alternating between contemporary themed horror and science fiction, and the early 1970s would see several more additions including some of their most fondly remembered productions, of which *The House That Dripped Blood* is one. While investigating the disappearance of flamboyant horror film actor and paranormal enthusiast, Paul Henderson (played by the then current television *Doctor Who*, Jon Pertwee), Detective Inspector Holloway (John Bennett) encounters the sad and sinister history of the film's titular building, the lonely Yew Tree House, whose former occupants – a tormented writer, a retired City stockbroker and a witch-haunted businessman – have all come to mysterious and gruesome ends while living on the premises.

For the final segment, the semi-comedic 'The Cloak', Holloway retraces the last days of Henderson and his beautiful co-star Carla (Pitt), who have taken on a short tenancy while filming at a nearby studio. Dismissive of the film company's sub-standard sets and wardrobe, Henderson visits a local costumer, the mysterious von Hartmann, played with great élan by Geoffrey Bayldon (whose horror credentials go back to a cameo role in Fisher's *Dracula*), where he purchases what the ghoulish proprietor claims to be a genuine vampire's cloak with supernatural abilities of its own. True to form, at the stroke of twelve, the sinister cloak works its power, transforming the hapless actor into one of the most comical of British vampires thanks to some typical *Navy Lark*-style antics by Pertwee, who finds that his lack of reflection in the dressing room mirror is more than made up for with an amusing set of fangs and the arresting ability to levitate at midnight. Soon, von Hartmann's body is discovered in a coffin buried in the cellar of his burnt-out shop, and Henderson, now horrified that he has inherited the undead costumer's mantle, plans a similar fate for his vampirised garment. Unfortunately for the horror star, he had not counted on the beautiful Carla being one of the undead herself – 'We liked your films so much, that we wanted you to become one of us!' – and Pertwee soon finds himself a fully-fledged vampire, rising from his coffin in the film's closing moments to be dispatched in traditional style by the investigating Holloway, who himself falls foul of the voluptuous Carla, now transformed into a bat!

For Ingrid Pitt, a minor role in Anthony Schaffer's alternative horror masterpiece *The Wicker Man* (1973) was to ultimately guarantee her a place in horror's pantheon of the immortals, but it was to the blood-drenched world of Hammer that she ultimately owed her fame. In later years, Pitt concentrated on writing and producing several genre-related books including *The Ingrid Pitt Bedside Companion for Vampire Lovers* (1998), *The Ingrid Pitt Bedside Companion for Ghosthunters* (1999) and an autobiography, *Life's a Scream* (1999), as well as running her own 'Pitt of Horror' memorabilia company. She died in London on 23 November 2010 aged 72 and is buried in South West London in the same cemetery as Montague Summers.

The undead again provided a humorous interlude, albeit interlaced with gruesome goings on, for Amicus two years later in 1973's *The Vault of Horror*, directed by Roy Ward Baker and starring amongst others a bearded pre-*Doctor Who* Tom Baker, Terry-Thomas, Michael Craig and Curt Jürgens. As with the previous year's *Tales from the Crypt*, Milton Subotsky based his screenplay on original stories published by Entertaining (EC) Comics in the early 1950s, linking the set with a simple scenario of a group of strangers stranded in a basement room discussing their most disturbing nightmares: in reality each of the five is a discarnate soul, doomed to retell his story until the end of time as a penance for his wicked ways on Earth. In the opening tale 'Midnight Mess', Daniel Massey stars as the villainous Harold Rogers who murders his sister Donna (played by Massey's real-life sister, Anna, both children of Raymond Massey by his second wife, stage actress Adrianne Allen) in order to obtain the entire share of their late father's estate. Unfortunately for Harold, his sister lives in an isolated town suffering from a plague of mysterious vampire-like deaths and the murderous sibling ends up as a human optic, strung up by the feet to provide fresh blood on tap for the midnight diners at the local vampires' favourite restaurant. The comic book violence is well handled by Ward Baker, who transfers the vampire myth effectively into a modern-day setting through a clever use of double sets and camera positioning: at one point Massey is shown eating surrounded by other diners while in an adjacent mirror he appears alone at his table, a scene stylistically reminiscent of Polanski's ballroom reveal from *The Fearless Vampire Killers* and achieved technically in the same way that the director had transformed Ralph Bates into Martine Beswick for Hammer's *Dr Jekyll and Sister Hyde* two years before.

Although not the best of Amicus' portmanteau series, *The Vault of Horror* shows how effective contemporary horror can be in juxtaposing supernatural elements with ordinary commonplace situations and happenings, and Rosenberg and Subotsky would ultimately perfect the presentation the following year in what was to be their most assured and finest feature, the classy four-episode *From Beyond the Grave* (1974). Using the underlying principal that money is the root of all evil, the film follows the misfortunes of several disparate customers as they search for bargains at Temptations Ltd, an eerie backstreet antique shop run by the seemingly mild-mannered Peter Cushing, who repays acts of wrongdoing by providing each purchase with an unusual and deadly novelty item. Directed by Kevin Connor, the screenplay (by Raymond Christodoulou and Robin Clarke and originally titled *The Undead*) uses original material by English ghost story writer, Ronald (R.) Chetwynd-Hayes (1919–2001), whose debut sci-fi novel *The Man from the Bomb* appeared in 1959.

David Warner, whose most notable horror role was to come two years later as the doomed photographer Jennings in Richard Donner's 1976 classic *The Omen*, is the first bargain hunter through the door in 'The Gate Crasher', buying an antique mirror for a knock-down price by falsely claiming the heirloom is a cheap reproduction. The looking glass is not only the genuine article but, unfortunately for Charlton (Warner), contains the blood-drinking ghost of a seventeenth-century buccaneer (the 'Face' played by Marcel Steiner), which quickly makes its presence known following an impromptu séance in the young man's flat. Soon Charlton is drawn into the supernormal world behind the glass, procuring victims to satiate the vampire's bloodlust and enable it to break free from its antique prison. In return, he becomes one of the legion himself and takes the phantom's place in the mirror, waiting for the appropriate time to begin his own reign of terror. When new tenants in the flat suggest holding a séance, Charlton's face appears in the looking glass and the audience knows what will be coming next.

Played straight, with most of the film's humorous touches transferred in this instance to a single story involving a Madame Arcati-style spiritualist, *From Beyond the Grave* is a fine tribute to Subotsky's muse, Ealing's seminal *Dead of Night*: its final story, 'The Door', in which Jack Watson plays the sinister aristocrat, Sir Michael Sinclair, a Jacobean occultist who survives death in a ghostly room created through a mixture of blood sacrifice and Black Magic, owes much to director Robert Hamer's 'haunted mirror' episode in the original picture, and is in fact the finest part of Conner's collection.

By 1974, however, not all of British screen vampires were as serious as that presented by Milton Subotsky in what was to be his penultimate portmanteau horror. With Lee flatly refusing to return to the Dracula role, coupled with Hammer's uninspired use of the character in *The Legend of the 7 Golden Vampires*, the Count was ripe for a send up, courtesy of screen icon David Niven and director Clive Donner, who together spoofed both Stoker and the entire undead genre in World Film Services' *Vampira*, known in America as *Old Dracula* in an attempt to cash in on the success of Mel Brooks' *Young Frankenstein*.

Scripted by English screenwriter and sometime actor, Jeremy Lloyd, famous for his bawdy television sitcoms *Are You Being Served?* (1972–85) and *'Allo 'Allo!* (1982–92), the film follows the misfortunes of the aristocratic Count Dracula (Niven) who has been forced to open his famous Transylvanian castle to the public in order to obtain a fresh supply of the rare blood group that will bring his beloved wife Vampira (Teresa Graves) out of suspended animation. When a party of *Playboy* magazine's 'Most Biteable Playmates of the Month' arrive for a photo shoot, it seems that the

Count's problems are solved; however, being made in the Blaxploitation climate of the early 1970s (which had already served up William Marshall as *Blacula* in 1972), Donner and Lloyd plumb the depths and give the proceedings a *Love Thy Neighbour* flavour: following a blood transfusion, both Dracula and his bride turn black!

If *From Beyond the Grave* had perfected the portmanteau presentation of the serious horror tale, then Milton Subotsky's final genre offering was altogether a completely lighter affair. Sword and Sorcery Productions' *The Monster Club*, an Amicus film in all but name, appeared in 1981. It took the association with the works of R. Chetwynd-Hayes one step further, linking three of the writer's original stories with a cameo performance by veteran actor John Carradine as the author himself, who finds he has become a temporary member of the institution of the film's title after an impromptu encounter on a London street with the elderly vampire Eramus, played by another horror veteran, and Roger Corman favourite, Vincent Price. As well as two other tales featuring a lonely whistling demon and a sinister fog-bound village filled with Sawney Bean-style cannibals, Subotsky's central 'Vampire Story' stars Richard Johnson as a Lugosi-inspired refugee, on the run from a comical Donald Pleasance and his bungling vampire-hunting assistants, played by Neil McCarthy and Anthony Valentine. A light-hearted affair, the episode sees the vampire killer Pickering (Pleasance) being ultimately staked by his own men after falling foul of the vampire himself, while Johnson survives a similar fate by conveniently donning a stake-proof vest under his cloak!

Featuring roles for a number of former Amicus regulars both in front and behind the camera (actors Geoffrey Bayldon and Patrick Magee, plus make-up artist Roy Ashton), the producer also wrote himself into his own script as the vampire's tormented young son, Lintom Busotsky. Subotsky continued to work in both film and television sporadically throughout the 1980s, amongst other projects co-producing an adaptation of Ray Bradbury's notable science fiction series, *The Martian Chronicles*. He died in June 1991 aged 69; his former partner, Max Rosenberg, survived him by some twenty years, dying in Los Angeles aged 89 in 2004.

With little exception, rather than exploit the trend for a contemporary setting as favoured by Subotsky and Rosenberg, the vampires that stalked British cinema screens in the opening years of the decade had all but returned to a more traditional Gothic environment for their bloodletting. In 1970, Simon Raven's *Doctors Wear Scarlet* had been filmed as *Incense for the Damned* by Lucinda Film Productions on location in Greece and under the dreaming spires of Oxford, with a steely Peter Cushing as Dr Goodrich and Imogen Hassall as the blood-crazed succubus, Chriseis. Patrick Mower, who had played Dennis Wheatley's Black Magic-obsessed playboy, Simon Aaron for Hammer in Terence Fisher's masterly *The Devil Rides Out* (1968) two years before, here continued his acting trend as tormented academic Richard Fountain, while *Avengers* stalwart Patrick Macnee and a pre-*Wicker Man* Edward Woodward, then known for his television spy role Callan, added support to the proceedings.

Directed by Robert Hartford-Davis, who ultimately dissociated himself from the project to the extent of completely removing his name from all release prints (including an American version known as *Blood Suckers*), the end result is an uninspiring travelogue whose clumsy presentation of the original novel's perverted sexuality leaves a lot to be desired – a scene depicting the death of one of the vampire cult's early victims during an LSD-fuelled orgy, filmed separately for French release editions, was included as an extra for the film's DVD release in 2003.

As well as *Incense for the Damned*, Cushing had also added much needed presence to London-born director Vernon Sewell's oddball quasi-vampire offering *The Blood Beast Terror* (known in its American release as *The Vampire Beast Craves Blood*), one of the first of short-lived Tigon British Film Productions series of Hammeresque horror offerings. It was released in 1968 with a decidedly English supporting cast that included Robert Fleming, Roy Hudd, Glynn Edwards, and Wanda Ventham, who played the human form of the titular monster – a giant carnivorous Death's Head moth, created through the madcap experiments of Fleming's fanatical entomologist villain, Dr Mallinger. True to form, Cushing sides with the forces of good, in this instance the genial Inspector Quennell of Scotland Yard, called in to investigate a series of gruesome murders in a remote corner of the Home Counties. Decidedly 'B'-movie fair, the film has its highlights: Sewell's location work creates a convincing Victorian atmosphere for the proceedings; the players achieve some interesting characterisations, particularly television actor Kevin Stoney in a sinister turn as a sadistic butler; and although the final monster reveal is disappointing, effects technician Roger Dicken (who would later puppeteer the famous *Alien* 'chest-buster' sequence for director Ridley Scott) excels with the blood-drenched chrysalis of Ventham's *Bride of Frankenstein*-like monster mate.

Tigon, founded by exploitation producer Tony Tenser in the mid-1960s, is most remembered today for genre classics such as Michael Reeves' *Witchfinder General* (with Vincent Price in the title role), *The Curse of the Crimson Altar* (both 1968), and the violent psycho-shocker *The Haunted House of Horror* starring former teen idol Frankie Avalon. Its best horror offering, and a candidate for one of the greatest British horror films of all time, is the astonishingly atmospheric *Blood on Satan's Claw* (1971), a Kubrick-like foray into seventeenth-century 'folk horror' involving the possession and increasingly violent corruption of a group of young village children by a sinister blood-drinking homunculus.

Outside of their ongoing *Dracula* series, Hammer Films, now based permanently at Elstree in Hertfordshire, ultimately took a traditional route for their final quartet of vampire-related features that, despite the inevitable clichés and production limitations, contain some of the studio's most imaginative contributions to the genre, thanks in the main to the involvement of a raft of independent producers and writers keen to test their metal under the famous film name. However, the weakest of the four (and altogether one of Hammer's most derided productions) had already been given the green light by Jimmy Carreras while its original inspiration was still in production. Confident that *The Vampire Lovers* would be a success, Tudor Gates was commissioned to write a sequel which went before the cameras in July and August 1970, two months before *Lovers* was released and at the same time that Peter Sasdy was helming *Countess Dracula* at Pinewood.

To Love a Vampire, a film that never was, initially promised to be an interesting mixture of the old and the new, a quasi-*Brides of Dracula* scenario with Hammer stalwart Terence Fisher lined up to direct what would be his first post-18-rated 'X' feature, and Peter Cushing returning to the Karnstein story, in this instance going against type in the role of the doomed schoolmaster, Giles Barton. With the entire film cast and extensive location work planned at Hazlewood House, Kings Langley, producers Harry Fine and Michael Style ultimately suffered a double blow that threatened to halt the entire production: a fortnight before filming was due to commence, Fisher was hit by a car outside Richmond railway station and was hospitalised with a broken leg, at the same time that star Peter Cushing was released from his contract to care for his wife Helen, who was dying of emphysema at their home in Whitstable. At the eleventh hour, Jimmy Sangster, fresh from his directorial debut *The Horror of Frankenstein*, agreed to step in, at the same time suggesting Ralph Bates as Cushing's replacement. It was to be a decision that both actor and director would live to regret.

Again set in nineteenth-century Styria, *Lust for a Vampire* (as it was eventually renamed at the behest of the producers) follows the adventures of philandering novelist Richard LeStrange (Michael Johnson), who takes a trip to nearby Karnstein Castle as inspiration for a new book on the supernatural. In the ruins he encounters three attractive women (an echo of Harker and his vampire brides) who, it transpires, are in fact flesh and blood students from an exclusive all-female finishing school, visiting the area in the company of their history teacher, Giles Barton. At the academy, LeStrange becomes infatuated with a new student, the beautiful Mircalla Herritzen, niece of the Countess Herritzen (Barbara Jefford), and bluffs his way into temporary employment as the school's English literature tutor in order to be close to her. Unfortunately for the besotted writer, he has unwittingly chosen the anniversary of the Karnstein vampires – who return to their ancestral home on a cycle of forty years – to carry out his lovemaking and Mircalla (played by Danish model Yutte Stensgaard) is unsurprisingly the seventeenth-century vampiress Carmilla Karnstein, who has been resurrected from her coffin of bones with a torrent of blood in the opening reel, and is subsequently presided over by Count Karnstein himself, another obligatory man in black played on this occasion by former Radio One disc jockey and sometime sculptor and sheep farmer, Mike Raven (real name Churton Fairman). In this instance, Raven really was the 'Man in Black' as his few lines of dialogue were dubbed in their entirety by Valantine Dyall, while for good measure, shots of Christopher Lee's eyes from *Dracula Has Risen from the Grave* were used as close-ups.

Soon the academy's attractive young students, together with its staff, are falling under Mircalla's sway, and as a result much of the proceedings are taken up with naked dormitory romps, midnight skinny dipping and similar nudity, interspersed with gory neck-biting as the beautiful blond takes her fill, while nearby woods and a disused well become a convenient dumping ground for several bloodless corpses, including that of history master Barton, a closet occultist whose desperation to learn the secrets of the undead ultimately proves his undoing. Eventually the school's gym mistress, Janet (Suzanna Leigh), who has fallen in love with the lusty LeStrange herself, alerts the local police to the deadly goings-on and a vigilante mob supported by a passing bishop march on Karnstein Castle intent on burning the evil building to the ground. Inside the ruins the vampires wait, confident that despite the flames their spirits will return on the occasion of the next anniversary. As LeStrange braves the blazing inferno to rescue Mircalla, a burning rafter falls from the roof and stakes her through the heart, ending the bloody reign of terror, and as the love-struck writer makes his escape to the waiting arms of Janet, the credits roll over a final view of the burning castle, in reality a recycled model sequence spliced in from the close of *Scars of Dracula*.

For Jimmy Sangster, *Lust for a Vampire*, his penultimate film for Hammer, was a depressing experience marred by on-set clashes with producer Michael Style, a less than adequate budget and uninspiring performances from both Ingrid Pitt substitute Yutte Stensgaard and Ralph Bates (here hopelessly miscast and almost unwatchable). However, the final nail in the Karnstein coffin lid is the inclusion of a song sequence 'Strange Love', overlaid onto a sex scene between LeStrange and Mircalla by Harry Fine in the hope of repeating the success of B.J. Thomas' Academy Award-winning 'Raindrops Keep Fallin' on my Head' from the 1969 Paul Newman-Robert Redford Western, *Butch Cassidy and the Sundance Kid*. Unfortunately for Hammer, despite Harry Robinson's attractive music, Frank Godwin's lyrics were no match for Hal David and Burt Bacharach, and the result was to drive Sangster under his seat with embarrassment at a screening at the Hammersmith Odeon six months after the production wrapped, on 18 August 1970.

Sangster scripted and directed his final Hammer horror, *Fear in the Night*, another of his signature psycho-shockers, later the following year. His twenty-fifth film for the company, it also marked nearly a quarter of a century's involvement of his working life up until the age of 45 with a studio that he would later look back on with fond memories. He later spent several years in America, script editing, amongst other projects, William Castle's *Ghost Story* television series as well as writing original screenplays for both the big and small screens, including episodes of *Ironside*, *Cannon* and *Wonder Woman*, together with several novels, among them the James Reed detective trilogy; an autobiography, *Do You Want It Good or Tuesday?* was published in 1997.

A fan favourite at horror film conventions in Britain and America, Sangster was philosophical about the post-war horror boom that he played an enormous part in bringing into being. '[A]s I see it, the Hammer era has gone,' he wrote in the epilogue of his *Inside Hammer* memoirs in 2001:

> And by the Hammer era, I mean the Gothics, the movies that made the company what it was. And they aren't popular any more. Other people have tried making them ... spending on one picture nearly as much money as Hammer spent during its entire existence. None of them have been box office hits, with the freak exception of Coppola's *Dracula*. As for the 'psycho' cycle that I started at Hammer, that's still going, but it was already going long before Hammer moved in that direction.

Jimmy Sangster, the architect of Britain's twentieth-century horror renaissance, died on 19 August 2011, aged 83.

Although their follow up to *The Vampire Lovers* left a lot to be desired, Harry Fine and Michael Styles were nothing if not persistent in their exploitation of the Karnstein story, and by the beginning of 1971 the pair had persuaded Michael Carreras that there was still potential for success in Le Fanu's work. As a result, Tudor Gates was once again brought on board to produce a new screenplay for which, as with the previous inclusion of Yutte Stensgaard, there were specific requirements: in this instance, suitable roles for Peter Cushing, returning to filmmaking for the first time following the death of his wife and, most challenging of all, the Maltese Collinson twins, Mary and Madeleine, who had come to Harry Fines' attention through a nude *Playboy* centrefold: neither woman had acted before or even spoke good English. Surprisingly, the resulting *Twins of Evil*, directed by John Hough and filmed at Pinewood in March and April 1971, is not only a fine tribute to Gates' imaginative scriptwriting (given the tall order of the brief) but is easily the best of the Karnstein trilogy of films and one of the highlights of Hammer's final years; a fourth instalment, *The Vampire Virgins*, thankfully never made it beyond a draft outline.

For his final *Carmilla* story, a violent mixture of undead bloodletting and religious persecution, Gates returned to the familiar environs of Karnstein Castle, now home to world-weary libertine Count Karnstein (Damien Thomas) whose dabbling with Black Magic and Satanism soon create the necessary conditions for another plague of vampirism, in this instance the unwitting resurrection of his famous ancestor, here brought back to life via a human sacrifice carried out on the lid of her mouldering tomb. In familiar fashion, blood seeping through the stonework quickly reanimates the shrouded skeleton within and Carmilla, now reduced to a brief cameo appearance by German-born actress Katya Wyeth, rewards the Count for his trouble by turning him into a vampire like herself. Karnstein's baptism into the legion of the damned coincides with the arrival in the nearby village from Vienna of two orphaned twins, the beautiful and identical Maria and Freida Gellhorn, who have come to live with their uncle, Gustav Weil (Cushing), a fanatical Puritan minister and leader of a horse-riding brotherhood of local zealots who patrol the countryside, capturing and burning suspected witches with a religious impunity matched only by the Count's favouritism and protection of Styria's ruling emperor.

The adventurous Freida soon takes a midnight trip to the castle where she joins the ranks of the undead, unleashing a wave of bloody killings in the misty Karnstein woods that include the Count's busty serving wench Gerta (Luan Peters), fawning manservant Dietrich, played by *Jeeves* actor Dennis Price, together with one of Weil's own young Puritan brothers. Eventually a local school teacher, Anton (David Warbeck), realises that the Karnstein curse has returned to stalk the village – particularly when finding he has taken the bloodthirsty Frieda to bed instead of Maria and that his pretty young partner casts no reflection in the bedroom mirror – and persuades the witch hunter and his cronies that the stake and the sword are the only true methods of dealing with the undead menace.

In a well-staged climax, Weil's Brotherhood, together with a village mob, storms the castle and the vampire Count and his fledgling bride are finally destroyed, but not before Karnstein has put paid to his earthly nemesis, burying an axe in Weil's back before throwing his body off a balcony for good measure. Well made, with convincing sets and solid performances from the entire cast, particularly Cushing as the Hopkins-like witch-hunter, *Twins of Evil* occasionally plumbs the depths with some crude sexual symbolism, but remains one of the best offerings from the studio's later collection of horrors with several classic shock sequences, particularly the gruesome fight scene between the vigilante mob and Karnstein's mute servant Joachim (Roy Stewart, familiar to classic series *Doctor Who* fans as the giant Toberman in the 1967 Troughton story, 'Tomb of the Cybermen'), although Cushing's steely beheading of vampiress Freida, unwittingly sent to her death by the wily Count, is perhaps the film's most memorable moment.

Four brief months separated the wrapping of Hough's *Twins of Evil* and the start of filming on what was not only Hammer's next undead offering but arguably their most dark and disturbing supernatural feature of all. *Vampire Circus*, directed by newcomer Robert Young and scripted by American writer Judson Kinberg from a story outline by co-producer Wilbur Stark, is a bleak and graphic masterpiece whose doom-laden claustrophobic atmosphere stems from an unremitting and unprecedented display of brutality and sexual violence present even from the very outset. Its catalogue of horrors, including child murder, beheadings, wild animal attacks, pestilence and gang rape-style beatings, made even Hammer's former chairman Jimmy Carreras uneasy, and although good does eventually triumph, it's salvation (as in William Friedkin's impending *The Exorcist*) is a long hard-worn fight that leaves a trail of bodies and gruesome images in its wake. Filmed on location at Black Park and at Pinewood using standing sets employed in *Countess Dracula* and *Twins of Evil*, as well as a refurbished church interior first employed in Peter Sasdy's *Taste the Blood of Dracula*, *Vampire Circus* is the second of a loose trilogy of period late productions from Hammer (beginning with *Twins of Evil* and ending the following year with *Captain Kronos*) that showed an attempt to inject new life and variation into a now well-worn theme, and as such ultimately remains the dark heart of the three.

A film within a film, an epic twelve-minute pre-credit sequence, beautifully scored by composer David Whitaker, generates not only an entire back story but all of the material that subsequently plays out in the main part of the feature. In recent months, the eastern European village of Schtettel has suffered a wave of child abductions for which a local nobleman, the Gilles de Rais-like Count Mitterhaus (Robert Tayman) is a prime suspect. After witnessing his wife, Anna, who has fallen under the Count's spell, entice one of the Schtettel children away into a nearby forest, local schoolmaster Albert Mueller (played by television *Sexton Blake* actor Laurence Payne) persuades the village Burgermeister (Thorley Walters) to mount a raid on Mitterhaus' castle, where they find Anna and the undead Count making love next to the child's bloodless corpse. Following a violent struggle, the vampire lord is felled by Mueller with a stake through the heart and his castle destroyed with kegs of gunpowder, but not before the dying Mitterhaus has cursed both the village and its inhabitants – 'Schtettel will die, your children will die, to give me back my life' – which becomes a mantra for the bloody events to come. As the castle burns, Anna Mueller flees the villager's wrath and drags the Count's body to an underground crypt, where it lies in state as the passing years gradually transform the shunned building above into an overgrown ruin.

A decade and a half later, Schtettel, now in the grip of the Black Death, lies isolated and under quarantine by the Serbian government: survivors from the original raid declare it to be proof of the Mitterhaus prophesy coming true, but a local physician, Dr Kersh (Richard Owens), refuses to believe in both curses and vampires, and with the help of his young son Anton (John Moulder-Brown) breaks through the surrounding blockade in an attempt to reach the city and obtain medical supplies. Strangely, a travelling carnival, the eerily-titled Circus of Nights, has managed to cross the barricades and soon provides some much needed relief for the plague-ridden inhabitants, representing, as David Pirie has noted, 'all the qualities of sensual wonder and suppressed erotic excitement which the villagers have blocked'. Unfortunately for Schtettel, the circus is in fact a wandering band of itinerant vampires – including the Count's shape-shifting cousin, Emil – that has left a bloody trail of death in its wake across the region, and which has arrived in the village for the sole purpose of bringing the Mitterhaus curse down on the houses of the three village families most responsible for the vampire lord's destruction: the dopey Burgermeister and his daughter Rosa; Hauser, a local dignitary and his two sons, Jon and Gustav; and schoolmaster Mueller and his daughter Dora, who has recklessly run the blockade from the city to be with both her father and her young sweetheart, Anton Kersh. Soon Hauser's sons are dead, enticed into the sinister Hall of Mirrors (in reality a supernatural portal into the castle's bat-infested dungeon crypt) by the circus' acrobatic twins, Heinrich and Helga (played by Robin Sachs and English rose, Lalla Ward), while a village family, tricked by the carnival dwarf Michael into believing they will be shown a route through the cordon, are savagely torn apart by vampire Emil (Anthony Corlan) transformed into a panther.

The Burgermeister, who has seen a vision of Mitterhaus in one of the carnival mirrors, attempts to shoot the circus animals but dies of a heart attack after a confrontation with Emil, leaving Rosa to become another blood sacrifice to rejuvenate the sleeping Count. The following night, the vampire twins pursue Dora Mueller, Mitterhaus' last remaining target, but a crucifix on her necklace drives them away. The relief is, however, only temporary, as the circus' gypsy leader (Adrienne Corri) – a supernaturally transformed Anna Mueller – removes it from her throat and Dora is taken to the castle ruins as the final offering that will bring the vampire lord back to life. In a bleak finale whose body count rivals the closing act of *Romeo and Juliet*, Hauser, Mueller and Dr Kersh, who has returned from the city with soldiers and medicine to combat the plague (now identified as a rabies epidemic spread by bats breeding in Mitterhaus' tomb), burn the carnival caravans and shoot dead the circus strong man (Green Cross Code and Darth Vader actor, Dave Prowse) before tracking the vampires to their lair where Dora is saved by Emil's unplanned slaughter of the gypsy shape-shifter, Anna.

Young Anton Kersh confronts and defeats the resurrected Count Mitterhaus (beheaded with the bow-string from a crossbow) and, together with his father and sweetheart, escapes the ruins which are finally put to the torch by the long-suffering Schtettel villagers. The fight is a hard one for both mortals and vampires: Hauser, Mueller, Emil, the twins Helga and Heinrich, dwarf Michael, the circus' animal performers, as well as Anna Mueller and Hersh's soldier bodyguards, all die, although a final shot of a solitary bat escaping from the ruins hints at the possibility of further horrors to come.

Described in Hammer's promotion at the time of its release in early 1972 as 'The Greatest Blood-Show on Earth', and subsequently with insight by Howard Maxford (in the 1996 *Hammer, House of Horror*) as 'one of Hammer's last true moments of glory', *Vampire Circus* overcame production problems and financial overruns (none of which are apparent in the finished film) to deliver the genre myth's core elements of sex and blood with both shocking power and much-needed originality. Aside from the obvious voyeuristic thrills of the undead leads' naked romps with their chosen victims, the vampires' perverted sexuality is more apparent here than in any other Hammer horror, from the near paedophilic overtones of Anna Mueller's orgasmic swoon at the Count's opening child murder, to the explicit demonstrations of sexual symbiosis between beasts and humans, as displayed in the relationship between the circus tiger woman Serena and her real-life counterpart.

Visually impressive given the usual demands of the Hammer budget, in this instance compounded by novice director Robert Young's lack of financial acumen during the course of the five-week shoot, the shape-shifting transformations of Emil and the acrobatic twins are particularly well realised by cinematographer Moray Grant in conjunction with effects regular Les Bowie, while composer David Whitaker's powerful yet lyrical score provides an effective and welcome variation to the traditional Hammer sound.

Now regarded as something of a cult favourite, Robert Young's debut underperformed at the box office, forcing Michael Carreras, who had co-produced the picture with independent Wilbur Stark, to look around for other ideas. It was an impossible task and Hammer never would (or even could) reproduce screen horror as darkly and with such assurance as they had achieved in the autumn of 1971 with *Vampire Circus*. Although several further undead projects were announced in the early 1970s – *Kali: Devil Bride of Dracula* (1971 and 1974), *Vampire Hunters* (1972), *Village of Vampires* (1973) and *Vampirella* (1975) amongst many other unrealised films – only one further vampire film would be made in what little time was left for Michael Carreras and his team before the famous house of horror all but closed its doors for good.

Conceived as the first in an ongoing series of supernatural adventures for both film and television, Brian Clemens' *Captain Kronos – Vampire Hunter*, filmed at Elstree in the spring of 1972, contained as much outlandish wit and burlesque-style comic book action as *Vampire Circus* had sexual obscenities and doom-laden depravity. Centred around the rollicking escapades of two nineteenth-century 'professional' vampire slayers, the swashbuckling Aryan hero of the title, played by German heart-throb Horst Janson, and his wily hunchbacked assistant, Professor Grost (John Cater), Clemens (a prolific scriptwriter best known for the television series *The Avengers* (1961–9) and *The Professionals* (1977–83)) intended to give a *Doctor Who*-style edge to future proceedings by having the duo appear in different time periods (*chronos* being the Greek equivalent of 'time') where they would continue to battle the undead menace wherever it was to be found as revenge for the deaths of the Captain's own mother and sister who, it transpires, have fallen victim to the scourge of vampirism while Kronos was away fighting for the Prussian Imperial Guard.

For their initial outing, the pair was let loose in more or less familiar period territory, being summoned to the isolated hamlet of Durwood by an old friend, former army surgeon Dr Marcus (John Carson), where one by one the young and pretty female villagers are being mysteriously transformed into hideous old women by an eerie black-cowled figure. Grost quickly identifies a species of vampire that robs its victims of youth – of 'life itself' – and the duo begin to scour the woods and fields for their enemy, employing a quirky mixture of science and folklore for the purpose: the burying of boxes containing dead toads is the most memorable, stemming from the old country knowledge concerning vampires and deceased amphibians contained in the couplets of an amusing rhyme (invented by Clemens for the purpose). The trail soon leads to nearby Durwood Hall where Paul and Sara Durwood (Shane Briant and Lois Dane), children of the late master swordsman Hagan, arouse suspicions by appearing to have the unnatural abilities of effortless good looks and perpetual youth. The beautiful pair are in fact red herrings as their mother, Lady Durwood (Wanda Ventham), a cousin of the Styrian Karnsteins, is the real culprit, who has hidden her supernatural lack of ageing behind a false mask while working to bring her dead husband back from the dead. In a rousing finale, Kronos, armed with 'God's blade' (a sword forged from a churchyard cross), engages the undead Hagen (ace fight arranger William Hobbs) in a duel to the death, and with the life-sucking vampires eventually reduced to mouldering skeletons, the duo set off across the countryside in search of fresh adventures.

Despite specifically commissioning a vampire story from Clemens and his team (co-producer Albert Fennell and composer Laurie Johnson), Michael Carreras was unhappy with the result and delayed the release of *Kronos* for eighteen months: it eventually saw the light of day in April 1974 and quickly passed into obscurity amongst a raft of Satanic-themed films that began appearing in the wake of *The Exorcist*, which had hit cinema screens in Britain and America the previous year.

Now highly regarded by devotees, Hammer's final non-*Dracula* feature has much to recommend it, particularly Clemens' quirky additions to the established vampire lore and a fine supporting cast, particularly Carson as the doomed and vampirised Dr Marcus, staked, hanged and burnt in the name of science as the slayers work to identify the method of destruction needed to wipe out the Durwood scourge; love interest for the Captain was provided by *Dracula A.D. 1972*'s shapely Caroline Munro as the gypsy girl, Carla, and Clemens also wrote in a cameo role for his ex-*Avengers* stalwart, Ian Hendry, as the troubled duellist, Kerro.

Where they had once lead the field as pioneering innovators of British screen horror, by the mid-1970s Hammer were now themselves following the trends set by others. The studio's final horror feature, a contemporary adaptation of Dennis Wheatley's 1953 *Black Magic* novel *To the Devil a Daughter*, with, appropriately, Christopher Lee in the lead role as evil de-frocked priest Father Rayner, appeared in 1976, but by the end of the decade, a poorly received remake of Hitchcock's *The Lady Vanishes* was the final nail in the coffin and Michael Carreras, owing in excess of £800,000, called in the receivers. The company was bought by former production executive Roy Skeggs who quickly helmed *Hammer House of Horror*, a thirteen-episode television series for which a number of Hammer regulars took part, both in front and behind the camera, including stars Peter Cushing and Denholm Elliot, writer Anthony Hinds (as John Elder), musicians James Bernard and Philip Martell, and directors Don Sharp, Alan Gibson and Peter Sasdy. An assortment of familiar themes including devil worship, spirit possession, witchcraft and lycanthropy, an undead episode was conspicuously absent as had been the situation on the big screen for the previous half-decade: in the passing of Hammer (effectively dormant until a financial resurrection took place in the late 2000s, by which time the original casts and production crews were long gone), the screen vampire had lost its greatest champion.

Clearly out of fashion in a post-Hammer world, the British vampire film's subsequent appearance has been sporadic but nonetheless bloody. In 1974, the year that effectively saw Hammer shut up shop on the genre with *Kronos* and *The Legend of the 7 Golden Vampires*, Essay Films, a small independent production company, contributed *Vampyres*, an erotic piece of homespun filmmaking against which Roy Ward Baker's *The Vampire Lovers*, then less than four years old, pales into insignificance in terms of its presentation of bloody violence and sexual exploitation.

Directed by Spanish painter José Ramón Larraz and filmed entirely on location in and around Hammer's old stomping ground of Oakley Court at Bray, the Vampyres of the title are two bisexual lovers, Fran and Miriam (Marianne Morris and Anulka Dziubinska), shot to death by a mystery assassin in the opening reel, who return from beyond the grave as undead hitchhikers, preying on passing motorists who are taken back to the pair's crumbling Gothic mansion to be used for both sex and food. One particular victim, Ted, played by Murray Brown, finds himself trapped inside the haunted house where he becomes gradually weakened by the sultry Fran, who drinks the blood from a wound on his arm during the course of their nightly orgies. A young holidaying couple, John and Harriet (Brian Deacon and Sally Faulkner), who have unwisely parked their caravan in the overgrown grounds, gradually become drawn into the mystery, particularly Harriet whose fascination with Fran and Miriam results in her discovery of the sleeping vampires in an abandoned wine cellar in the vaults under the house. Eventually Ted manages to escape and goes to the caravan for help, but the deadly pair attack and the holidaymakers are killed. In a final twist, it transpires that Ted, who survives and is discovered in his car the following morning by an irate landowner, is in fact the original murderer who, in returning to the scene of the crime, has unwittingly become haunted by the bloodthirsty ghosts of his own victims.

A sex film with the weakest of plots, *Vampyres* contains some surprisingly chilling moments: the tension generated during Harriet's exploration of the silent and seemingly abandoned house is well handled by Larraz, while scenes of the vampire couple both waiting silently by the roadside as well as fleeing through a nearby churchyard in their billowing cloaks, have an eerie dream-like quality, enhanced by cinematographer Harry Waxman's effective use of the rural English country settings. The director of a number of horror and thriller films during the 1970s and 1980s, José Larraz holds the record as the only filmmaker brave enough to combine the disparate subjects of sex vampirism and that peculiar native British pastime of caravanning!

Another of Hammer's regular filming locations, which saw a brief return to former times, was Black Park at Wexham when, in 1979, American stage actor Frank Langella became the new face of *Dracula* for both Universal Pictures and *Saturday Night Fever* director, John Badham.

Based as per the Lugosi original on the Deane/Balderston stage play, *Dracula* boasted prominent roles for Sir Lawrence Olivier as Van Helsing and Donald Pleasance as Jack Seward in a highly romanticised screenplay that took huge liberties with Stoker's original narrative, including, amongst other things, scrambling several of the novel's principal character relationships. A number of Cornish locations, including St Michael's Mount and Tintagel, stood in for Whitby and Carfax Abbey, while the film shared its release with two other *Dracula*-themed pictures at the complete opposite ends of the undead spectrum: Werner Herzog's *Nosferatu the Vampyre*, with Klaus Kinski as Dracula, and Stan Dragoti's horror comedy, *Love at First Bite*, that starred the perpetually suntanned George Hamilton in the top vampire role.

In 1983, Tony Scott, whose younger brother Ridley redefined the science fiction/horror genre for a new generation with his pioneering *Alien* (1979), directed Catherine Deneuve and David Bowie in a big screen adaptation of American novelist Whitley Strieber's *The Hunger* (1981), which saw the stylish couple as a pair of predatory vampires posing as classical music teachers in modern day New York. When John Blaylock (Bowie) begins a process of unstoppable accelerated ageing, he seeks help from Susan Sarandon's Dr Sarah Roberts, who is at the forefront of studying genetic ageing in primates. However, Blaylock's condition quickly becomes critical and he is reduced to a withered but undying husk which his wife Miriam (Deneuve) locks away in a steel casket, along with the many other mummified undead lovers she has collected down through the centuries. Miriam and Roberts' subsequent lesbian affair provides a *Carmilla*-like atmosphere, and after the doctor chooses suicide rather than vampiric immortality, the film's final reel shows Miriam relocated to central London in the company of new and willing victims.

In *The Hunger*, Scott swaps the cult-like attractiveness of vampirism as presented by Terence Fisher under Hammer and replaces it with a likening to another all too familiar twentieth-century addiction, that of drug dependency and heroin addiction.

For the final two entries in our survey we again cross briefly into the 1980s in the company of cult film favourite Ken Russell, whose controversial adaptation of Aldous Huxley's 1953 novel *The Devils of Loudun* was being filmed at Pinewood (*The Devils* with Oliver Reed and Vanessa Redgrave) at the same time that Hammer were laying down the first two entries in their Le Fanu Karnstein series at nearby Elstree.

Born in Southampton in 1927, a former actor and freelance photographer, Russell came to prominence as a television director at the BBC during the 1960s, where he helmed a series of biographical essays on the lives of several notable English and foreign composers, including Bruckner, Elgar, Debussy and Delius. His maverick reputation was cemented during the 1970s with a number of prominent big-screen productions including *Women in Love* (1969), *The Music Lovers* (1970), *Mahler* (1974) with Robert Powell in the title role, as well as the film version of The Who's epic rock opera *Tommy* (1975). *The Devils*, however, was the most troublesome in terms of its relationship with the BBFC censors and despite the existence of a number of edited versions, has never been seen in its entirety since its release in May 1971.

In 1988, Russell filmed his own screenplay of Bram Stoker's *The Lair of the White Worm*, retaining the novel's Derbyshire location but reworking much of the original plot which centred on the discovery (by Scots archaeologist Peter Capaldi) of a mysterious snake-like skull, unearthed during the course of the excavation of a Roman villa in the grounds of a rural bed and breakfast run by two sisters, Eve and

Mary Trent (Catherine Oxenberg and Sammi Davis). Amanda Donohoe played the title monster's blue-skinned snake goddess servant, masquerading as the aristocratic dominatrix, Lady Sylvia Marsh, and in addition to his usual arsenal of religious and sexual imagery (which includes a tableau of Ursuline nuns gang-raped by a cohort of Roman legionnaires at the foot of a living statue of Christ), Russell manages to apply a passing vampire-like quality to certain aspects of the proceedings, particularly the somewhat comical scene of a fanged policeman snake-charmed into submission by the kilted Capaldi playing the bagpipes.

Two years before, Russell had brought the British vampire film full circle with his bold and stylish recreation of Byron's 1816 summer of horror at the Villa Diodati, scripted by Welsh screenwriter Stephen Volk, best remembered for BBC television's controversial 1992 *Ghostwatch* documentary, *Gothic* (1986), which starred Gabriel Byrne as Lord Byron, Julian Sands as Percy Shelley, and Natasha Richardson as Mary Shelley. With his grotesque and leech-like Polidori (Timothy Spall) licking the blood from the self-inflicted wounds opened up by Byron's cynical mockery, Russell engineered the genesis of Lord Ruthven and the entire vampire industry in a convincingly fevered atmosphere of nightmarish imagination that the late Ingrid Pitt has described as the 'total horror movie' [original emphasis].

As we have seen, both the post-war revival of Gothic horror together with the modern spread of the undead legend have been solid British affairs and the medium of the cinema has been perhaps the vampires' most powerful ally. Belief in vampires and vampirism may be, as Christopher Frayling has described it, 'as old as the world', but the general public's knowledge and understanding of the subject in our present time is based primarily on the visual history transmitted over the course of the period we have been examining in the previous three chapters, the Hammer phenomenon and its aftermath in particular. By the beginning of the 1970s, this power, together with the occult revolution of the previous decade, was starting to leave its mark, no more so than in one particular suburb of north London: a case of life imitating art, or something far darker?

10

The Strange Story of the Highgate Vampire

(1965-Present)

For psychic investigators, ghost hunters and aficionados of the supernatural, the environs of Highgate in North London have today an inseparable association with the world of the occult and the paranormal. A fashionable suburb, the village has a history of settlement stretching back to Roman times, in past centuries benefiting from its location on the trade route into the city from the north. In 1565, under a Royal Charter granted by Elizabeth I, Highgate School was established by Sir Roger Cholmeley, Lord Chief Justice and Recorder of London. Despite being admitted into the County of London in 1889, Highgate retains much of the character established in the sixteenth and seventeenth centuries when, as local author and medium Patsy Langley has noted, it became 'an attraction for the aristocracy and the genteel'. Many fine buildings were erected during the Georgian period and these, together with later Victorian additions, are now both coveted and protected by conservation areas established by Haringey and Camden Councils and the Highgate Society. This is the Highgate that Bram Stoker would have known, but as we have already seen, there is no clear evidence that the area had a direct influence during the writing of his famous novel.

In the early 1680s, Sir William Ashurst, one of the founding subscribers of the Bank of England and later Lord Mayor of London, acquired what became known as Ashurst House, a large three-storey property in extensive grounds, situated on the south side of Highgate High Street. A drawing of the building in the archives of the Guildhall Library, dating from the early 1820s, shows a substantial period residence with an imposing gabled entrance and a high dormered roof surmounted by a cupola, built no doubt to take advantage of the fine views out over London from Highgate Hill. Sir William died in 1720 and ownership of Ashurst House passed to surviving members of his family; it was subsequently sold in the mid-1700s and later owners rented the estate for many years before finally turning the building into a private school. In 1830, now semi-derelict, it was sold to the Church Commission who demolished the building and built a new church, St Michael's, to a design by architect Lewis Velliamy, a pioneer of the neo-Gothic style whose drawings for the project were exhibited at the Royal Academy in 1831; construction began the following year, taking an impressive eleven months to complete. The church is today most famous for its association with the poet Samuel Taylor Coleridge, author of *The Rime of the Ancient Mariner* (1798) and, aptly enough given what follows, the vampiristic *Christabel* (1797–1800), who worshipped and is buried here.

Surplus to requirements, the former gardens of Ashurst House to the south of the new St Michael's were sold off and in 1836 the site was purchased by The London Cemetery Company, a private consortium established under the auspices of the recently created Cemeteries Act of 1832. The new legislation allowed profit-making companies to build private cemeteries in and around London to alleviate problems associated with the disposal of the city's dead, and between 1832 and 1841, seven substantial burial grounds (christened the 'magnificent seven' by architectural historian Hugh Meller in the early 1980s) were created: Kensal Green (1832), West Norwood (1837), Abney Park (1840), Nunhead (1840), Brompton (1840), Tower Hamlets (1841), and Highgate Cemetery, which opened in 1839 and occupied a large tract of sloping land opposite Waterlow Park on the west side of Swains Lane, a narrow, single carriageway road which runs north-south from Highgate High Street. In 1854, the cemetery was extended with the opening of a second section to the east of Swains Lane, the two being linked by an underground coffin tunnel beneath the roadway to ensure that once blessed in the chapel, a casket was always kept within consecrated ground. The chapel itself was unusual, being divided into two halves: an Anglican chapel on one side of a central archway and a 'dissenters' chapel on the other, where funerals of all other faiths took place – to ensure maximisation of profits, no one, whatever their particular religion or belief, was turned away. In total, Highgate Cemetery covers 37 acres of ground and today is statistically the last resting place for approximately 167,000 people occupying 52,000 graves.

For fifty years, Highgate became one of the most fashionable places in London to be buried, leading the Victorian era's fascination with funerary splendour and excess. Elaborate vaults, graves and monuments began to line the winding pathways crossing the side of Highgate Hill, many demonstrating the Victorian passion for cemetery symbolism. The older West Cemetery, now most often associated with occult happenings, vampirism and Black Magic practices, contains the iconic Circle of Lebanon – a sunken corridor of characteristic vaults created around one of the original trees from the garden of Ashurst House – and the equally well known Egyptian Avenue (both Grade I listed buildings), as well as the graves of many notables, including Australian politician Sir Charles Cowper, author John Galsworthy and the eminent Michael Faraday, who was one of the first scientists to attempt to debunk the Victorian craze for table-tipping. Arguably Highgate's most famous occupant, German philosopher Karl Marx, author of *Das Kapital* (1867), was buried in the East Cemetery in 1883, a period in time which saw the fortunes of the famous burial ground begin to fail, a decline initiated by the re-legalisation of cremation in the late 1880s followed by the Cremation Act of 1902, compounded by the subsequent slaughter of the First World War, which tamed the previous generation's 'cult of death' exuberance for grand burials and monuments. Un-consecrated areas of the site, including the stonemason's yard, were sold off for housing development in an effort to raise funds, but Highgate's financial crisis continued. The passing of the years also saw the cemetery grounds themselves grow wild and untended, the riotously tumbling tombs and statues overtaken by an unchecked jungle of trees, grass and weeds, creating the ideal conditions in which stories of phantoms and strange happenings flourish. By the time Peter Underwood included the location in his pioneering *Haunted London* in 1973, Highgate presented 'a chilling scene of utter ruin and decay where vaults yawn in the shadows and gravestones crumble beneath one's feet'.

Unsurprisingly, by the mid-1960s, accounts of supernatural encounters in and around both sections of Highgate Cemetery had been common knowledge for a number of years. For pure ghost hunters, the East Cemetery had acquired what could best be described as a more traditional haunted reputation than the association with vampires and Black Magic that its westerly counterpart would soon acquire by the end of the decade. The east plot is now the resting place of many noted actors, artists, writers and thinkers – as well as Marx, Patrick Wymark, Sir Ralph Richardson, Paul Foot, Douglas Adams, and Anna Mahler, daughter of the great composer, are all buried here. Peter Underwood was able to interview two witnesses who claimed to have seen the ghost of an old crone, with thin streaming hair, simultaneously from different vantage points, moving quickly amongst the overgrown tombs before vanishing away: local tradition identifies this as the restless shade of a mad woman, searching for the graves of her murdered children; another apparition, a shrouded skeletal figure with long bony fingers, is said to appear silently beside the main gateway into Swains Lane.

Ghost stories and accounts of strange experiences associated with the older West Cemetery have also been recorded and according to some Highgate residents were well known to many local people within living memory. David Farrant, a local man whose name is now synonymous with strange happenings in the area in the late 1960s and early 1970s, recalled such tales as 'a definite story' learnt from a young age. 'There were always rumours of a ghost there,' he recalled during an interview in 2012. 'I was born in Highgate and even as a child I used to hear these stories about ghosts in the village, in village pubs and Highgate Cemetery.'

The second half of the 1960s saw the beginning of one of the most intriguing and infamous periods in Highgate's long and colourful history, and specifically its connections with Satanistic rituals and the cult of the undead. In July 1965, Brian Bourne, an ex-Army officer originally from Exeter, was walking his dog along Swains Lane around eight o'clock one evening on his way to a local party. As he drew near to the West Cemetery's top gate, located in the north-east corner of the burial ground at the start of the high perimeter wall flanking the roadway, he became aware of an unnatural stillness in the atmosphere accompanied by a sudden drop in temperature. In the centre of the footpath a short distance ahead, Bourne saw what appeared to be a mass of dark liquid flowing down the brick wall of the cemetery and which began forming into a dense black pool. As he stood watching, the amorphous mass suddenly rose up and seemed to come together into a frighteningly tall black shape which quickly towered over him. 'My overall impression was that it was a black figure wearing dark garments,' he stated in an account published in the Highgate Vampire Society's *Suspended in Dusk* newsletter several years later in 1997. '[There was n]o face. Where eyes would have been if it were human, there were just two red pits, red glows ... This wasn't a ghost, this was an entity ... It simply was not human.' Bourne fled with his dog – which reacted by growling at the apparition – back up Swains Lane to the safety of The Flask public house in nearby Highgate West Hill opposite St Michael's Church, where he sank two much-needed brandies.

Brian Bourne's experience was the first of a number of alleged incidents that were to take place in Swains Lane in the vicinity of the West Cemetery's north-east gate over the next few years. Early in 1967, a young couple, Thomas O'Loughlin and his fiancée, were passing the same spot following a night out, when they both seemed to see an unidentified figure with an unpleasant face looking out at them through the iron bars; as they stood watching, the figure appeared to fade away and was gone. Intrigued by the incident, O'Loughlin returned to the cemetery several nights later accompanied by a male friend, with the intention of carrying out a light-hearted ghost hunt amongst the tombs. As they explored the old West Cemetery by torchlight, both men later claimed to have heard a sinister 'booming sound' and to have caught a glimpse of a dark shape that crossed the pathway in front of them. Frightened, they both ran back to the point along the boundary wall where they had entered and climbed back onto the road. Upset by the incident, when asked to show where the sighting had taken place, O'Loughlin subsequently refused to return.

More incidents took place during the course of the following year. Peter Underwood, at the time president of the long established Ghost Club, heard first-hand accounts from two people who claimed to have seen a ghostly – and by implication, vampiric – figure moving about inside the West Cemetery during the course of night-time visits. One man reported finding a trail of blood leading into a vault where he and a companion had seen a dark figure enter, while two other visitors described seeing a similar apparition which seemed to rise up from the ground and then move off 'with incredible speed and swift, long strides' along one of the overgrown pathways. Around the same time, fresh accounts of ghostly happenings in and around buildings in the Highgate village area became common knowledge after reports began appearing in the local press. George Sample, the landlord of the Ye Olde Gatehouse pub at the top of Highgate High Street, told a reporter from the *Hampstead and Highgate Express* that doors inside the building often opened mysteriously by themselves and footsteps were heard crossing rooms known to have been empty at the time; this is the same hostelry where the apparition of a tall cloaked figure wearing an Elizabethan-style hat was apparently seen by a customer in an upstairs corridor in October 1966.

Residents in a post-war estate of council flats known as Hillcrest, located off North Road, half a mile from Highgate Cemetery and built on the site of a former Victorian convent for unmarried mothers, also reported the appearance of a tall dark figure that appeared on occasion in and around the grounds. In July 1969, a local resident returning home to a house in Priory Close, claimed to have seen an approaching figure running soundlessly along Swains Lane which was visible for several seconds before vanishing. In his *Haunted London*, Underwood also gives brief mention of an incident (reported to have taken place in January 1970) concerning motorist Paul Fluckiger, who (while waiting in his car, which had broken down in Swains Lane opposite one of the cemetery gates) saw a sinister apparition with wild eyes and bared teeth, that peered out at him through the iron railings before vanishing away at a seemingly non-human pace into the darkness.

It was into this arena of local mystery that a young David Farrant stepped in the spring of 1967 after returning from a teenage backpacking tour of Europe. Born in 1946, Farrant's mother, a spiritualist, had stimulated an interest in the world of the unseen and in 1964, at the age of 18, he had been initiated into the pagan religion of Wicca. The same year, Farrant paid his first visit to Highgate Cemetery and saw first-hand much evidence of vandalism and localised damage amongst the once fine Victorian tombs: many vaults and graves by this time had been broken into by lead thieves, with coffin lids lifted and the contents disturbed, the cemetery authority's ineffectual repairs only adding to the atmosphere of desolation and abandonment that was clearly prevalent at the time. On his return from Spain, Farrant became interested in new reports of unusual happenings in and around Highgate village and became part of a small group of local friends, known today as the British Psychic and Occult Society (BPOS), who met on a semi-regular basis to discuss instances of hauntings and other ghostly phenomena.

In 1969, Farrant sought out and interviewed two people whose recent and unusual experiences in the vicinity of the cemetery had come to his attention. An elderly woman from the nearby Holly Lodge estate, while walking her dog one evening along Swains Lane, claimed to have been frightened by the appearance of a tall dark figure with evil-looking eyes which floated towards her from a point inside the West Cemetery's top gate before vanishing. As with the incident of Brian Bourne, the lady's dog reacted in a similar way, howling and refusing to move while the apparition was visible, its behaviour returning to normal once the figure had disappeared. In his *Beyond the Highgate Vampire*, first published in 1991, Farrant describes speaking with a second person, a male accountant (given the pseudonym 'Thornton' in the book) who he describes as encountering a ghostly figure, on this occasion inside the West Cemetery, one afternoon in daylight. After visiting the Circle of Lebanon and then retracing his steps back to the Swains Lane chapel, he became lost and spent some time walking around in an attempt to find the way out. At one point, Thornton suddenly became aware of a presence close by and, turning, came almost face to face with a tall black shape which seemed to radiate what has been described as a 'hypnotic force' that began almost immediately to drain him of mental and physical energy, very much in the manner of a psychic attack. The incident lasted for several minutes before the apparition abruptly disappeared and the accountant found himself gradually returning to normal.

In the account published by David Farrant, Thornton described the figure as being clearly malevolent and felt that in some way it had sought him out as he had been walking around inside the gloomy cemetery. Before the year was out, Farrant would claim to have his own sinister encounter with the paranormal, one that would precipitate, as he would later describe it, 'one of the most chilling accounts of vampirism in the twentieth century' that even today, many years after the events, continues to hold an increasing number of both sceptics and believers in its sway.

Although contemporary accounts suggest more than one event taking place, David Farrant has subsequently placed importance on a single incident which he says occurred in his presence during the winter of 1969/70, a time when he and his fledgling group of psychic investigators were taking more than just a casual interest in the many reports of strange happenings in the local area. On the night of the Winter Solstice – Sunday, 21 December 1969 – the shortest day of the year, Farrant elected to hold a night-time vigil inside the West Cemetery in the hope of catching sight of the sinister apparition himself. In *Beyond the Highgate Vampire*, the novice researcher described his experience in the following way:

> Around 11 p.m. on the proposed night, I set off for the cemetery. It was a bitterly cold night and the surrounding area was deserted. Walking down the narrow lane that ran alongside the cemetery, there was a sudden awareness of some 'alien presence'. This was difficult to define, except in so far that there was a distinct impression of being no longer alone. Passing the top gate and preparing to scale this … [s]uddenly, something caught my eye and looking up, just inside some [five] yards from the gate and clearly visible, was a tall dark shape.

The apparition appeared to be some 7 or 8ft tall, almost as high as the cemetery gates themselves, with two eyes which were clearly visible, described in other interviews as appearing like red pinpoints of light. So vivid and realistic was the figure that Farrant's initial reaction was that it was simply a hoaxer dressed up in a Halloween-style costume, but at the same moment, the area around the top gate seemed to turn 'icy cold' and, like the accountant Thornton before him, he felt immediately under some form of psychic attack. Drawing on his knowledge of Wicca, Farrant describes mentally uttering a Cabalistic incantation for protection and the black figure suddenly vanished. The whole incident is said to have lasted between four to five seconds.

A short while later, with no doubt both the unnaturalness and the malevolence of his recent encounter still on his mind, Farrant contacted the local *Hampstead and Highgate Express* and under the title 'Ghost walks in Highgate', his letter appeared in the newspaper on 6 February 1970. By this time, two other members of Farrant's group had allegedly seen the ghostly figure for themselves but were unwilling to make their experiences public. Farrant subsequently decided to take ownership of these encounters and for convenience include them in with his own, but there are still inconsistencies in the published account, an example of the problems and controversy which has been part of the case practically from the very beginning:

> Some nights I walk home past the gates of Highgate Cemetery. On three occasions I have seen what appeared to be a ghost-like figure inside the gates at the top of Swains Lane. The first occasion was on Christmas Eve [*sic*]. I saw a grey figure for a few seconds before it disappeared into the darkness. The second sighting, a week later, was also brief. Last week the figure appeared, only a few yards inside the gates. This time it was there long enough for me to see it much more clearly, and now I can think of no other explanation than this apparition being something supernatural. I have no knowledge in this field and I would be interested to hear if any other readers have seen anything of this nature.

The following week (13 February), the local readership responded and four brief accounts of strange happenings in and around Highgate Cemetery were published. '[M]any local people have seen Mr Farrant's ghost in Highgate Cemetery,' Kenny Frewin of Mountbatten House, Hillcrest, subsequently a life member of the British Psychic and Occult Society, commented. 'The ghost will sometimes appear nightly for about a week, and then not be seen again for perhaps a month. To my knowledge the ghost always takes the form of a pale figure and has been appearing for several years'. A spiritualist reader, Nava Grunberg, then known as Nava Areili and like Frewin latterly a member of the BPOS, also claimed to have seen a similar apparition the previous year, as did Audrey Connely who, in the company of her fiancé, saw a 'most unusual form' around the same time. A fourth correspondent confirmed the tradition of a Victorian-looking apparition appearing in and around the West Cemetery area, adding that a local superstition told of the bells in the disused chapel in Swains Lane ringing 'mysteriously' by themselves as a sign that the ghost was abroad.

Clearly enjoying the 'ghost story for Christmas' atmosphere that Farrant's initial letter had established, the editor of the *Ham and High* made a front page appeal for more stories, qualifying the request by saying 'to those who think it is a golden opportunity to spoof us with spooks, we warn that we will check the authenticity of all letters received'. The following edition of 20 February 1970 contained five more letters and a further editorial appeal for additional experiences. Amongst this second postbag were further accounts of a mysterious form glimpsed moving around inside the West Cemetery, including an apparition that frightened two nurses returning home from a nightshift along Swains Lane; one reader, Marianne Fowler of Holly Lodge Mansions, claimed to have encountered a ghostly cyclist in the roadway outside Highgate Cemetery that (in the following week's edition) was named by another correspondent as being known locally as the 'White Ghost'.

Although genuine psychical experiences cannot and should not be discounted, it must be said that, leaving aside deliberate hoax letters (two of which appeared in the following edition of 27 February), Highgate Cemetery's unique appearance and atmosphere – then as now – no doubt provided a fertile breeding ground for the imaginative mind that may be behind many of the experiences reported in the *Hampstead and Highgate Express* at the time. Writing in his book *Raising the Devil* (2000), in connection with the Highgate case, American folklorist Bill Ellis felt that:

> … the most impressive detail [of the various newspaper accounts] is the sheer amorphousness of the Highgate traditions; apart from the ghostly cyclist, hardly two informants gave the same story. Yet in all, young people seem compelled to walk by or even enter the cemetery in male/female couples or in unisex groups. The idea that 'Something is supposed to happen' is coupled with the lack of a definite threat …

Thus suggesting that the sinister-looking locations generate their own mythology of ghostly and supernatural associations and that in this case, 'the Highgate legends fit into a much larger tradition of cemetery visits and dares.'

Tellingly, in the immediate months prior to David Farrant's experience on the night of the Winter Solstice, a film crew from Hammer spent an autumn day filming location sequences in key areas inside the West Cemetery, including Egyptian Avenue and the Circle of Lebanon, for their forthcoming feature *Taste the Blood of Dracula* which, as we have already seen, was released in the spring of 1970 in what would be the aftermath of the most public phase of the entire Highgate Vampire affair. In *Hammer Films on Location* (2012), film historian Wayne Kinsey includes the reminiscences of actor John Carson who, together with Geoffrey Keen and Peter Sallis, took part in several scenes. 'The most eerie thing that happened was when we filmed in Highgate Cemetery,' Carson later recalled.

> The other cemetery [i.e. the West] is now totally neglected and overgrown. It's on a steep hill and many of the graves … have been plundered and broken into and they've been rooted into by sycamore saplings. We filmed there on a wet and misty day and we needed no artificial help to create the atmosphere. We didn't need smoke machines or anything like that. It was very spooky indeed. We all felt it, and we were very glad to get out of the place.

One Highgate resident who responded to the *Ham and High's* initial letters on the cemetery ghost was Elizabeth Wegner. 'I read your four letters in reply to the original letter of Mr Farrant,' she commented. 'I find this distressing, because I live at the bottom of Swains Lane, not far from the cemetery. Although I have not seen a ghost myself, I find it interesting that so many people have,' adding, 'the story of the ghost behind the gates should be seriously looked into.' This investigation was soon to arrive, but neither she nor the people of Highgate could have envisaged how it would pan out and also what lasting legacy for the area it would in fact ultimately leave behind.

As stories of ghosts and strange happenings flitted through the newspaper pages and narrow streets of Highgate, evidence of more tangible and sinister happenings in the locale began to come to light. Amongst the tomb vandalism and general decay in the West Cemetery, David Farrant and others became aware of clear signs that the area was being used as a meeting place for Black Magic practitioners and similarly Satanic-orientated activity. During the course of one visit, Farrant and his friends discovered that a particularly secluded mausoleum in the very heart of the cemetery had been converted by what has been described as 'professional Satanists' into a cult-like temple: the vault, resembling a small chapel where the coffins were concealed below ground level, had been broken into and pentagram-like markings and other symbols painted on the marble floor. The burnt-down stubs of several thick black candles made it clear that some form of ritualistic activity, possibly a necromantic rite, had taken place. Farrant noted that a heavy marble bust had been moved into a position close to the markings on the floor, as though whoever was involved was attempting to establish contact with the spirit of the tomb. The possibility that this activity was in some way connected with or had some direct bearing on the appearances of the sinister black figure in Highgate Cemetery was made at the time and has been repeated in a number of accounts of the case that have appeared in the ensuing years, to the effect that the malevolent apparition seen by David Farrant and a number of others was either an evil 'entity' purposely summoned up by Satanic activity, or that these same rituals had accidentally disturbed some existing presence that up until that time, nameless and unidentified, had lain dormant and undisturbed amongst the graves.

An undercurrent of occult and pseudo-Black Magic activity in Britain during the preceding eight or nine years had almost guaranteed Highgate an appointment with the mysterious and clandestine world of devil worship and Satanism, with churchyard desecrations and similar vandalism involving the removal of buried remains and evidence of ritualistic ceremonies creating headlines and column inches in both the local and national press. In March 1963, a skeleton was removed from an eighteenth-century vault at the derelict church of St Mary's at Clophill in Bedfordshire, while the following month the discovery of several mutilated cows' heads and a horse skull around a makeshift altar in a wood at Caddington on the outskirts of nearby Luton was also linked to 'Black Magic raiders'. Later the same year, four youths were charged with attempting to dig up a skull from a churchyard at Coleshill near Amersham in Buckinghamshire; while in September 1963, a local bricklayer discovered a human effigy together with a sheep's heart pierced with hawthorns nailed to an oak door at an ancient monument in Castle Rising, Norfolk. Three months later, near Pevensey in Sussex, a bellringer was involved in a scuffle with four robed men who were discovered reciting 'incantations' around lighted candles in the chancel of Westham parish church, while the *Daily Mirror* for 6 January 1964 reported on the Revd Ernest Streete, who had pronounced a curse on the ''Black magic' wreckers' who had smashed gravestones and drawn magical signs on the floor at St Nicholas' church at Bramber, Sussex. In August 1964, the Bishop of Southwark carried out a service to re-hallow the church of St Giles in Camberwell, South London, where intruders had carried out 'blasphemous rites' involving stolen wafers and holy water at the high altar, as well as tampering with coffins recently excavated by builders extending the church crypt. At an isolated churchyard at South Malling, near Lewes in Sussex, in August 1967, on a date coinciding the with pagan festival of Lammas, a 100-year-old skeleton was removed from a grave and several bones taken away, while the following year one of the decade's most high-profile incidents of grave robbing took place on Halloween night, 31 October 1968, at Tottenham Park Cemetery, Edmonton, North London, when intruders opened three coffins in a communal grave and drove a 6ft-long iron stake through the breast of one of the female corpses inside.

David Farrant had noticed several incidents of similar vandalism and disturbance to buried remains at Highgate during visits prior to his experience in 1969: 'Vaults had been broken open and coffins literally smashed apart,' he wrote several years later. 'One vault near the top gate … was wide open and one could see the remains of a skeleton where it had been wrenched from a coffin. Another vault on the main pathway had been thus entered and one of the coffins inside set alight.' Clearly the opportunity for necromantic rites and similar divination was unprecedented at Highgate Cemetery at the time, but how much of this level of desecration was actually the work of a Satanic cult is unclear.

Whatever the origins of the malevolent figure seen in Highgate's West Cemetery during the cold winter of 1969/70, events in the locale were about to take a bizarre and unprecedented change of direction. On Friday, 27 February 1970, the *Hampstead and Highgate Express* published what was undoubtedly the most startling headline in its then 110-year history. The now infamous 'Does a wampyr walk in Highgate?' announced the arrival into the proceedings of 25-year-old photographer and exorcist Sean Manchester, who we have already encountered previously in connection with the future case of the Kirklees Vampire. Manchester's presence altered the dynamics of the proceedings completely as what he would soon describe as the 'official' investigation into the Highgate affair quickly began to gather momentum. It was a local phenomenon that the editor of the *Ham and High* felt was too good to pass over and in a lengthy front page article introduced readers to the new happenings in the following way:

> We don't want to frighten you, but the ghost of Highgate Cemetery might just be – a vampire.
>
> So says ... Sean Manchester, president of the British Occult Society. He claims to have carried out 'extensive research and investigation into the matter.'
>
> Mr. Manchester ... said: 'The phenomenon reported by Highgate people in letters to the Ham and High is not merely the apparition of an earth-bound spirit, which is relatively harmless, but much worse – that of a wampyr or, as it is more popularly known, a vampire.'
>
> His theory is that the King Vampire of the Undead, originally a nobleman who dabbled in black magic in medieval Wallachia, 'somewhere near Turkey,' walks again.
>
> 'His followers eventually brought him to England in a coffin at the beginning of the 18th century and bought a house for him in the West End,' said Mr. Manchester. 'His unholy resting place became Highgate cemetery.
>
> When parts of Britain were plagued by vampirism centuries ago, the Highgate area was the centre of a lot of activity. It has been ever since.
>
> And now that there is so much desecration of graves by satanism [*sic*], I'm convinced that this has been happening in Highgate cemetery in an attempt by a body of satanists [*sic*] to resurrect the King Vampire.'
>
> Unlike the British Society for Psychic Research [sic], the British Occult Society – which has no formal membership, but has correspondence from '50 to 100 interested people' – believes in 'countering magic by magic.' Some adherents have spent nights in Highgate cemetery.

The leader closed with what has now become one of the article's most often cited quotations. 'We would like to exorcise the vampire by the traditional and approved manner,' Manchester told the newspaper, ' – drive a stake through its heart with one blow just after dawn between Friday and Saturday, chop off the head with a gravedigger's shovel, and burn what remains. This is what the clergy did centuries ago. But we'd be breaking the law today.' In his book, *The Vampire Hunter's Handbook* (1997), written over a quarter of a century after the events in North London, Manchester claims he was misquoted at the time of his interview:

> What I actually state, and have always stated, is that Ashurst House was sold and leased to a succession of tenants of whom one was a mysterious gentleman from the Continent who arrived in the wake of the vampire epidemic that had its origins in south-east Europe [...] This does not have quite the same sensationalist impact as 'King Vampire from Wallachia'.

Whatever the truth of the matter concerning the tenancy of Ashurst House, the 'King Vampire' of Highgate was soon to leave the desolate confines of its last resting place forever as an ensuing media circus would quickly create what has subsequently grown to become one of the most controversial benchmarks in post-war British occultism.

Over the weekend of 28 February–1 March, Sean Manchester and David Farrant met up in Highgate Cemetery, their encounter being recorded for posterity by a reporter from the *Ham and High*. Farrant had written to the newspaper a second time the previous week, his letter appearing in the same issue as the arresting 'Wampyr' headline. 'You can imagine how relieved I was to discover by the response in the letter columns that I am not alone in witnessing the spectre that haunts Swains Lane,' he stated. 'Moreover, that other readers' descriptions of the ghost correspond exactly with my experiences has left me stunned, though glad that my sanity can no longer be held in question.'

The two men spent some time in the West Cemetery, Farrant pointing out the spot to Manchester where he claimed to have seen the apparition on the night of the Winter Solstice. Both men felt the presence of dead foxes in the cemetery was somehow connected with the appearances of the eerie phantom figure: Farrant had encountered the body of a dead fox on a visit in late 1969, which was found lying in the middle of one of the main paths with no obvious sign of injury, and Manchester revealed to the reporter who accompanied them that several others, again with 'no outward sign of how they died', had been discovered in recent weeks in the same location. In a front page article, 'Why do the foxes die?', published in the *Hampstead and Highgate Express* on 6 March 1970, Manchester was quoted as saying, 'These incidents are just more inexplicable events that seem to compliment my theory about a vampire'. Part of an interview with David Farrant, who, for the moment at least, seemed to be in agreement with Manchester's theories, also appeared in the same piece: 'Much remains unexplained,' he admitted, 'but what I have recently learnt all points to the vampire theory as being the most likely answer,' adding, 'Should this be so, I for one am prepared to pursue it, taking whatever means might be necessary so that we can all rest.'

Soon reports began filtering through to both investigators of more strange happenings in and around the gloomy North London cemetery. Around the time that Farrant's first letter was published, a male student from the North London Polytechnic was walking along Swains Lane one evening when he was allegedly confronted by a phantom form close to the top gate and thrown to the ground in the manner of a physical psychic attack. What appeared to be a tall figure dressed in black quickly vanished through the cemetery wall at the same moment as a car with full headlights came into view up the hill. The incident was in fact to be mirrored the following year when, in 1971, a nurse returning to the Whittington Hospital up the hill towards Highgate High Street claimed to have been thrown to the ground by an invisible force in the vicinity of the cemetery gates, at the same time as she had become aware of a tall dark figure with a 'deathly white face' approaching from out of the cemetery itself. The apparition allegedly vanished in the headlights of an approaching car, the driver of which took the distressed woman to Highgate police station. Subsequently a search of the area was undertaken but nothing out of the ordinary was found and it should be noted that the cemetery walls at this point along the lane where the 'attack' took place are over 14ft high.

As well as assaults by seemingly ghostly figures, the continued presence of Black Magic followers in the eerie West Cemetery added a further worrying aspect to the proceedings. David Farrant has described receiving several threatening letters 'all signed in blood' from unidentified persons demanding that further investigation and publicity in and around the cemetery should cease immediately. 'There was little doubt that these letters were from genuine Satanists,' he later noted, '[F]or one thing, the secret magical signs that adorned the letters could only have been known to people with a great deal of knowledge of the Magical Arts.' Farrant and his friends chose to ignore the threats and as public awareness of events at Highgate showed no sign of decreasing in the ensuing weeks, evidence of genuine Satanic activity in the cemetery began to lessen as the perpetrators eventually abandoned the site and moved elsewhere.

Inevitably, the increasingly Draculaesque events at Highgate – real, imagined or otherwise – were to slip the confines of the London suburbs and become part of the national psyche. During the second week of March 1970, following the *Ham and High's* latest front page article on the cemetery mystery, a small film crew from Thames Television visited Highgate to cover the story for the *Today* programme, a regional news magazine broadcast on weekday evenings across London and the south-east. Both Farrant and Manchester were contacted to take part in filmed interviews for the programme, while television reporter, Sandra Harris, was taken on a tour of parts of the cemetery, including the eerie Circle of Lebanon, to see the haunt of the 'vampire' for herself. Beyond the overgrown and tumbling tombs' atmospheric 'camouflage of time' was clear evidence of the vandalism and desecration that had plagued the area in the preceding months, as the film crew quickly came across a Victorian-era coffin lying broken and discarded on one of the pathways with the lid removed, exposing the skeleton inside. David Farrant appeared on camera and described his own encounter with the cemetery apparition: 'It certainly wasn't human,' he confessed, adding in response to Harris' prompting as to whether he felt threatened by the vision, 'I did feel it was evil … I actually saw its face, and it looked like it had been dead for a long time.' Sean Manchester also appeared and again stated his, and the belief of the British Occult Society, that a vampire was responsible for the recent spate of ghostly sightings and animal deaths. For a solution to the problem, one had to go beyond the pale: an exorcism, he stated, was the only way of removing the undead menace from society. The interview is notable for containing the first recorded rumblings of what would eventually develop into decades of rivalry and bitterness between the two men. When asked about his views on Farrant's activities, Manchester replied by saying: 'He goes against our explicit wish for his own safety … he does not possess sufficient knowledge to exorcise successfully something as powerful or evil as this King Vampire, and may well fall victim as a result.' The filming session itself was not without some drama of its own that befitted the report's gloomy and atmospheric location: at one point as the crew prepared a set up outside the cemetery's now enigmatic top gate, one of the cameramen collapsed clutching his throat and was taken by car to the nearby Whittington Hospital. All present, including reporter Sandra Harris, were shaken by the incident.

Shortly after six o'clock on the evening of (appropriately enough) Friday, 13 March 1970, Harris' report into the affair of the Highgate Vampire was broadcast on the *Today* programme. Locals in the area were given a heads-up earlier in the day by the *Hampstead and Highgate Express* whose article 'The ghost goes … on TV' was given prominent space on the front page. 'Cameras from Thames Television visited Highgate Cemetery this week to film a programme about its celebrated ghost,' the newspaper noted, 'but they could not go ghost hunting. The *Today* film team was not allowed inside and had to use the cemetery gates as a background for interviews.' Mentioning Farrant by name, the article stated his intention 'to visit the cemetery again, armed with a wooden stake and a crucifix, with the aim of exorcising the spirit', and also made mention of Sean Manchester's opposition to the plans. 'We also issue a similar warning to anyone with likewise intentions' Manchester stated, but neither he, Thames Television, nor the editor of the *Ham and High* could have predicted what a watershed moment the short news item would eventually prove to be.

Within hours of the *Today* broadcast, Swains Lane was thronging with scores of visitors who, inspired by suggestions of an 'official vampire hunt' amongst the tombs, were eager to encounter the modern undead for themselves. By ten o'clock, police were unsuccessfully attempting to control a vast crowd who had converged on Highgate village, and in scenes reminiscent of the public hysteria surrounding press reports of the haunting of Borley Rectory fifty years before, groups of drunken youths climbed the iron gates and began roaming around inside the cemetery. Subsequent press interest quickly focused on the appropriately named Alan Blood, a 25-year-old school teacher from Chelmsford, who had travelled over forty miles from Essex to North London together with a group of his own students. 'Mr Blood Hunts Cemetery Vampire', the *London Evening News* informed its readers the following day, claiming that the 'vampire expert' had made the night-time journey to seek out what he described as an 'undead Satan-like being'. The *Hampstead and Highgate Express* also carried an interview with Blood the following week, by which time the thrill of running the undead to ground had somewhat waned: 'I have taken an interest in the black arts since boyhood,' he admitted, 'but I'm by no means an expert on vampires.' The precedent for mob-handed ghost hunts in London had in fact been set decades before when on Halloween night, 31 October 1895, the *Illustrated Police News* reported on a crowd of over 300 people who had descended on a cemetery in Hackney after reports of strange activity amongst the graves. In his biography of Bram Stoker, Dan Farson likens the night-time events at Highgate to the 1849 invasion of Paris' Montparnasse cemetery, when a crowd of policemen and soldiers lay in wait for the deranged Sergeant Victor Bertrand, whose repeated assaults on several female corpses had caused panic throughout the city, earning him the nickname of 'Le Vampyr'. Wounded by rifle-fire, Bertrand, a necrophiliac who claimed he committed his crimes while in a trance, spent a year in prison. At Highgate, order was eventually restored in the early hours, but the following night police were again called, eventually escorting a small group of teenagers out of the West Cemetery.

Interestingly, sixteen years before, on 23 September 1954, a similar mass hysteria, again connected with vampirism, had gripped the south side of Glasgow, giving rise to the urban legend of the Gorbals Vampire, a frightening 7ft-tall apparition with iron fangs who, according to the local rumour which had precipitated the panic, had abducted and murdered two local children. Police officers called to the city's Southern Necropolis situated in Caledonia Road close to the south bank of the River Clyde had been startled to find groups of schoolchildren and infants, some as young as 4 and in total numbering several hundred, combing the graves and mausoleums armed with an assortment of sticks, sharpened staves of wood and penknives, all summoned by a city-wide playground rumour mill rife throughout the day. What in reality created the wild scene is still a matter of debate even today: at the time local outrage put the blame fair and square at the feet of the corrupting influence of imported American comics such as *The Vault of Horror* and *Tales From the Crypt*: EC Comics' *Dark Mysteries* the previous year had run a strip drawn by artist Hy Fleishman entitled 'The Vampire with Iron Teeth' which most likely was the specific culprit. However, an old Glaswegian poem 'Jenny wi' the Airn Teeth', written by Alexander Anderson in 1879, was well known in schools across the city, but it was ultimately the lurid and sensationalist comic strips which took the rap and the following year gave rise to the Children and Young Persons (Harmful Publications) Act 1955, introduced by Major Gwilym Lloyd George, which sought to prohibit the sale of material thought corruptible to young children's minds.

Not surprisingly, in the aftermath of the Friday the thirteenth invasion, local patience with continued accounts of strange happenings in and around Highgate was beginning to wear thin, and the issue of the *Hampstead and Highgate Express* for 20 March 1970 was the last to devote space to the subject for several months. Under the heading 'Latest ghosts', the newspaper's published postbag contained a petulant letter from an S. Levitt of Lisburne Road, which no doubt summed up the feelings of a certain proportion of the weekly readership:

> Mr. Manchester is painting such a horrific picture of his Highgate vampire that one might now be willing to settle for meeting one of the many peaceful ghosts commuting to and fro across the cemetery … Pears Encyclopaedia says a vampire is a spectre in human form that rises from its grave at night, sucks blood from sleeping humans and then returns to its grave. This being so, it is time the British Occult Society emerged from behind its screen of threats and warnings and gave us some facts. For example, let them answer the following question: Have any of them come into unmistakable contact with a vampire as described above?

As well as its interview with Alan Blood, the newspaper also offered what appeared to be a more down-to-earth explanation for much of the undead hysteria reported in recent weeks. Under the headline 'I was the vampire', Barry Edwards, a 24-year-old mail clerk from Peckham, claimed that he had been mistaken for the Highgate ghost while making an amateur ciné film, suitably titled *Vampires at Night*, inside the West Cemetery for his Hellfire Film Club. Edwards had been rushed onto the *Today* programme earlier in the week in an attempt to restore calm after the results of the previous edition's claims of undead happenings in N6, but although he may have been responsible for some of the reported incidents, clearly not all of the happenings, such as the experiences of David Farrant and his friends, can be explained in this way. Predictably, Edwards' claims were quickly countered by Sean Manchester, who rushed to the defence of a supernatural explanation in the same edition, and although the editor no doubt revelled in the boost in sales the recent run of ghostly tales had afforded the newspaper (over 18,000 copies sold, the highest circulation in the *Ham and High's* history to date), similar reports quickly became conspicuous by their absence in the weeks to come.

Interestingly enough, Edwards was not the only filmmaker who had been using the cemetery for location work during the same period. In early 1970, Andy Milligan, a screenwriter and cinematographer from Saint Paul, Minnesota, whose ultra-low budget sexploitation features have earned him a posthumous reputation as one of the worst horror film directors of all time, filmed the opening scene of his modern vampire tale, *The Body Beneath*, in and around the Circle of Lebanon, whose then starkly untended and dilapidated condition is amply demonstrated despite less than two minutes of screen time. The amateur nature of Milligan's off-the-wall direction (described in specific terms by horror writer Stephen King in connection with an earlier offering – *The Ghastly Ones* (1968) – as 'the work of morons with cameras') is readily apparent from the outset: three green-faced vampire women wearing chiffon shrouds reduce what was no doubt intended to be a Stoker homage to cheap parody. Although Milligan's storyline of an undead priest organising a family reunion is instantly forgettable, by the time the film was released in September 1970, Highgate's growing association with vampirism and the occult was clearly reflected in both the cinema trailer (which mentions the cemetery by name) as well as the front of house poster's 'Filmed in the graveyards of England' tag-line.

Less than six months after the *Today* fiasco, the 'vampire cult' returned to the pages of the *Hampstead and Highgate Express* and surrounding newspapers following a gruesome discovery which took place in early August 1970. Two 15-year-old schoolgirls walking through the West Cemetery in the vicinity of the Circle of Lebanon mausoleums came across a charred and headless corpse lying in the grass close to the open doorway of a vandalized tomb. Details of the violation, together with 'signs of a satanic ceremony', reignited newspaper interest in the possibility of Black Magic practices in the area, and the incident was quickly linked (by Sean Manchester) to the disturbing world of Satanism and vampires. Interviewed by the *Ham and High* for their edition of 7 August 1970, Manchester identified the incident as being a necromantic ritual, the object of which was to increase the strength and power of the Highgate Vampire, the 'Evil One', whose disciples planned 'to spread the cult [of the undead] in the hope of corrupting the world'. Despite distancing himself from Farrant's activities for the proceeding five months, the two men broadly agreed that Satanic activity was then currently at the root of the Highgate phenomena.

Some time after midnight on Monday, 17 August 1970, David Farrant was arrested while attempting to leave the West Cemetery by the Highgate police who, along with the cemetery groundsmen, had stepped up surveillance of the area in the wake of the headless body incident earlier in the month. A short time later, at Hornsey Road police station, he was charged with 'being in an enclosed area for an unlawful purpose' and bailed to subsequently appear at Clerkenwell Magistrates' Court. In contemporary press reports and in subsequent interviews, Farrant has described being interrupted carrying out a séance in the company of a psychic medium with the intention of making contact with the cemetery 'entity' and establishing its purpose; and in an interview recorded in 1997, he describes deploying candles and incense and a process of casting circles upon the ground using a length of cord attached to a wooden stake that were discovered on his person at the time. However, as anyone who makes more than just a superficial examination of the Highgate case will discover, this together with other statements made by both David Farrant and Sean Manchester have and continue to be challenged by both sides, helping to fuel a controversy still undiminished despite the passing years.

While Farrant waited for his case to be heard, the cemetery soon made the headlines again, in this instance in connection with more alleged clandestine activity in Highgate. In an article for 28 August 1970, the *Hornsey Journal* reported on the continued involvement of self-appointed exorcist Sean Manchester, who had taken it upon himself to cleanse the cemetery of supernatural activity with a service of exorcism. The possibility of exorcising the Highgate 'ghost' as it was then, had been mooted several months previously by a correspondent to the *Hampstead and Highgate Express*; now it seemed that this much-discussed ceremony had finally been carried out in response to the recent Satanic outrage in the eerie Circle of Lebanon. 'A secret ritual at Highgate Cemetery by members of the British Occult Society has, they say, exorcised the evil powers invoked when a tomb was desecrated,' the *Journal* stated. 'Seven crucifixes, four white candles, and four cups of Holy Water from a Catholic Church, were used in the 15-minute ceremony … by four men and a woman who met on an August afternoon near the entrance of a vault where a headless woman's corpse had been found. Incense was burned and holy water was sprinkled near the vault, and the banishment of evil powers, including words in Greek, Latin, Hebrew and English, was read by Mr Sean Manchester' who was pictured wearing a nosegay of laurel leaves and holding a crucifix. 'When we suspect that [Satanic] meetings have happened we exorcise the place afterwards,' Manchester was quoted as saying. When asked to comment on Farrant's recent night-time arrest in the cemetery, the exorcist noted: '[He] was lucky the police got to him. Had he met with the Satanists first, I feel that we would not have heard more of him'. It was a throwaway line that was to garner a chilling significance just over a year later.

After some delay, David Farrant's case was heard on 29 September 1970. The prosecution alleged that Farrant was caught vampire hunting with a cross and wooden stake in Highgate Cemetery, vandalizing coffins in the process. A verbal statement, allegedly made shortly after his arrest, was read out in court and subsequently picked up on by press reporters:

> At midnight I went with the cross and the stake to St Michael's churchyard to look for the vampire. Had the police not arrived when they did my intention was to make my way to the catacombs to search for it. I would have entered the catacombs and inspected the coffins in my search, and upon finding the supernatural being, I would have driven my stake through its heart.

After destroying the Highgate Vampire, this modern-day Van Helsing would then have simply 'run away'. Farrant denied making the statement and claimed that the 'wooden stake' had actually been used to mark out circles on the ground as part of a serious psychic investigation being carried out in the locale. The magistrate, Mr D.J. Purcell, accepted this denial and the case was dismissed: the cemetery, he said in summing up, was not an 'enclosed area' in the strict legal sense of the words and Farrant was just as entitled to pursue a hobby of 'vampire hunting' as were others who spent 'vast sums of money trying to locate the Loch Ness Monster.'

Not surprisingly, the popular press quickly picked up on the event: 'Return of the Vampire Hunter' screamed the *Daily Mirror* for 30 September 1970, claiming that '[f]earless Allan [*sic*] Farrant was back on the trail of his deadliest enemy ... the dreaded vampire of London's Highgate cemetery'. After being acquitted of what amounted to an 'eerie midnight expedition' among the tombs, the *Mirror* concluded by saying that, '[a]s he left the court yesterday the intrepid hunter said defiantly: "I won't rest until I catch this vampire."' Similarly, the *Daily Express* of the same date ('Vampire hunter: I won't rest until HE does...') reported on Farrant's steadfast determination in circumstances that '[s]tudents of Count Dracula would recognise immediately.'

As Farrant returned to Highgate, more publicity surrounding the Highgate Vampire was quick to follow. Within days of the acquittal at Clerkenwell, both he and rival Sean Manchester were persuaded to take part in filmed interviews at Highgate for BBC Television whose *Twenty Four Hours* news magazine was reporting on the cemetery's lure for vandals, devil worshippers and vampire hunters alike as part of a compilation of what it described as 'a case history of the occult'. Both men carried out reconstructions of recent events, Manchester re-enacting his recent exorcism ceremony, while Farrant was pictured stalking the undead amongst the overgrown graves, wooden cross and stake in hand. Closing his report, presenter Laurence Picethly gave a dismissively down-to-earth summing up of recent events, 'The owners of Highgate Cemetery – United Cemeteries Ltd – regard Mr Manchester, his society, and freelance vampire hunters like Farrant as a thoroughgoing nuisance,' he concluded. 'The rituals, the publicity, the court case, have attracted to Highgate all kinds of undesirables and disrupt the tranquility of the tombs.' In the cold light of day and keen to provide as little incentive as possible for another midnight invasion, it was important to make tales of the undead as absurd as possible. 'Mr Manchester and his associates,' Picethly stated for the record, 'count among the last surviving relics of an age when every flicker in the dark was reported to be a vampire.'

The *Twenty Four Hours* programme aired on Thursday, 15 October 1970. Earlier the same week, Farrant, again with his now familiar home-made cross and stake, had taken *London Evening News* journalist, Barry Simmons, and a staff photographer on a midnight tour of the West Cemetery in another staged vampire hunt; Simmons' article, 'Midnight vigil for the Highgate Vampire', appeared the day after the BBC broadcast. 'Black magic circles are doing terrible things in the cemetery,' Farrant confided:

> I am sure there is a spectre of some kind. I saw it once. It seemed about eight feet tall and seemed to float above the ground [but] I don't believe in vampires in the commercial sense of the word. I don't think they suck people's blood. If we see the vampire I don't think it will hurt you physically. But it will give you a horrible fright.

After a predictably lively Halloween, when police were again out in force to keep droves of sensation seekers at bay, the Highgate horrors quickly fell from the radar and it was to be midway through the following year before the case was to hit the headlines again.

In the relative calm afforded by a distinct lessening in media attention, David Farrant continued to visit the site as part of his ongoing investigation into the cemetery mystery. In the first volume of his autobiography, *In the Shadow of the Highgate Vampire* (2009), Farrant describes a meeting on 21 June 1971 in order to carry out what he describes as being 'one of the most dangerous magical rituals in existence'. This was an apparent attempt to make contact with the malignant cemetery apparition, and, according to Farrant's account during the course of the ritual, a hazy black shape identical with the one glimpsed on the night of the Winter Solstice in 1969 was seen to materialize inside a triangular design drawn on the ground. At this point, one of the female members of the group screamed and collapsed, upon which Farrant performed 'a rite of banishment', causing the sinister figure to disappear.

As well as Farrant and his associates, freelance vampire hunters and similar supernatural adventurers continued to find a fascination with Highgate and its now notorious burial ground. The following month, on 24 July, two youths holding a vigil equipped with wooden stakes, sandwiches and a Thermos of coffee who were inside the West Cemetery, were arrested by patrolling policemen and committed for trial at the Old Bailey: like Farrant before them, John White and Simon Wiles made the pages of the national press ('Vampire hunters grabbed by a "ghost squad"', *Daily Mirror*, 29 September 1971) and were also acquitted. Less than three months later, on the night of 7 October 1971, David Farrant was again detained by policemen searching the cemetery grounds after returning to perform an occult ritual. By this time, Farrant had swapped an interest in ghost hunting for sex magic in order to control both internal and external psychic forces by – as he himself later described it – 'utilising subconscious sexual energy'. He was released without charge, but several photographs taken by Farrant at the time, two of which showed a naked assistant, Martine de Sacy, would ultimately prove to have disastrous consequences. The high police presence in the area at the time was in fact not only due to the need to root out alleged vampire hunters and similar unwelcome visitors. Only days before, a constable patrolling the West Cemetery had discovered a fatally injured man bleeding to death amongst the graves. Peter James Clement, a mental patient and former antique dealer who had absconded from the Priory Hospital in South London where he was being treated for depression, had multiple stab wounds to his throat and chest and died a week later in the Whittington Hospital. A subsequent inquest recorded a verdict of suicide (Clement had apparently confessed to the policeman who found him that he had inflicted the injuries himself) but, then as now, it is tempting to believe that Sean Manchester's earlier prediction about the dangers of night-time encounters with Satanic covens and devil worshippers may in fact have come true, particularly as (albeit anecdotal) evidence exists that the injured man had several stab wounds in his back, a physical impossibility for a suicide victim. In later years, Manchester, like David Farrant, would also cast doubt on the official verdict of Clement's death, but in a totally different way, by stating that the incident was yet 'another vampiric outrage' that, despite his recent efforts at banishment, showed clear proof that 'the malign supernatural still held sway in Highgate's haunted Victorian graveyard'.

Over the next three years, Farrant's increasing attempts to elevate himself to what he would later describe as being 'one of Britain's leading occultists' would bring him into ever increasing contact with the law. In October 1972, he and an assistant, Victoria Jervis, were arrested while attempting to summon a ghost in the churchyard of St Mary's at Monken Hadley in Barnet and subsequently fined £10 (with £10 costs) for indecency using an obscure and rarely used Ecclesiatical Act. A further arrest occurred in December the following year at a semi-derelict house in Avenue Road, Crouch End (described in the local press at the time as 'The House of Dracula'), when Farrant and a naked acolyte, 24-year-old Barnet labourer John Pope, were discovered during a police raid inside a magical circle drawn on the floor of an upstairs room. The presence of a ritual plate of hot coals enabled Farrant and Pope (who later changed his name by deed poll to Pope de Locksley, claiming ancestry with Robin Hood) to be charged with arson – the house had previously been damaged by fire – but this was subsequently dismissed by a Crown Court jury in early March 1974. By this time, however, David Farrant was already on remand in Brixton Prison on suspicion of violating buried remains in Highgate Cemetery together with charges associated with Black Magic, some of which would ultimately prove to be inescapable. On 14 January, a 160-year-old corpse, partially mummified and missing its head and part of one leg, had been found by a local architect propped up in the driver's seat of his car, which had been left parked and untended in Swains Lane. Farrant had been arrested and taken to Kentish Town police station and subsequently, while the young occultist was in custody, additional charges were proffered, namely vandalism and desecration of several vaults inside the cemetery catacombs as well as sending threatening voodoo doll effigies to two London police detectives: to support the former, police prosecutors produced several photographs found during a search of Farrant's Muswell Hill flat, including the stills of Martine de Sacy taken in the Cory-Wright mausoleum over two years before, claiming that the Satanic markings on the floor had been drawn by the two magicians; Farrant himself admitted sending the sinister dolls, in reprisal to allegations made by John Pope, who claimed he had been beaten up by police following an arrest on an indecency charge on New Year's Day, 1974.

What would become known as the 'Nude Rites' trial opened in Court No.2 at the Old Bailey on 11 June 1974 in front of Judge Michael Argyle, who had risen to notoriety in 1971 after sentencing three editors of the satirical *Oz* magazine to imprisonment with hard labour for publishing a controversial cartoon strip of Rupert Bear. Defending himself, Farrant fared little better: despite being acquitted of the 'body in the car' charge (Anthony Field from Islington, North London, subsequently given a ten-year sentence for armed robbery, admitted vandalising the cemetery 'for a laugh'), the young occultist was found guilty of threatening the police and for vandalism inside Highgate Cemetery; the sentence from Judge Argyle was four years and eight months in prison. 'It was the first fully-fledged witchcraft trial to return to the English courts after several centuries,' Farrant reflected in his memoir, *Out of the Shadows*, published in 2011, 'but all the ingredients relating to Satanism and black magic, "nude orgies" and "invoking the devil" to the detriment of the Christian Church, were all still there.'

In the opening to an account of the 'vampire hunt in Highgate Cemetery' in his book *The Possessed* (1995), author and former crime journalist, Brian McConnell, states: 'It began with a reader's question in a newspaper about apparitions in the cemetery in 1970 and ended four years later in an Old Bailey trial in which the same reader, an alleged Devil-worshipper, was convicted of grave desecration'. If that had actually been the case, the story of the Highgate Vampire would by now have lain forgotten by all but its main protagonists for nearly four decades, a 'silly season' media sensation gradually receding into obscurity. In reality, the most astonishing phase of the case of the Highgate Vampire had only just begun.

In 1975, Peter Underwood, now well on the way to establishing himself as one of Britain's leading paranormal writers, issued *The Vampire's Bedside Companion*, a new examination of what publisher Leslie Frewin cited as 'a riveting compendium of new facts and fiction on the "undying" theme of vampirism'. As well as four original vampire stories by writers James Turner, Peter Allan, Richard Howard and Crispin Derby, Underwood's book included chapters on such vampiric topics as the origins and writing of Stoker's *Dracula*, the 'vampire talisman' of Montague Summers, a psychological interpretation of the undead myth, as well as the recent phenomenon of vampire hunts in modern London. Now an obligatory inclusion in all new published collections and accounts of vampires and vampirism, the Highgate case had in fact first appeared in print as early as 1971 in the introduction to *The Undead*, a collection of fictional stories (including *Dracula's Guest* and Carl Jacobi's 1933 masterpiece *Revelations in Black*) edited by university lecturer James Dickie; in 1973, English writer Basil Copper, known for his Lovecraftian tales such as *Shaft Number 247* (1980) and *Beyond the Reef* (1994), included the seminal extended essay 'Nights in Highgate Cemetery' as the closing chapter of his *The Vampire In Legend, Fact & Art*.

For his *Bedside Companion*, Underwood compiled his own brief chronology of events at Highgate before handing over the reins of this 'startling account of present-day vampirism' to a guest author: 'Ever since I became aware that Highgate Cemetery was the reputed haunt of a vampire, the investigations and activities of Mr Sean Manchester commanded my attention,' he wrote by way of an introduction. 'I became convinced that, more than anyone else, this psychic consultant and President of The British Occult Society, knew the full story of the Highgate Vampire.' A previous correspondent of both Underwood and Tom Perrott, then chairman of the Ghost Club, Manchester's eponymously titled essay on the Highgate case ultimately proved to be the longest non-fiction chapter in the book, dovetailing media reports and other published experiences with his own record of the recent cemetery investigation.

In his account, Manchester cites the alleged experience of Thomas O'Loughlin and his fiancée in 1967, together with another incident involving two local schoolgirls from Highgate's La Sainte Union Convent, as being his introduction to mysterious happenings in Highgate – in fact, Manchester's writings are the primary source for both incidents. In his essay, Manchester describes a vision of corpses rising from their graves that the two young women are said to have witnessed while walking down Swains Lane past the top cemetery gate, after spending an evening with a girlfriend. One of the schoolgirls, Elizabeth Wojdyla, a Polish Catholic, gave a full account of her experience, as well as details of several recent nightmares in which she felt 'something evil' with a deathly white face was trying to get into her bedroom at night through a closed window.

During the summer of 1969, several months before the explosion of local media interest in the cemetery haunting, Manchester was contacted by Wojdyla again. Now aged 19 and living in a small rented flat in the Highgate area to which her boyfriend, a young Scotsman named Keith Maclean, was a reasonably frequent visitor, the Polish girl reported that in recent weeks the nightmares, involving being menaced by a sinister presence of 'a man with the expression of an animal', had returned; Manchester himself describes Wojdyla as looking highly pale and unwell at this time and subsequently learnt that she had become prone to sleepwalking episodes, on one occasion being discovered at night by Maclean standing in a trance-like state outside the top gate of Highgate Cemetery. As well as the alleged somnambulism and anaemia, the young woman also displayed two bite-like marks on the side of her neck, a photograph claiming to depict the same and darkened by the publisher to enhance the swellings, was included as an illustration by Underwood in his book. Keith Maclean is described as entering Elizabeth's bedroom one night after hearing her cry out, and finding specks of fresh blood on her pillow.

Now convinced that a vampire, in his words 'a supernatural being, belonging neither to the living nor the dead, who emerges from the nightmare world of the undead to quaff fresh blood whereby it is nourished and revitalised' was responsible for the young girl's malady, Manchester instructed Maclean to procure and deploy 'the ancient and carefully approved vampire repellents' both around the Polish girl's bedroom and on Wojdyla's person: these included a silver cross and a linen wrapper of salt around her neck, verses from the Bible placed under her pillow, while the bedroom window was to be 'sealed' with a crucifix reinforced with garlic flowers. This entire ritual was allegedly played out, not as one would expect in a seventeenth-century Transylvanian peasant's cottage or on a Hammer set at Bray, but in a small flat in a fashionable suburb of 1960s North London, in a year when hippies flocked to Woodstock and Apollo 12 astronauts walked on the Moon.

In just over a week, Elizabeth showed signs of a return to health and her mysterious anaemic condition began to subside. Maclean found the sinister bite marks faded after being bathed with holy water, so that by the time David Farrant had his strange experience on the night of the Winter Solstice, the young Polish girl had been returned to 'her happy, normal self and all was well'. Of her eerie night-time intruder, there was no sign. Interviewed by actor Anthony Head for the Discovery television programme *True Horror* in 2004, Maclean supported Manchester's version of events as described in 'The Highgate Vampire' in 1975. 'I hadn't included the possibility of it being a vampire because I hadn't even thought of that, or realised the existence of vampires,' he confessed, 'but then when Bishop Manchester spoke to me and explained about the legions of the undead, thereafter everything fitted and totally made sense. I believe it was a vampire – I don't have any doubt about that.'

Following publication of the 'Wampyr' article at the end of February 1970, Manchester describes being contacted by the sister of an attractive 22-year-old woman (given the pseudonym 'Lusia' in this and subsequent publications) who, like Elizabeth Wojdyla, was displaying similar symptoms of being molested by a vampire-like presence. Like the Polish 'victim', Lusia had allegedly been found wandering in the vicinity of Swains Lane, and on examination also possessed the characteristically sinister 'Seal of Dracula' pin-prick marks on the side of her neck. One sleepwalking episode, said to have been witnessed by both Manchester and the girl's sister, ended inside Highgate Cemetery itself after Lusia had led them through the broken railings at the rear of St Michael's Church – the same location where David Farrant was later filmed entering by the BBC – and through the overgrown burial ground to a locked and gated vault in the cemetery catacombs. A photograph of the girl taken standing outside the tomb in daylight was also included in the *Bedside Companion* book.

In his essay, Manchester describes a further series of events, said to have taken place on the night of the Friday the thirteenth invasion, when an 'official vampire hunt' took place involving a party of 100 people. Examining the catacombs where Lusia had taken him, which according to the account involved being let down on a rope through an opening in the roof, Manchester claims to have discovered three empty coffins which were quickly cleansed with a combination of holy water, salt and a metal cross. By this time, the police presence inside the cemetery had made further investigation impossible, but according to the published account, shortly after two o'clock in the morning, a 'low booming vibration', seemingly identical to that heard by Thomas O'Loughlin and his companion in the same area in 1967, was both heard and felt by a small party of hunters (including Manchester himself) who had stayed behind to watch over the catacombs until dawn.

'The Highgate Vampire' concludes with a fuller account of the alleged exorcism ceremony carried out in August 1970 in the wake of further desecrations in the Circle of Lebanon tombs. It was here that one afternoon, according to his own account, Manchester and a small group were drawn (following another of Lusia's sleep-walking episodes) to the Wace mausoleum, one of the inner circle of tombs to which the vampire hunters were able to gain access by prising open the heavy iron door. Inside, lying in an unmarked coffin at the very back of the vault, was a body 'which appeared neither dead nor alive', having the appearance of a newly buried corpse but in a crypt that had been sealed for nearly a century. As Manchester prepared to stake the undead creature, the group's nerve broke, forcing the party to retreat to the tomb entrance. It was here that the self-styled president of the British Occult Society allegedly performed a service of exorcism, after which the entrance to the mausoleum was bricked up; a crucifix was hung behind the inner doors and garlic added into the builder's cement. 'The purpose of this account has not been an attempt to vindicate the reality of the vampire,' Manchester concluded, but was, in his own words, 'a report of a series of events which actually took place in twentieth-century England.'

Ten years after his collaboration with Peter Underwood, Sean Manchester brought the case of the Highgate Vampire once more into the public eye. By this time, David Farrant, who had been released from prison in July 1976, had distanced himself from the cemetery happenings, his soured relationship with Manchester instigating what has been described by one commentator as 'one of the most lengthy and bitter feuds in the history of psychical research'. The two men met in 1977 when Farrant gave a lengthy tape-recorded interview about his background and involvement in the Highgate case, heavily edited extracts of which have been made public in recent years by Manchester's Vampire Research Society.

Changes at Highgate Cemetery itself had already taken place by this time: in August 1973, the West Cemetery was closed to all members of the public other than those with buried relatives, finally halting much of the wanton damage and vandalism that had been rife for the best part of a decade. One thing that was not to change, however, was Highgate's reputation as being the haunt of supernatural evil.

In 1985, Manchester published *The Highgate Vampire* through the British Occult Society imprint. Sub-titled *The infernal world of the undead unearthed at London's famous Highgate Cemetery and environs*, the book is an extended version of the original *Bedside Companion* essay, now revised and expanded into a full-length monograph and illustrated with many original photographs, including several of the second vampire 'victim', Lusia. No doubt aware of the controversy that would be generated by much of its contents, the author defended his work from the very outset: 'This book will undoubtedly shock and be hotly denounced,' Manchester wrote in the cover blurb, 'but it cannot be dismissed', adding, 'Dare we risk ignoring a force whose strength lies in the fact that no one will believe it?' Revisiting the events of 1967 to 1970, Manchester extended his examination of the case to cover a broad period beginning in the winter of 1973 through to the summer of 1982, at the start and end of which are described two separate incidents which have given this phase of the Highgate Vampire case much of its later posthumous notoriety.

The first of these took place in December 1973 when Manchester and his associates became interested in a large derelict house on the borders of Highgate village where, according to local rumour, '[s]omething evil was said to have taken residence and now stalked the lonely corridors'. Appropriately enough, this 'once magnificent neo-gothic house' was the very 'House of Dracula' in Avenue Road, Crouch End, where 'King of Black Magic' David Farrant together with John Pope were arrested for arson around the same time, and which had featured in a contemporary illustrated article in the *Hornsey Journal*. Visiting the house accompanied by two assistants, a male colleague named Arthur together with a female clairvoyant, Veronika, Manchester describes confronting a sinister 'corpse-like apparition' and in the cellar of the house encountering a heavy wooden coffin in which lay the same undead being that the occultist and his party had allegedly attempted to exorcise in the Circle of Lebanon three years before. After being dragged in its casket out into the overgrown back garden, the vampire creature was destroyed in the traditional manner, after which the coffin and its now decayed contents were cremated on a bonfire. As well as a photograph of the coffin in-situ inside the basement room, Manchester also reproduced two stills, allegedly taken by his colleague, of the decomposing vampire 'moments after exorcism'. Subsequently, the scene of this dramatic showdown, now literally transformed into the 'House of Dracula', was to be demolished and a block of modern flats built on the site, although part of the existing building's front façade still survives as a reminder of its sinister past associations.

By late 1978, however, a familiar pattern was beginning to repeat itself, this time three miles north-west of Highgate in parts of Finchley and Hampstead Garden Suburb. As domestic animals – mainly pet rabbits but also in one instance two domesticated goats – began falling victim to a mystery night-time attacker who left bodies mutilated and seemingly drained of blood, Manchester and the British Occult Society were soon generating newspaper headlines ('Animal Deaths – Vampire Theory', *Finchley Press*, 13 April 1979) that again linked these gruesome incidents with 'the infernal world of the undead'. Although an RSPCA inspector and a local vet felt the killer was most likely a stray dog, the incidents, which continued into the following year before eventually petering out, have never been fully explained.

By January 1980, Manchester began narrowing the search for what he believed to be another undead creature to the New Southgate area, specifically the Great Northern London Cemetery (now renamed as New Southgate Cemetery), a large burial ground established in the 1850s that at one time had its own railway connection from Kings Cross to a terminus adjacent to the graveyard specifically for the transportation of coffins and mourners. By the early 1980s, the Great Northern was being threatened by developers, and as plots of land were lined up to be sold for house building, Manchester launched a 'Save the Cemetery' campaign, which involved delivering a petition to Downing Street as well as standing as a local by-election candidate for Brunswick Park under the pseudonym of George Byron. These efforts were carried out in order to gain time to complete his latest vampire investigation, as by now the British Occult Society (eventually dissolved by Manchester in 1988) had established that the new undead's lair lay somewhere amongst the threatened graves: this was Lusia, the Highgate Vampire's original victim who had died in the mid-1970s of a leukaemia-like illness and had been buried there by her family. In the closing pages of his account, Manchester describes carrying out another exorcism ceremony, this time alone, one midsummer evening, during which the undead Lusia was finally staked and destroyed. Whether this encounter took place physically or on a psychic level is unclear – Lusia is described at one point as having transformed herself into a monstrous spider 'the size of a full grown cat' – but as written, the author implies that the incident actually took place in the real world. A second revised edition of *The Highgate Vampire* appeared in 1991, for which many of the original photographic illustrations, including several portraits of Lusia, were replaced by hand-drawn artwork. Also omitted was a lurid *Exorcist*-style dream sequence involving a vision of Lusia masturbating with a wooden stake 'which leaves her spurting blood out of every orifice at the moment of orgasm'.

Access for the curious to Highgate's West Cemetery is today restricted to guided tours operated and run by the Friends of Highgate Cemetery Trust, a charity that took over the ownership and running of the graveyard in 1988. Despite the change of circumstances from the heyday of vampire hunts in the 1970s, strange happenings are still reported with some regularity from in and around the area. In August 2005, Martin Trent, a local man who at the time had lived on the nearby Holly Lodge estate for several years, described seeing the apparition of a man 'quite tall and dressed in dark, drab, nondescript clothing' outside the East Cemetery gates as he returned home down Swains Lane after an evening out. As he drew level, the figure seemed to speak (in an 'old fashioned' manner) although the sound of its voice appeared as a whisper in the man's ear rather than being projected across the street in the normal way. After walking approximately fifty yards further down Swains Lane to the junction with Oakeshott Avenue, Trent looked back and saw the figure was now on the opposite side nearest to the West Cemetery. As he watched, it appeared to glide across the road at right angles, pass through the East Cemetery gates and disappear. Seven years later, in June 2012, three members of the North London Paranormal Investigations (NLPI) group claimed to have encountered a tall black figure like that of an undertaker outside the West Cemetery chapel shortly after ten o'clock in the evening. Described as being 'gaunt and pale', the apparition showed no malevolence and vanished almost as soon as the group was aware of its presence. The present author heard Martin Trent and NLPI member Mickey Gocool, a former policeman, describe their experiences at a public lecture on the Highgate Vampire at The Green public house in Clerkenwell on 23 September 2013.

Today, over forty years after its beginnings during the winter of 1969/70, the case of the Highgate Vampire continues to both fascinate and divide public opinion. Since 1991, David Farrant has issued a number of revised editions of his *Beyond the Highgate Vampire* book, continually challenging Sean Manchester's version of events while at the same time disassociating his own experiences from having any connection with a Stoker-inspired world of supernatural vampirism. In his writings on the subject, Farrant has subsequently explored the possibility of a connection between ley-lines and the appearance of unexplained phenomena in the Highgate area, including sightings of phantom figures, and has expressed his belief in the reality of malignant 'entities' – the incubus and the succubus – as an explanation for vampire-like happenings. In 1997, David Farrant took over the running of the Highgate Vampire Society, a membership-based organisation established by local author and historian Jennie Lee Cobban, which aims to become an ongoing repository for much of the published and verbal testimony concerning the Highgate case.

Other authors and researchers who have been drawn to the Highgate story include Peter Underwood (*Exorcism!*, 1990), American writer Rosemary Ellen Guiley (*Vampires Among Us*, 1991), Bill Ellis, an associate professor at Pennsylvania State University (*Raising the Devil*, 2000), American journalist Carol Page (*Bloodlust*, 1991), English horror writer Ramsey Campbell (*Ramsey Campbell, Probably*, 2002), Patsy Langley (*The Highgate Vampire Casebook*, 2007) and Matthew Beresford whose *From Demons to Dracula* appeared in 2008. In 1997, Sean Manchester issued his *The Vampire Hunter's Handbook*, a rebuttal of criticisms levelled against his activities which at the same time demonstrated the complex political and personal issues that the case, then as now, continues to generate. Bishop Manchester's last filmed public interview, after which he stated he would no longer discuss the subject of Highgate with the media, took place in 2011 on the forty-first anniversary of the publication of the notorious 'Wampyr' headline; an edited version was subsequently included in an episode of Vision TV's *The Conspiracy Show* covering the subject of vampirism, which originally aired on Canadian television on 1 April the same year.

Now, with the advent of the Internet, the Highgate Vampire, like many other paranormal cases including hauntings such as Borley Rectory, has made the leap into cyberspace, enabling camps of both sceptics and believers to trade blows through forum boards, blog posts and webtalk radio programmes. As such, one thing is certain: it will be many years before the real truth behind the strange story of the Highgate Vampire will ever be known for sure.

11

Undead Television: Vampires in British Broadcasting (1968–2010)

As we have seen, from the shadowy beginnings of Murnau's *Nosferatu* in 1921, the cinematic film has articulated and defined the vampire myth in the public consciousness more than any other medium. In Britain from the late 1960s through until the mid-1980s, a period when the small screen was at its most influential in shaping the identity of the public at large, home-grown television drama's relationship with supernatural literature effected what is now in many ways a golden era in which some of the most highly regarded and lasting presentations of the genre were being produced and broadcast. In 1968, Jonathan Miller scripted and directed a much admired teleplay of the 1904 M.R. James classic, *Oh, Whistle, and I'll Come to You, My Lad*, the first of several BBC adaptations of James' stories in a *Ghost Story for Christmas* series that loosely spanned the 1970s, finishing with Leslie Megahey's 1979 version of Le Fanu's *Schalken the Painter*. In 1976, six screenplays by *Quatermass* author Nigel Kneale were turned into a memorable series, *Beasts* by ATV for Independent Television, while the same year the BBC began a regular summer season of late night 'double bills' that introduced both the classic Universal black and white horror features together with modern Hammer films offerings to a home audience, often for the first time. During this period a number of vampire-related dramas were broadcast on both BBC and ITV television and in this chapter we will look briefly at their contributions to the overall evolution of British vampirism. As with much of the twentieth-century fiction discussed in this book, it is another area where the presence of Bram Stoker's immortal creation casts a long and imposing shadow.

Between January 1966 and February 1970, first ABC and subsequently Thames Television broadcast a seminal series of supernatural teleplays, twenty-four in total, under the all-embracing title *Mystery and Imagination*, that included dramatisations of works by such noted writers as M.R. James (*Lost Hearts*, *The Tractate Middoth*, *Number 13* and *Casting the Runes*), Edgar Allan Poe (*The Fall of the House of Usher*), Mary Shelley (*Frankenstein*) and L.P. Hartley (*Feet Foremost*). Today only eight of the original two dozen stories are known to exist as video recordings, with the result that an early adaptation of Le Fanu's *Carmilla* directed by Australian television director Bill Bain and starring Jane Merrow in the title role has been lost. In November 1968, at a time when Christopher Lee still dominated the role on the big screen, Thames concluded the programme's fourth season with a mostly studio-bound version of *Dracula* which, thankfully, does survive and despite limitations of both budget and screen time, remains a stylish and innovative presentation of Stoker's story. As a bearded Count Dracula, Denholm Elliot effects one of the most striking entrances for the King of Vampires – wearing sunglasses while playing Beethoven's 'Moonlight Sonata' on a grand piano – and Charles Graham's script makes a number of interesting changes to the original, among them omitting the characters of Quincy Morris and Arthur Holmwood and combining the lunatic Renfield and Jonathan Harker into one. Notable for featuring Nina Baden-Semper as the first black vampire bride, director Patrick Droomgoole's production includes Bernard Archard as an underrated Van Helsing and contains several subtle and effective touches: Corin Redgrave as Harker, channelling Dracula's voice as he keeps the vampire hunters at bay is an arresting moment, and Susan George's punctuation of Lucy Weston's ordinary speech with a series of snarling gestures cleverly conveys both her infatuation with and the emotional corruption of the arch vampire; while her orgasmic shrieks as Lucy finally succumbs to Elliot's night-time attack easily surpass those of Veronica Carlson, who enjoyed similar treatment by Christopher Lee in Hammer's *Dracula Has Risen from the Grave* the same year. As Dracula, Denholm Elliot is both urbane and commanding, while the vampires' central incisors, modelled on those of a vampire bat, make an impressive visual alternative to the familiar and conventional arrangement normally afforded to the cinematic undead both then and now.

It would be nearly ten years before BBC Television attempted a small screen adaptation of Stoker's masterpiece, but despite the delay in following their independent rivals, Philip Saville's *Count Dracula*, broadcast in two lengthy episodes in December 1977, with French actor Louis Jourdan in the title role, still remains (despite some minor changes) the most faithful and literally accurate presentation of the story to date. Filmed on location in St Mary's churchyard at Whitby and London's Highgate Cemetery, and with Alnwick Castle in Northumberland standing in for Castle Dracula, the production benefits from the BBC's growing excellence in period costume drama, and captures both the violent nightmare and sensual eroticism of the novel. Minor revisions include making Mina (Judi Bowker) and Lucy (Susan Penhaligon) sisters and amalgamating the character of Arthur Holmwood into that of Richard Barnes' Quincy (named Quincy P. Holmwood in the script), but despite the slight detours, Gerald Savory's screenplay adheres closely to Stoker's linear narrative and contains all of the great set pieces that other writers continue to either omit or reshape, including Dracula's bat-like crawl down the castle battlements, the stormy arrival of the *Demeter* at Whitby, Lucy's bloody staking, Mina's blood exchange with the Count, and the final chase to Castle Dracula and the vampire's ultimate destruction on the edge of twilight.

Fresh from his performance as publisher Peter Manson in London Weekend Television's controversial adaptation of Andrea Newman's *Bouquet of Barbed Wire*, Frank Finlay gives Van Helsing both charm and steely determination, while Jourdan captures the supernatural and physical menace of Stoker's creation to perfection, epitomised in the 'blaze of basilisk horror' glance as Harker (Bosco Hogan) discovers Dracula and his vampire brides sleeping in the castle crypt, a scene that conveys the vampires' bloated, leech-like repletion after their meal of infant blood with greater power and repulsive disgust than any other screen adaptation.

The year 1977 had in fact been a good year for Gothic horror on mainstream British television. *Supernatural*, an eight-part BBC series scripted by Robert Muller, starring amongst others Robert Hardy, Billie Whitelaw, Denholm Elliot, Jeremy Brett and Gordon Jackson, had transposed a number of the genre's key motifs including werewolves, vampires and *Frankenstein*-like resurrection onto the small screen through a collection of mainly studio-based colour teleplays set around the activities of the Club of the Damned, a Victorian gentleman's society whose singular route to membership is the successful recounting of a true and original tale of blood-curdling horror. The stakes for potential candidates are high: those who pass the test join fellow members by the fireside, while unsuccessful entrants are allegedly never seen again. 'Dorabella', subtitled 'In Love with Death', the series' closing story, owes much to Byron's *Augustus Darvell*, onto which Muller grafts a distinctly *Carmilla*-like menace in the form of the eponymous vampiress of the title, played by Ania Marson. Philip Hambleton (David Robb) on this occasion is the one vying for Club of the Damned status, recounting a narrative said to have taken place 'a long time ago, before the railways began to spread like spiders' tentacles across the entire continent of Europe'. Together with a travelling companion, the world-weary Walter von Lamont (Jeremy Clyde), Hambleton encounters the mysterious Dorabella in a wayside inn where Walter quickly becomes infatuated with her ethereal presence. Abandoning their proposed journey, Walter insists on travelling north to Dorabella's castle where the couple will be married, taking with them a large gilded trunk, the woman's only piece of luggage: Dorabella is never seen by day and at each wayside inn along the way, bodies are soon discovered mutilated and drained of blood. Eventually, the love-sick Walter suffers the same fate at the hands of the vampire woman and her equally undead father (John Justin), leaving Hambleton to tell the tale, he himself cursed as one of the walking dead.

Despite somewhat lacklustre direction, courtesy of Simon Langton, 'Dorabella' contains some effective moments which remain uncomfortably in the mind, notably the mysterious smoking trunk together with its maggot-ridden contents, the vampiress' ability to temporarily transfer her powers to ordinary people, and Robb's final chilling reveal as one of the grinning and white-eyed undead. Never repeated since its initial broadcast, *Supernatural* survived for many years on bootleg videos circulated amongst aficionados until its official release on DVD by the British Film Institute in November 2013.

One television series which has included vampires in one form or another on several occasions is the long-running and ever popular *Doctor Who*, first broadcast on 23 November 1963 with London-born and former *The Army Game* actor William Hartnell in the title role. Hartnell's Doctor briefly encountered a clockwork Count Dracula (Malcolm Rogers) in the 1965 Dalek-themed story 'The Chase', but it was not until 1971 that the series included a more recognisable vampiric menace, albeit with heavy science fiction overtones, with the psychedelically-inspired 'The Claws of Axos', scripted by Bristol-based writers Bob Baker and Dave Martin, and with the flamboyant Jon Pertwee playing the time-travelling hero. Originally titled 'The Gift' and later 'The Vampire From Space', the story revolves around a seemingly benign alien race – the Grecian-sculpted gold-skinned Axons led by Bernard Holly – who offer a solution to the growing food crisis on Earth in exchange for time and energy to refuel their beleaguered spaceship. In reality, the Axons are sinister intergalactic parasites intent on draining the very life out of the planet and who, in their 'undead' form, are revealed as impressively grotesque tentacled monstrosities. The Doctor, however, ultimately saves the day, thwarting the evil menace by projecting both the aliens and their spacecraft into a conveniently engineered and, for the unfortunate Axons, never-ending time loop.

Writer Terrance Dicks, who acted as script editor for 'The Claws of Axos', was to provide the programme with its most overtly vampire-themed story nearly a decade later with 1980s four-part 'State of Decay', broadcast at a time when actor Tom Baker was coming to the end of his record-breaking seven-year term as the Doctor. Originally written in early 1977 as 'The Vampire Mutation', when then producer Philip Hinchcliffe together with script consultant Robert Holmes were keen to include more Gothic-themed horror as part of the Time Lord's staple diet, Dicks' script was shelved when BBC Head of Drama, Graeme McDonald, felt there could be potentially unfavourable comparisons with Philip Saville's *Count Dracula*, which at the time was being prepared as a large-scale Christmas television extravaganza.

In November 1979, new producer John Nathan-Turner decided to resurrect Dicks' story which, under the guidance of script editor Christopher Bidmead, was re-crafted as a stylish blend of hardcore science fiction and medieval Hammeresque pastiche and the completed scripts went into production in May the following year. For his revised story, Dicks presented a clever evolution of the traditional myth format: Aukon (Emrys James), Camilla (Rachel Davies) and Zargo (William Lindsay) are astronauts, trapped in the parallel universe of E-Space and turned into undead feudal lords by the presence of the Great One, the last of a race of giant space vampires, who lies in suspended animation in an underground chamber in readiness for the Time of Arising when the results of innumerable blood sacrifices amongst the local peasant population will give it new life. A youthful fan of Hammer Horror, Dicks incorporated many of the familiar touchstones such as the Gothic castle and village inn setting but justified their appearance by providing both rational and scientific explanations: Aukon's castle is in fact the space travellers' rocket ship, the Hydrax, whose nose cone, when activated by Baker's Doctor, is transformed into a gigantic metal stake which kills the Great One as it prepares to reanimate; while the ship's crews' quarters and fuel tanks double as Highgate-like catacombs and vats of blood respectively.

For his atmospheric 1989 Second World War story 'The Curse of Fenric', writer Ian Briggs created a new vampire monster, the blood-drinking Haemovores, barnacle-encrusted zombies that emerge from the sea off the Yorkshire coast to enact an ancient Viking curse, itself brought to life by Dinsdale Landon's Turing-like scientist Dr Judson, whose 'Ultima' code-breaking machine is used to translate an ancient inscription discovered in the crypt of a country church. Here, the familiar Dracula figure is replaced with the eponymous Fenric of the title, an ancient evil that evolved during the creation of the universe and is present throughout all history, while the Haemovores themselves are revealed as the veritable origins of the vampire myth itself, minion-like servants of Fenric transported by a time storm from the end of the world to ninth-century Transylvania, where their appearances create the legend of the undead.

The penultimate story of classic *Doctor Who*, 'The Curse of Fenric', starring former comedian Sylvester McCoy, contains some memorable and genuinely frightening moments, in particular the Haemovores themselves as they advance through a mist-enshrouded churchyard, while the killing of an elderly village woman by two teenage vampire evacuees remains one of the series' most shocking and darker moments. Resurrected for a twenty-first-century audience in 2005, *Doctor Who* has returned to the theme of the undead on one occasion to date, namely writer Toby Whithouse's 'The Vampires of Venice', set in a sixteenth-century Venetian girls' school with Matt Smith as the Doctor and broadcast on 8 May 2010.

The enduring fascination of the vampire theme continues to appeal to new writers, and its inherent flexibility allows it to be easily combined with contemporary trends and fashions. Far less long-lived than *Doctor Who*, the ITV series *Demons*, broadcast in a single season in 2009, combined the tradition and characters of Bram Stoker with the modern fantasy phenomenon of author J.K. Rowling, with Christian Cooke waking up in a post-Harry Potter world to his inheritance as the last of the Van Helsings, battling a hidden retinue of demonic monstrosities and hoodie-wearing werewolves beneath the streets and alleyways of modern-day London.

The same year that John Nathan-Turner began resurrecting vampires for *Doctor Who*, the BBC's long-running drama presentation *Play for Today* examined the effect of horror and fantasy films on the minds of the young in the one-off teleplay 'Vampires', written by Dixie Williams and broadcast in early January 1979. A late-night showing of Hammer's *Dracula: Prince of Darkness* proves to be a divisive experience for two Merseyside schoolboys whose father has died in a car accident two years before: whereas Davey (Paul Moran) is repelled by the gruesome images, his brother Stuart Perry (played by real-life sibling Peter Moran) becomes caught up in a fantasy world that quickly begins to impinge on reality. Playing truant from school, Stu becomes convinced that a genealogy researcher in a local cemetery is a vampire who has killed the class teacher by frightening her to death, and instigates a mass vampire hunt among the gravestones in a scene clearly reminiscent of the Gorbals Vampire hysteria of the mid-1950s. Finally returning to his house late in the evening, Stu is horrified to see his own mother – who in reality has been beaten up by her latest boyfriend – apparently transformed into one of the fanged undead and in the play's closing scene finds comfort from the growing nightmare by going to sleep next to his brother holding a crucifix.

As well as drama, a number of factual documentaries have successfully examined the shadowy world of the undead where, as might be expected, Stoker and his vampire Count are given especial prominence. In 1974, Dan Farson, then in the throes of researching for his forthcoming Stoker biography, visited Transylvania for BBC Television and in the subsequent one-off *The Dracula Business* (broadcast 6 August), reported on both the origins of his great-uncle's seminal tale as well as the exploitation of both the fictional character and his bloodthirsty real-life counterpart. The fortieth anniversary of the post-war re-establishment of Hammer Films was marked by BBC2 in the summer of 1987 with the landmark documentary, *Hammer: The Studio That Dripped Blood*, a lengthy retrospective that featured contributions from many of the company's leading players and actors including Anthony Hinds, Jimmy Sangster, producer Aida Young, Michael Carreras, James Bernard, as well as film icons Peter Cushing, Christopher Lee and Ingrid Pitt. Similarly, in 1996, Christopher Frayling both scripted and presented what remains to date the definitive television examination of the evolution of *Dracula*, again for the BBC, with *Nightmare: The Birth of Horror*, one of four extended documentaries on the seminal Gothic classics that also included episodes on *Frankenstein*, Robert Louis Stevenson's *The Strange Case of Dr Jekyll and Mr Hyde* (1886) and Conan Doyle's *The Hound of the Baskervilles* (1902). As well as Romania, the programme visited many of the landmark locations in the story's genesis including Cruden Bay, Whitby, Highgate Cemetery and the Lyceum Theatre. Three years before, in January 1993, Frayling also took part in London Weekend Television's arts magazine *The South Bank Show*, which used the recent release of Francis Ford Coppola's *Bram Stoker's Dracula* to revisit familiar territory in the company of screenwriter James Hart and writer and editor Stephen Jones, together with actor Christopher Lee, literary aficionado Tina Rath and vampire hunter and exorcist Sean Manchester.

As well as literature, music is another facet of the arts that has become a platform for the shadowy world of the undead. 'Listen to them – the children of the night. What music they make!' announced Dracula in 1897, as the wolves howled around his castle fortress. In the next part of our survey we look briefly at some of the post-war British musicians and composers who have also been inspired to walk with the children of the shadows.

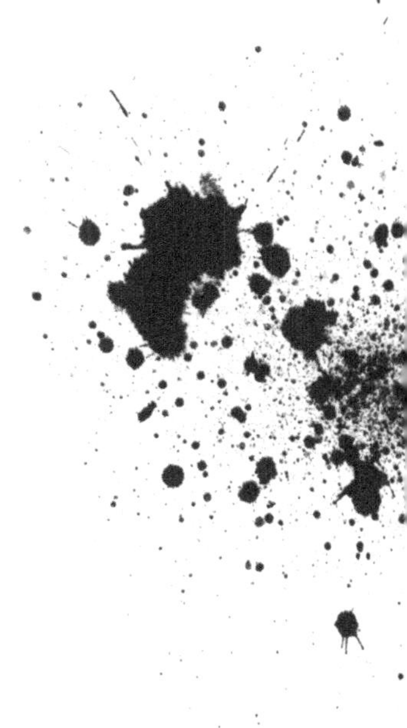

12

The Music of the Night

(1960-2000)

Down the years, from the time of the evolution of the literary vampire in the decadent luxury of the Villa Diodati, Western musical culture has shown both a fascination and aptitude for the world of the supernatural and the macabre. In Leipzig in 1828, Heinrich Marschner, one of a number of composers inspired by Polidori's writings, conducted the first performance of his own *Der Vampyr*, a Romantic opera with a libretto by his brother-in-law, Wilhelm Wohlbrück. Unlike other vampire-themed operas of the time, *Der Vampyr* has proved to be something of a survivor: in 1992, BBC Television broadcast a dramatised performance with English baritone Omar Ebrahim in the title role, with a new modern libretto by London-born lyricist, Charles Hart.

Many nineteenth-century musicians were inspired by the dark side of human nature and the mysterious possibilities of an unseen world beyond the grave. Goethe's epic two-part tragedy *Faust*, completed in its entirety in 1831, has captured the imagination of a number of famous composers: Berlioz (*La damnation de Faust*, 1846), Gounod (*Faust*, 1859) and Mahler (*Symphony No. 8*, 1910); Robert Schuman completed an oratorio, *Scenes from Goethe's Faust*, in 1853, while Liszt produced four works for various forces composed between 1861 and 1883 under the embracing title, *Mephisto Waltzes*. As a performer, violinist and composer Niccolò Paganini courted a Mephistophelean appearance; similarly, Tartini's *Devil's Trill Sonata* from the early 1700s is traditionally linked with the appearance of the Devil in the composer's dreams; while in 1874, Frenchman Camille Saint-Saëns conjured up a nightmare world of Halloween skeletons rising from their graves in his popular concert piece, *Danse Macabre*.

In Britain in the twentieth century, composers of so-called 'serious' music were all in all less inclined to follow their former Continental predecessors.

Ralph Vaughan-Williams alluded to 'the ghostly drummer of Salisbury Plain' in the slow movement of his *Symphony No. 9* (1958), and while musicians such as James Bernard, Elisabeth Lutyens and Benjamin Frankel (whose *Curse of the Werewolf* for Hammer holds the record as the first British serial film score) carved a living writing music for home-grown horror, the only large-scale work in the repertoire today with a supernatural theme remains Benjamin Britten's chamber opera, *The Turn of the Screw*, first premiered in Venice in September 1954.

Before the emergence of the metal and gothic rock genres in the 1970s and 1980s gave occultism and the paranormal – at least in the eyes of the general public – a centre of gravity in popular music, the world of vampires and the supernatural was very much the province of novelty records and Halloween humour. In 1961, The Moontrekkers, a London-based rock and roll group, released 'Night of the Vampire', an eerie instrumental written by the band's lead guitarist Gary Leport, which, despite BBC indifference, climbed to number 50 in the UK singles chart. The tune was recorded at Joe Meek's now famous Holloway Road studio and the producer, known for the otherworldly quality of his many hit records including The Tornados' 'Telstar' (1962) and the haunting 'Johnny Remember Me' by John Leyton, also from 1961, provided the number's closing banshee-like screams.

Meek, a troubled homosexual who committed suicide in 1967 at the age of 37, had an abiding interest in spiritualism and often conducted Ouija-board séances in his studio in the hope of contacting the spirit of Buddy Holly. In order to obtain authentic sounds for his songs, he set up a reel to reel tape recorder in a local churchyard at night and on one occasion recorded the sound of a cat which he claimed was a familiar that began speaking in a half-human voice. Another of Meek's artists was the eccentric David 'Screaming Lord' Sutch, the self-styled 3rd Earl of Harrow, known in later years for his satirical Official Monster Raving Looney Party by-elections, an early exponent of 'shock rock' whose lively theatrical antics including dressing in a top hat and cloak and emerging from a full-size coffin onto a stage littered with skulls and fake bodies. As lead vocalist for his group The Savages, Sutch augmented such singles as his popular 'Jack the Ripper' (1963) and 'She's Fallen in Love With the Monster Man' (1964) with the undead-themed 'Dracula's Daughter', also recorded in 1964, which featured the night-time activities of the heartbreaking and blood-sucking Vampire Mary.

Originally a traditional rhythm and blues band, Black Sabbath, widely regarded as one of the principal architects of heavy metal music, first adopted their signature doom-laden style in the late summer of 1969 after a queue of filmgoers lining up to see a horror film at a local cinema close to their rehearsal room in the working-class suburb of Aston in Birmingham opened the group's eyes to the public fascination with the world of death and horror. Named after Mario Bava's 1963 *Black Sabbath*, starring the legendary Boris Karloff, the group's dark lyrics and heavy distorted sound were the result of bass player Terence 'Geezer' Butler's fascination with the occult writings of Dennis Wheatley and the necessity (following an industrial accident to his fretting hand) of lead guitarist Tony Iommi to often tune down his guitar several semitones in order to make the strings easier to bend. When vocalist John 'Ozzy' Osbourne sang the opening line of their debut album's eponymous title track, 'What is this that stands before me?' and proceeded to describe a nightmarish black shape that Butler claimed he had woken to find materialised at the foot of his bed, the four Birmingham musicians created a sound world that instantly stripped away any last vestiges of humour and gave the world of the macabre a serious and compelling platform within the framework of popular music.

Despite the Satanic imagery, Sabbath's song writing has over the years been more at ease with depicting social issues, religious criticisms, warfare and drug dependency than outright supernatural horror. As a solo artist beginning in the early 1980s, Ozzy Osbourne, however, has courted a Crowlean image that includes direct pastiche of classic horror themes with albums like 1983's *Bark at the Moon*. Judas Priest, another Midlands hard rock band, also formed in Birmingham in the late 1960s, and who found major and lasting success as part of the post-punk New Wave of British Heavy Metal (NWOBHM), have often used science fiction and horror iconography within their music. Like Lord Sutch, an early song 'The Ripper' invoked the world of the psychotic serial killer, but vampirism has also found its way into the Priest canon: 'Night Crawler', from the 1990 *Painkiller* album, features a predatory bloodsucker, while the imagery of 'Love Bites' from the earlier *Defenders of the Faith* (1983) – 'Love bites you/Invites you/To feast in the night/Excites you/Delights you/It drains you to white/Love bites' – captures the eroticism of the feast of blood that has transcended the years since the 'penny bloods' of Varney and James Rymer. Other NWOBHM bands from the same period have also used vampiric imagery in varying ways. The globally successful Iron Maiden, formed in East London in 1975, tell the tale of a hapless youth enticed into the waters of a bottomless pool by a blood drinking water nymph in 'Still Life' from their 1983 album *Piece of Mind*, while the equally long-lived Saxon, originally from Barnsley in South Yorkshire, describe a Draculaesque menace amidst the grinding riffs and soaring solos of 'Bloodletter' from 1997's *Unleash the Beast*, and vampires also lurk in the darkness of 'Nighthunter' from the earlier offering, *Forever Free* (1992).

During the latter half of the 1980s, the New Wave of British Heavy Metal began to fragment into several different splinters or sub-genres as foreign musicians, particularly from America, Germany and Scandinavia, initially inspired by the UK scene, began to develop the music with influences of their own, and today amongst others, thrash metal, death metal, black metal, power metal, symphonic metal and even Viking metal have their own well-established bands and fan bases.

One British group that has adopted overtly vampiric themes both visually and musically is the aforementioned Cradle of Filth, an extreme metal band fronted by vocalist Dani Filth (Daniel Davey) and long-standing guitarist Paul Allender, originally from Suffolk, whose influences include Gothic literature, Lovecraftian imagery, and horror cinema as well as elements from within metal music itself including bands such as the noted pioneers of thrash and black metal, Newcastle's Venom. A debut album *The Principle of Evil Made Flesh* (1994) initiated an undead connection with its cover of twin blood-drenched vampire brides, a relationship which was reinforced by the group's next two releases, the Le Fanu-inspired *Dusk ... and Her Embrace* (1996), featuring genre songs such as the signature 'Funeral in Carpathia' and an atmospheric instrumental 'The Graveyard by Moonlight'; and *Cruelty and the Beast* from 1998, a concept album around the life of the 'Blood Countess', Erzsébet Báthory. Later material retaining the vampiric essence includes 'Cemetery and Sundown' and 'Lovesick for Mina' (*Thornography*, 2006) and 'Illicitus' from the 2012 album, *The Manticore and Other Horrors*.

Growing out of the 'Bromley Contingent', a journalistic description of the embryonic south London punk movement of the mid-1970s, Siouxsie and the Banshees, with their long-standing vocalist and song-writer Susan Ballion (stage name Siouxsie Sioux), transcended their angst-ridden origins to become one of the most experimental and long-lasting of British post-punk musicians. A number of songs from 1981's *Juju* onwards have both direct and indirect references to vampires and vampire-like subjects, both from a male as well as female perspective. Amidst the tribal rhythms of 'We Hunger' (*Hyæna*, 1984), the vampire satiates its thirst while gazing with envious eyes at the world of the living: 'Shanghaied on a locust flight/And the thirst from a vampire bite/Fills the emptiness inside/Consuming everything green eyed/We hunger'. Some commentators such as J. Gordon Melton have detected vampiric overtones in *Juju*'s brooding 'Night Shift' with its image of a black-clad stranger complete with '[a] bride by my side'; however, the song has more of a kinship with C.M. Eddy, Jr's *The Loved Dead* (1919) than Stoker's *Dracula* and follows the band's intention to record a concept album based on various aspects of the darker side of human existence. A later song, 'The Sweetest Chill' from the 1986 *Tinderbox* record, also invokes the image of an unseen nocturnal presence that may or may not be a visitor from the other side: 'Fearing you but calling your name/Icy breath encases my skin/Fingers like a fountain of needles/Shiver along my spine/And rain down so divine'. Far less ambiguous is 'The Dog' from the 1982 studio album *Strawberries* by another progressive British punk band, The Damned. Drawing on lead singer Dave Vanian's (real name David Lett) interest with vampire literature and Gothic imagery, the song is a musical portrait of the vampire child Claudia from Anne Rice's popular series of novels, *The Vampire Chronicles* (1976–2003). The books were also the inspiration for English musician Sting's (Gordon Sumner) 'Moon Over Bourbon Street' (1985) while Scottish singer Annie Lennox also used the same material for the 'Love Song For A Vampire', which was used on the closing soundtrack for Francis Ford Coppola's *Bram Stoker's Dracula*.

The British post-punk landscape of the late 1970s, as well as catalysing the NWOBHM generation, also gave rise to the Gothic rock movement that, like progressive punk and metal itself, has been a natural home for vampiric-themed music in the last quarter of the twentieth century. Bauhaus, formed in Northampton in 1979 and comprising vocalist Peter Murphy, guitarist Daniel Ash, and brothers Kevin and David Haskins on drums and bass guitar respectively, were one of the seminal bands of the period whose gloomy introspective lyrics and sparse guitar-driven sound ultimately proved influential to the growing scene. The haunting sonic landscape of the nine-minute debut single 'Bela Lugosi's Dead', recorded in a single take within weeks of the musicians coming together as a band, depicts an experimental sound amidst which the traditional vampire figure drifts eerily, courtesy of Murphy's sonorous eulogy: 'The bats have left the bell tower/The victims have been bled/Red velvet lines the black box/Bela Lugosi's dead'. Used as the soundtrack to a number of films and television programmes, Bauhaus are seen playing the song live as a nightclub band in the opening reel of Tony Scott's, *The Hunger*.

As the genre evolved during the course of the 1980s, a second wave of British Gothic rock bands began building on the tradition, both in terms of musical style and literary inspiration. *Beltaine* (1990), the first extended release from Cheltenham band Inkubus Sukkubus, contained the attractive 'Vampyre Kiss' – 'Feel no fear my love/For we were meant to be as one/Is not the moon much finer than the sun?/Let my cheeks be stained/By the yielding of your heart/And never more need we be apart' – while 'Intercourse With The Vampyre' with its prelude of driving strings featured on the band's fourth studio album, *Heartbeat of the Earth* (1995). *Vampyre Erotica* from 1997 continued the group's association with the sexuality of the undead myth: as well as the romance of the driving title track – 'I'll cheat you/I'll eat you/I'll maim you/I'll drain you/Come to me/Come to me/To the dark side where love sleeps' – the haunting 'Danse Vampyre', with its creepy ostinato suggestion of a Mahlerian funeral march depicts a similar landscape where 'Purest souls are slowly weakening/Screaming, crying, living, dying/Yearning breast descending, sighing'. Similarly Nosferatu, a contemporary group formed in London in 1988, have likewise covered familiar territory beginning with 'Vampyres Cry' from their debut album *Rise* (1993), and like their counterparts have demonstrated a continuing creativity and fascination with the subject matter that, like the vampires themselves, appears undiminished despite the passing years.

13

In the Shadow of Stoker: Modern Vampire Literature

(1975-2013)

For aficionados of vampire literature, the mid-1970s were to prove to be something of a watershed period, as two seminal works which have done much to fuel the continuing modern enthusiasm for tales of the undead were published within a year of each other. In 1975, Stephen King, following on from the success of his debut novel *Carrie* (1974), brought the essence of Dracula to small town America with his second major work, *Salem's Lot*. The following year, in April 1976, New Orleans writer Anne Rice published her debut novel, *Interview With the Vampire*, an expansion of an original short story composed in the late 1960s and written as an act of recovery in the aftermath of the death of her 4-year-old daughter, Michelle. Both books, through film and television versions, and in the case of Rice's novel an extended series of sequels, have proved successful in presenting the vampire myth within a contemporary time period and as such have paved the way for later and equally popular film and television vampires, in particular *Buffy the Vampire Slayer* (1997–2000) and *The Twilight Saga* (2008–2012). For the final part of our survey, we will look at some of the British authors who, like King and Rice nearly a century on from Stoker's bloody benchmark, have with imagination, humour and a dark fearful delight, continued to sustain, expand and reinvent the vampire myth both through the closing years of the twentieth century and on into the new millennium.

In Britain during the 1970s, the New English Library (NEL) provided a platform for many new writers and in many ways defined horror fiction for a large proportion of the paperback-reading public. Londoner James Herbert (1943–2013), whose bestselling *The Rats* appeared in 1974, proved influential in spearheading a resurgence of home-grown horror writing, particularly in the field of 'eco-horror', and the decade saw a growing multitude of previously benign creatures and insects including spiders, slugs, worms and bats beginning to modify their feeding habits and develop a taste for human flesh and blood. Despite several novels dealing with the subject of supernatural evil, including the Jamesian-influenced *The Survivor*, published in 1976, Herbert never wrote a directly vampiric novel, in the main content to expand on the theme of the urban apocalypse first mooted in *The Rats* and subsequently developed in other novels including *The Fog* (1975), *The Dark* (1980) and *Domain* (1984), as well as reinventions of the traditional haunted house scenario, as deployed in *The Magic Cottage* (1986), *Haunted* (1988) and *The Secret of Crickley Hall* (2006).

In 1974, the same year that Herbert launched his rat attack on modern London, NEL published *The Death Box*, the fourth in a series of supernatural adventures by Wilfred McNeilly who, under the pseudonym of Erroll Lecale, had created the Van Helsing-like psychic detective, Eli Podgram, known by his own *nom de plume* as The Specialist. For his latest outing, Podgram, who, like Dennis Wheatley's Duke de Richleau, often takes to the astral plane to fight against the forces of darkness, takes on a vampiric warlock named Dagmar the Black, Archduke of Szlig, released from a wooden chest recovered from the hold of a mysterious ship found drifting in the Sargasso Sea. Following a climactic duel in the shadowy Egyptology wing of the British Museum, Dagmar, about to release the Hounds of Hell to destroy his opponent, is finally slain in traditional fashion with a wooden harpoon.

McNeilly returned to the subject of an undead menace the following year in *Blood of My Blood*, the sixth and final instalment of the saga in which The Specialist, accompanied by his niece Anthea and the sceptical Professor Raymond Imrie, travel to Transylvania to investigate a series of sinister happenings in the depths of the hero's own ancestral home, Castle Podgram. The year 1975 also saw the release of another NEL vampire story, this time a little nearer to home, in the form of Ian Dear's minor pulp horror classic, *Village of Blood*. The hamlet of the title is the haunted village of Reston in Oxfordshire, populated by a Doomwatch-like band of inbred inhabitants that hide a terrible secret unwittingly revealed by the activities of a film crew on location to shoot a horror film financed by the local landowner, Lord Bellingham. In reality, Bellingham is plotting the return of an ancient evil, a heretical vampire burnt at the stake generations before, whose violent and bloody revenge attacks on the perpetrator's modern descendants are predicated in director Ken Mather's shooting script, a supernatural document drafted by the lord of the manor himself. Like Dagmar the Black, the resurrected vampire lord is dispatched in stock fashion, in this instance with a wooden spear, and Dear rounds off the proceedings with a Hammeresque conflagration that razes Bellingham Hall to the ground.

Another NEL stablemate and direct contemporary of James Herbert, Guy N. Smith has enjoyed a writing career spanning forty years and written over 100 books, the majority of which have been in the horror genre that has established his name. Born in the Staffordshire village of Hopwas in 1939, Smith, a journalist, countryman and former bank manager, was first published in a local newspaper at the age of 12.

Werewolf by Moonlight, released in 1974, a tale of modern lycanthropy set in the Welsh/Shropshire border country, established a distinctive style of contemporary home-grown horror with a strong rural setting, and was quickly followed by two further stand-alone novels, *The Slime Beast* (1975) and *The Sucking Pit*, issued the same year and later described by Stephen King as '[t]he all-time pulp horror classic title'. In 1976, NEL published Smith's *Night of the Crabs* 'in the tradition of *The Rats*' and it became a summer bestseller, allowing the author to leave banking and establish himself as a full-time writer. Describing a nightmarish invasion of the Welsh coast by an army of gigantic flesh-eating crustaceans, the book spawned six sequels beginning with 1978's *Killer Crabs*, and in the ensuing years the author has populated his pages with a vast array of suitably monstrous creations including werewolves, undead Nazis, ancient curses, voodooism, cannibalistic locusts and necromancy. Smith's idiosyncratic take on the vampire myth has resulted in two full-length novels and two short stories, one of each featuring Mark Sabat, an SAS-trained exorcist who first appeared in *The Graveyard Vultures* (1982). An occult master possessed by the evil spirit of his own Crowleyesque brother Quentin, Sabat's penchant for hardcore sex and ultra-violence stands him in good stead as he takes on a potentially deadly array of adversaries, both on Earth and, like McNeilly's Specialist, as a spirit form inhabiting the higher realms of time and space. For 1982's *The Blood Merchants*, the vampire element is provided by the Disciples of Lilith, a neo-Nazi cult whose army of brainwashed skinhead thugs dispatch their victims using a syringe-like weapon that drains the blood direct from the unprotected jugular vein. A pseudo-vampiric threat also features in a later novel, *The Knighton Vampires* from 1993, set in the Welsh village close to Smith's own home in the Shropshire borders, where a gang of drug smugglers initiate a series of gruesome murders as cover for an illegal trade in illicit narcotics. For the 1996 compilation *Dead Meat*, a short story 'Vampire Village' provided Sabat with a real undead encounter as he is lured into the German village of Verboten, where a horror-themed tourist attraction proves to be the hunting ground for a pack of predatory vampires; while for Stephen Jones' *The Mammoth Book of Dracula* (1997), Smith's short story *Larry's Guest* sees the hapless bachelor of the title playing host to the King of the Undead, whose coffin mysteriously appears in an abandoned garden air-raid shelter.

Another British author whose short stories populated the 1970s and 1980s with vampires was Ronald Chetwynd-Hayes, whose work we have already encountered in an earlier chapter in connection with Amicus Productions. Born in Isleworth, West London in 1919, Chetwynd-Hayes enlisted in the Middlesex Regiment in 1939 which saw him both evacuated at Dunkirk and subsequently returned to France in 1944 as part of the Normandy landings. From 1946 he worked as a buyer at Harrods and from the early 1950s onwards at Peerless Furniture as a showroom manager, writing and selling stories in his spare time: his first published short story appeared in *The Lady* magazine in 1953. In 1973, Chetwynd-Hayes became a full-time writer and editor, compiling several series of anthologies including *The Fontana Book of Great Ghost Stories* which ran for twelve volumes between 1973 and 1984, as well as issuing several collections of his own tales including *The Unbidden* (1971), *The Elemental and Other Stories* (1974), *The Monster Club* (1975) and *Tales of Fear and Fantasy* (1977).

In 1997, Stephen Jones brought together a collection of the author's vampire stories under the title *Looking For Something to Suck*, which showcases both the humour and imagination that Chetwynd-Hayes brought to a well-worn subject. For the title story, the author pares the vampire down to its absolute minimum, reducing Dracula to a sentient shadow, creeping and sliding through the darkness, avoiding the deadly contact of all sources of light in a constant search for human nourishment, draining its victims to little more than a literal bag of skin and bones. 'I've always got this terrible urge to send the whole thing up,' Chetwynd-Hayes once admitted in connection with the 'disarming' comedy elements that crept into a number of his tales, 'It just slips in. I have never been able to stop it.' *Rudolph* from 1987, otherwise known as Mr Acrudal, the son of Dracula, takes on a housekeeper who feeds him lashings of pig's blood and mince, the vampire's favourite dish:

> [H]e grabbed the spoon and began shovelling the mess in. It was a dreadful sight and sound. Slop-slub-lip-smacking with what missed the target dribbling down his chin. When the bowl was half empty he paused for breath and expressed sincere appreciation. 'The best blushie I've tasted in years, Miss Benfield. You are talented ... I knew by your smell that we'd haunted the same track.'

Eventually, Miss Benfield bears Rudolph a son, a human/vampire mutation known as a 'humvamp', in order to continue the Dracula line. Once the creature is born, however, its mother is abandoned and reduced to living the life of a fugitive, forever on the run from 'the pack', a never-tiring hit squad of undead predators. Chetwynd-Hayes is perhaps at his most inventive in *The Labrynth*, first published in *The Elemental and Other Stories* in 1974: a young couple, lost in the wilds of Dartmoor, unwittingly take shelter in a strange house occupied by a seemingly benign old woman, Mrs Brown, and her dog-like servant, Carlos, unaware that the building itself is a living vampire, grown out of the gravesite of an ancient warlock, Petros, whose undying brain lives on in the foul depths of the house's intestinal cellars, rooted into the earth and rock and nourishing the structure with the blood of its sacrificial victims. When the gruesome head is smashed with a boulder, the vampire house and its occupants are destroyed, and the sinister building is reduced to a pile of misshapen rocks.

The mid-1970s also saw another take on the traditional vampire format, in this instance by Colin Wilson whose futuristic novel *The Space Vampires* was published in March 1976. Inspired by the science fiction author A.E. Von Vogt's 1942 short story *Asylum*, Wilson crafted his own take on the Canadian's concept of 'energy vampirism' involving creatures or beings who drain their victims of the very force of life itself, rather than feasting on meals of human blood; a shift away from the traditions of the myth in much the same way that earlier authors became fascinated with psychic vampires towards the end of the nineteenth century.

Set in the far future, the astronaut crew from the spaceship *Hermes* encounter a vast castle-like alien craft, over fifty miles long, drifting lifelessly in deep space. Christened the Stranger by the world's press, the derelict contains the bodies of several humanoid beings, both male and female, that are brought back to the *Hermes* in suspended animation. Back on Earth, one of the female aliens returns to life, reducing a hapless reporter to a withered husk before escaping from a high security hospital out onto the streets of London. Wilson's hero, Captain Olof Carlsen, narrowly escapes a similar fate but becomes tainted with part of the vampire alien's essence. As with his other fictional novels, including *Ritual in the Dark* (1960), the Lovecraftian *The Mind Parasites* (1967) and the later *The God of the Labyrinth* from 1977, Wilson uses the story medium to share his own personal theories, in this case concerning the origins of the vampire myth and the exchange and transfer of consciousness – the author's 'energy undead' are able to parasitise themselves on individuals without destroying their hosts, although surprisingly the traditional clove of garlic is found to be effective in ridding a victim of its unwanted vampiric presence. In the story's closing pages, Wilson uses philosophy rather than a hammer and stake to destroy his extraterrestrial menace as the space vampires ultimately seek self-destruction following contact with a higher form of their own race, the Cthulhu-like Nioth-Korghai, hidden on Earth for hundreds of years, who reveal to the aliens the atavistic state into which they have fallen.

As well as reinventing the subject of vampirism and expanding it into other areas, a number of modern British writers have also found themselves returning to the genre's most influential source. In 1977, Peter Beresford Ellis (b. 1943), better known to fantasy and horror fiction readers as Peter Tremayne, published *Dracula Unborn*, a literary synthesis of Transylvanian history and Stokerian fiction that relates the swashbuckling fifteenth-century adventures of Mircea Dracula, the youngest son of Vlad the Impaler, as set down in an original manuscript by none other than Abraham Van Helsing. This was followed by *The Revenge of Dracula* (1978), a Victorian mystery involving a jade amulet that mixes the King of the Undead with a love story involving the reincarnation of an ancient Egyptian princess. In 1980, Tremayne added a third novel, *Dracula, My Love*, that gave the vampire count a pre-1897 romance all of his own as well as conveniently setting the scene for the events of Stoker's forthcoming novel: Dracula's love interest is a Victorian Scotswoman, Morag MacLeod, who is banished to Transylvania after having a child out of wedlock.

To Peter Tremayne's *Dracula Lives* trilogy, which also contains a short story, 'Dracula's Chair' (*The Count Dracula Fan Club Book of Vampire Stories*, New York, 1980), a sinister item of outwardly benign furniture recovered from Carfax Abbey that transports the narrator back in time and into the paralysed body of one of the Count's Victorian victims, can also be added several attempts by other British writers in recent years to provide the most famous literary vampire story with the sequel that its author never felt obliged to write.

In 2000, Sean Manchester brought James Harker, the grandson of Jonathan Harker, to late 1960s London, and combined aspects of the real-life events of the Highgate Vampire case with David Seltzer's *The Omen* (1976) to produce *Carmel: A Vampire Tale*, which sees Count Dracula, masquerading under the title of the Count de Ville, presiding over a scheme to bring about the age of the Antichrist, who will be born to Harker's daughter Calantha during a solar eclipse in the final days of the second millennium. Pitted against the forces of darkness is the Van-Helsing-like Lord Mamucium, a swashbuckling bishop, who takes on not only the vampiress of the title – in reality James Harker's undead wife – and Dracula himself, but also members of a Satanic cult, the Black Order of the Dragon, whose senior members are conveniently defeated during a sword fight duel on Hampstead Heath. Unaware of what publishers HarperCollins would confidently cite in 2009 as the 'official' sequel to Stoker's *Dracula*, namely *Dracula The Un-Dead*, co-written by the author's Canadian-born great grand-nephew Dacre Stoker together with New York writer Ian Holt, British author Kate Cary had already taken up the challenge of extending a classic with 2006's *Bloodline*: a paranormal romance set initially in the trenches of the Somme and later in the 'land beyond the forest', involving cavalry officer Quincy Harker, the vampire son of Jonathan and Mina Harker, and Mary Seward, daughter of Dr John Seward, whose Purfleet Sanitorium is being used as a convalescence home for injured soldiers. In 2011, Cary continued the saga with a sequel volume, *Bloodline: Reckoning*, while Scotsman Xander Buchan has brought a technology-savvy Count firmly into the twenty-first century, using e-mail, text messaging as well as Facebook and other social media in order to regain a foothold on the British Isles in his *Dracula Rekindled* (2011).

Not surprisingly some of the most influential and bestselling of modern British horror writers have also contributed to the never-ending canon of new and imaginative vampire literature. Edinburgh's Graham Masterton (b. 1946), a former editor of *Mayfair* and *Penthouse*, whose road to horror stardom began with *The Manitou* in 1976, has explored the subject of Romanian vampires in his novel *Descendant* (2006) whose Dracula-like leader, Duca, is resurrected in late 1950s London when a leaden casket containing his undead corpse is recovered from a wartime plane wreck in the mud of the Thames estuary. Two of Masterton's short stories with an overt vampire theme are of especial mention: 'Laird of Dunain', written for Stephen Jones' 1992 anthology, *The Mammoth Book of Vampires*, references an unusual vampiric trait considered by Stoker for *Dracula* which ultimately went unused, namely the sinister way that a vampire's portrait is impossible to capture on a canvas. When a painting student on an art course at Dunain Castle attempts to paint the Laird himself, whose ancestor cursed his bloodline into undead immortality at the Battle of Culloden, the Scotsman's features continue to remain deathly pale until blood from a cut is mixed in with the oils. Entranced by the vampire's spell, the luckless artist commits suicide in order to finish the painting but the laird gets his just deserts, ripped in half along with his portrait in an ending reminiscent of actor Tom Baker's demise from the closing 'Drawn and Quartered' episode of Amicus' *Vault of Horror*. 'Roadkill', penned for another Jones compilation, *The Mammoth Book of Dracula* in 1997, shows the Count surviving into the late twentieth century in a secret coffin space in the cellar of an old house, only to fall foul of Government red tape when his home is demolished to make way for a new ring road, trapping the vampire lord in his coffin under the tarmac for an eternity.

The Liverpool writers Ramsey Campbell and Clive Barker have earned their places in the pantheon with many published novels that showcase the imaginative thinking both have brought to the genre. Campbell (b. 1946), whose Lovecraftian debut writings *The Inhabitant of the Lake and Less Welcome Tenants* were published by August Derleth's Arkham House in 1964, has cited Le Fanu's *Carmilla* as one of his favourite supernatural stories. 'Conversion', a short story in Michael Parry's anthology *The Rivals of Dracula* (1977), neatly describes the account of a Transylvanian peasant who visits Castle Dracula to remonstrate with the Count over the death of his sister-in-law and returns home as one of the undead, while 1980s 'The Brood' are a sinister gathering of vampire-like creatures inhabiting the basement of a derelict Merseyside house, where they are fed with a constant supply of stray animals by a strange elderly woman. With his *Books of Blood*, Clive Barker (born in Liverpool in 1952) changed the horror landscape of the 1980s forever by describing a world of bizarre and brutal supernatural evil seemingly alive and hidden within the ordinary day-to-day urban landscape. His 1986 novella *The Hellbound Heart* spawned the successful *Hellraiser* franchise and as well as being an accomplished painter, Barker himself has both produced and directed a number of films including *Nightbreed* (1990), *Lord of Illusions* (1995) and *The Midnight Meat Train* (2008). 'Human Remains', first published in volume 3 of *The Books of Blood* in 1984, typifies Barker's style and introduces perhaps the most bizarre vampiric creature in the present book: a wooden Romanesque statue recovered from an archaeological dig by a rogue collector which bathes in human blood and gradually becomes the living doppelganger of a young male prostitute.

Like Barker and Campbell, a hidden subterranean world populated with unspeakable horrors (itself the essence of supernatural fiction in the Lovecraftian tradition) has proved attractive to other British writers, particularly those seeking to expand the vampire story outside of a hackneyed Stokerian environment. Doncaster-born author Simon Clark affected an interesting compromise with his Wagnerian horror novel *Vampyrrhic*, published by NEL in 1998. Here the fictional North Yorkshire town of Leppington, a near neighbour of Whitby, provides the story with a familiar anchor but Clark, like Lovecraft, takes his horror underground, combining ancient Norse mythology with a sinister family secret that populates a series of underground tunnels deep in the earth with a race of blood-drinking Valkyries, fed down through the years by the gory sluices of a Victorian era slaughterhouse which remains the town's principal employer. Clark's character-driven narrative, centred on the occupants of the Gothic-period Station Hotel, creates a *Salem's Lot*-style atmosphere that provides some genuinely eerie moments, particularly the attacks by several of the town's vampire inhabitants, and to date the story has spawned two sequels, *Vampyrrhic Rites* (2003) and *Whitby Vampyrrhic* (2009).

Brian Lumley (b. 1937), a former military policeman in the British Army who took up full-time writing in 1980, is another author whose first fledgling tales found their way into print through the press at Arkham House. Today, perhaps identified the most among late twentieth and early twenty-first-century British authors with modern vampire fiction, his first professionally written novel *Necroscope* (1986) having spawned a literary armada of Tolstoy-like proportions of which 2010s *Necroscope: The Plague-Bearer* is the seventeenth entry in the series. At the core of Lumley's writing is the character of Harry Keogh, born with a superior form of ESP that allows him to read the thoughts of the dead lying in their graves. Keogh, together with his descendants, wages a never-ending war against the Wamphyri, a parasitic alien race much in the vein of Lovecraft's *Cthulhu Mythos* (of which the author is an avowed devotee) and in whose terms the writer has successfully reinterpreted the vampire myth for a new generation of readers, incorporating many of its clichés but expanding the appeal to cosmic proportions with suitably fantastic parallel worlds and named hierarchies of frightening vampiric creatures. Outside of the *Necroscope* series, Lumley, like his contemporaries Fritz Leiber and Ramsey Campbell, has also expanded the Lovecraft *Mythos* itself, often centring the action – as with 1974s *The Burrowers Beneath* – around the *Doctor Who*-like occultist Titus Crowe; while the author's free-standing vampire stories, some of which cross over into the Lovecraftian arena, were first collected in a single volume, *A Coven of Vampires*, published in 1998. Of note amongst these are 'Necros' (1986), a holiday romance cut short by a grotesque blood-drinking homunculus, 'Back Row' (1988), which describes a bloodthirsty mutant loose in the stalls of a local cinema, and the *Mythos*-inspired 'The House of the Temple' (1980), whose principal occupant is a colossal vampiric tick that drinks the blood of an ancient race of stellar creatures from a distant galaxy, now hidden for centuries within the bowels of the earth.

With the medium of film and television still the most influential in introducing and shaping the public interest and education about vampires and vampirism, it seems appropriate to end both this chapter on modern fiction and our survey as a whole with the work of English cinema critic and historian Kim Newman, whose multi-part fictional series *Anno Dracula* has proved to be a major contribution to reinventing the undead myth within the frame of modern English literature. Newman, born in London in 1959, has cited Tod Browning's *Dracula* as his personal introduction to the world of film and horror fiction history, and has published a number of critical works examining the history and social impact of both: they include *Nightmare Movies* (1988), *Horror: 100 Best Books* (1988) and *The BFI Companion to Horror* (1996). As a fictional author, Newman has cultivated a personal style of alternate history which in the tradition of other works such as George Orwell's *Nineteen Eighty-Four* (1949) and Len Deighton's *SS-GB* (1978) has been applied with much imagination and humour to the world of the bloodsucking undead. First mooted in the novella 'Red Reign', contained in *The Mammoth Book of Vampires* in 1992, Newman subsequently expanded his story into *Anno Dracula*, published as a full-length novel by Simon & Schuster the same year. At the heart of this and subsequent sequels is the premise that Count Dracula did not perish at the hands of Abraham Van Helsing and his companions at the end of Stoker's novel and went on to not only survive but also to marry Queen Victoria, thereby spreading, as the undead Prince Consort, a vampire bloodline into English aristocracy, generating a Victorian social world where humans and vampires effect an uneasy coexistence. Into this arena of established nosferatu, the newly 'turned' undead and those still 'warm' or wholly human, Newman adds a vast cast of both genuinely historic as well as wholly fictional characters (both from the horror and fantasy genres as well as many other works including Dickens, Conan Doyle, H.G. Wells, Sax Rohmer, William Hope Hodgeson and Oscar Wilde), all of whom have a part to play and add interest and depth to the literary texture. For *Anno Dracula*, set mainly in Whitechapel in 1888, Stoker's Dr Seward is revealed to be none other than Jack the Ripper, viciously slaughtering vampire prostitutes as an act of revenge for the death of his beloved Lucy Westenra. In the novel's closing pages, Queen Victoria, reduced to a pathetic totem chained at Dracula's feet, is given the means (a silver-bladed scalpel) to commit suicide, thereby negating the Count's right to rule and driving him from the country and into exile. In 1995, Newman added a sequel, *The Bloody Red Baron*, set during the grim days of the First World War, which sees the vampire king, now Graf von Dracula, ruling Germany and intent on destroying the Entente Powers with a mighty squadron of aerial vampires led by Baron Manfred von Richthofen; while three years later a third instalment, *Dracula Cha Cha Cha* (1998), brought the action several decades forward to late 1950s Rome where, amidst a heavy atmosphere of Frederico Fellini and Ian Fleming, a murderer is on the loose as Dracula gets set to marry his sixth wife, the Moldavian Princess Asa Vajda.

After a long gap, Newman published (in September 2013) *Johnny Alucard*, a collection of previously issued novellas and original material, now set against a background of the entertainment and drug culture of the 1980s. In his opening chapter, 'Coppola's Dracula', Newman gives an alternate take on the madness of American multi-million-dollar filmmaking, consigning Francis Ford Coppola to make *Apocalypse Now* within the 'Anno Dracula' universe, with Martin Sheen as Jonathan Harker, travelling through the wilds of Ceauşescu's Romania to hunt down and destroy Marlon Brando as Count Dracula who, insane and holed up in his Carpathian fortress, has become a figurehead for the Transylvanian Movement, revolutionaries who hope to re-establish a pure vampire homeland for the world's undead. With the vampire more identifiable now than ever before in today's society with the irresistible forces of blood, sex and death, we close with the last words of Newman's Jonathan Harker who, after his traumatic journey into self, returns to the outside world cursed with its shadow:

> Harker, face still red with Dracula's blood, is back in his room at the inn in Bistritz. He stands in front of the mirror.
>
> HARKER's Voice: They were going to make me a saint for this, and I wasn't even in their fucking church any more.
>
> Harker looks deep into the mirror.
>
> He has no reflection.
>
> Harker's mouth forms the words, but the voice is Dracula's.
>
> The horror … the horror …

Two hundred years of the British vampire – the horror indeed.

About the Author

PAUL ADAMS was born in Epsom, Surrey, in 1966. Brought up on a diet of Hammer Films and British pulp-horror literature, a major preoccupation with the paranormal began in the mid-1970s. Employed as a draughtsman in the UK construction industry for nearly thirty years, he has worked in three haunted buildings but has yet to see a true ghost. As well as the history of psychical research, his main interests at present are in materialisation mediumship and the physical phenomena of spiritualism. He has contributed articles to several specialist paranormal periodicals and acted as editor and publisher for *Two Haunted Counties* (2010), the memoirs of Luton ghost hunter, Tony Broughall. Adams is the co-author of *The Borley Rectory Companion* (2009), *Shadows in the Nave* (2011) and *Extreme Hauntings* (2013), and has written *Haunted Luton and Dunstable* (2012), *Ghosts & Gallows* (2012), a study of British true-crime cases with paranormal connections, and *Haunted St Albans* (2013). He is also an amateur mycologist and viola player and has lived in Luton since 2006. Website: www.pauladamsauthor.co.uk

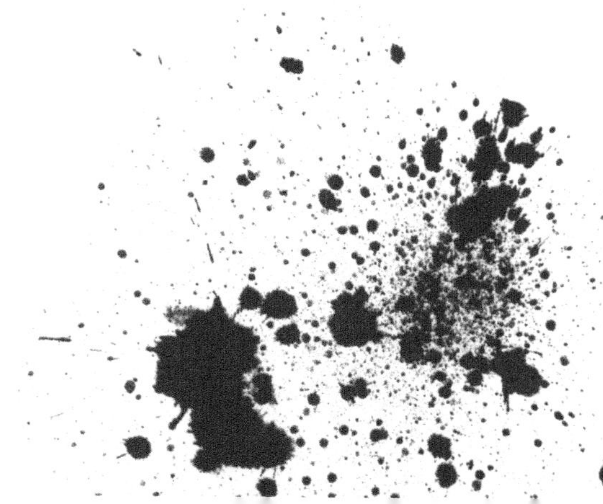

Bibliography and Further Reading

Adams, Paul and Brazil, Eddie, *Extreme Hauntings: Britain's Most Terrifying Ghosts* (The History Press, Stroud, 2013)

Cammell, C.R., *Aleister Crowley* (Richards Press, London, 1951; New English Library, London, 1969)

Carrington, Hereward and Fodor, Nandor, *The Story of the Poltergeist Down the Centuries* (Rider & Co., London, 1953)

Copper, Basil, *The Vampire in Legend, Fact & Art* (Robert Hale & Co., London, 1973)

Dawidziak, Mark (ed.), *Bloodlines: Richard Matheson's DRACULA, I AM LEGEND, and Other Vampire Stories* (Gauntlet Publications, Colorado Springs, 2006)

Dalby, Richard (ed.), *Dracula's Brood* (Crucible, Wellingborough, 1987)

Dello Stritto, Frank J. and Brooks, Andi, *Vampire Over London: Bela Lugosi in Britain* (Cult Movies Press, Houston, 2000)

Dickie, James (ed.), *The Undead: Vampire Masterpieces* (Pan Books Ltd, London, 1971)

Ellis, Bill, *Raising the Devil: Satanism, New Religions, and the Media* (The University Press of Kentucky, Lexington, 2000)

Farrant, David, *Beyond the Highgate Vampire* (British Psychic & Occult Society, London, 1991)

——————, *David Farrant: In the Shadow of the Highgate Vampire* (British Psychic & Occult Society, London, 2009)

——————, *David Farrant: Out of the Shadows* (British Psychic & Occult Society, London, 2011)

Farson, Daniel, *The Man Who Wrote Dracula: A Biography of Bram Stoker* (Michael Joseph Ltd, London, 1975)

Fodor, Nandor, *On the Trail of the Poltergeist* (Citadel Press, New York, 1958)

Frank, Alan, *The Movie Treasury: Monsters & Vampires* (Octopus Books Ltd, London, 1976)

Frayling, Christopher, *Vampyres: Lord Byron to Count Dracula* (Faber & Faber Ltd, London, 1991)

Gauld, Alan & Cornell, A.D., *Poltergeists* (Routledge & Kegan Paul, London, 1979)

Gaute, J.H.H. & Odell, Robin, *The Murderers' Who's Who* (George G. Harrap & Co. Ltd, London, 1979)

Glut, Donald F., *True Vampires of History* (HC Publishers, Inc., New York, 1971)

Haining, Peter (ed.), *The Vampire Omnibus* (Orion Books Ltd, London, 1995)

Hall, Mike, *Haunted Places of Middlesex* (Countryside Books, Newbury, 2004)

Huckvale, David, *James Bernard, Composer to Count Dracula: A Critical Biography* (McFarland & Co., London, 2006)

James, M.R., *Collected Ghost Stories* (Wordsworth Classics, Ware, 1992)

Kaplan, Stephen, *Vampires Are* (ETC Publications, Palm Springs, 1984)

Kinsey, Wayne, *Hammer Films: The Unsung Heroes* (Tomahawk Press, Sheffield, 2010)

Kinsey, Wayne & Thomson, Gordon, *Hammer Films on Location* (Peveril Publishing, Barnby, 2012)

Langley, Patsy, *The Highgate Vampire Casebook* (British Psychic & Occult Society, London, 2007)

Lee, Christopher, *Tall, Dark and Gruesome* (Victor Gollancz, London, 1997)

Manchester, Sean, *The Highgate Vampire* (British Occult Society, London, 1985; Gothic Press, London, 1991)

——————, *The Vampire Hunter's Handbook: A Concise Vampirological Guide* (Gothic Press, London, 1997)

Markham, Len, *Ten Yorkshire Mysteries* (Countryside Books, Newbury, 1995)

Masters, Anthony, *The Natural History of the Vampire* (Mayflower Books Ltd, St Albans, 1974)

Maxford, Howard, *Hammer, House of Horror: Behind the Screams* (B.T. Batsford Ltd, London, 1996)

McConnell, Brian, *The Possessed: True Tales of Demonic Possession* (Headline Book Publishing, London, 1995)

Melton, J. Gordon, *The Vampire Book: The Encyclopaedia of the Undead* (Visible Ink Press, Canton, 1999)

Morrison, Robert & Baldick, Chris (eds), *John Polidori: The Vampyre and Other Tales of the Macabre* (Oxford University Press, Oxford, 1997)

Newman, Kim (ed.), *The BFI Companion to Horror* (Cassell, London, 1996)

North, Dan (ed.), *Sights Unseen: Unfinished British Films* (Cambridge Scholars Publishing, Newcastle, 2008)

Pirie, David, *The Vampire Cinema* (Quarto Publishing Ltd, London, 1977)

Pitt, Ingrid, *The Ingrid Pitt Bedside Companion for Vampire Lovers* (B.T. Batsford Ltd, London, 1998)

Rymer, James Malcolm, *Varney the Vampire* (Wordsworth Editions Ltd, Ware, 2010)

Sangster, Jimmy, *Do You Want It Good or Tuesday?: From Hammer Films to Hollywood – A Life in the Movies* (Midnight Marquee Press, Baltimore, 1997)

——————, *Inside Hammer* (Reynolds & Hearn Ltd, London, 2001)

Silver, Alain & Ursini, James, *The Vampire Film* (The Tantivy Press, London, 1975)

Sleight, Graham, *The Doctor's Monsters: Meanings of the Monstrous in Doctor Who* (I.B. Taurus & Co. Ltd, London, 2012)

Smith, Timothy d'Arch, *The Books of the Beast* (Mandrake, Oxford, 1987; 1991)

Summers, Montague, *The Galanty Show* (Cecil Woolf, London, 1980)

——————, *The Vampire: His Kith and Kin* (Kegan Paul, Trench, Trubner & Co. Ltd, London, 1928)

——————, *The Vampire in Europe* (Kegan Paul, Trench, Trubner & Co. Ltd, London, 1929)

Underwood, Peter, *Exorcism!* (Robert Hale Ltd, London, 1990)

——————, *Haunted London* (George G. Harrap & Co. Ltd, London, 1973)

——————, *The Vampire's Bedside Companion: The Amazing World of Vampires in Fact & Fiction* (Leslie Frewin, London, 1975)

Wilson, Colin, *Afterlife* (George G. Harrap & Co. Ltd, London, 1985)

——————, *Beyond the Occult* (Bantam Press, London, 1988)

——————, *A Criminal History of Mankind* (Granada Publishing Ltd, London, 1984)

——————, *Poltergeist!: A Study in Destructive Haunting* (New English Library, London, 1981)

Wilson, Colin & Pitman, Patricia, *Encyclopaedia of Murder* (Arthur Barker Ltd, London, 1961)

Wilson, Colin & Wilson, Damon, *Unsolved Mysteries: Past and Present* (Headline Book Publishing, London, 1993)

Index of Names and Titles

Abominable Snowman, The, 108
Account of the Principalities of Wallachia and Moldavia, 54
Ackroyd, Peter, 22
'Adam' (murder case), 78
Adams, Douglas, 158
Adams, Fanny, 112
Addams, Dawn, 137
Addinsell, Richard, 116
Adrian, Max, 118
Adventure of the Sussex Vampire, The, 71
Adventures with Phantoms, 72
Afterlife, 36
Ahmed, Rollo, 95
Aickman, Robert Fordyce, 38
Aleister Crowley, 96
Alexander, Marc, 29, 31
Alfred the Great, 137
Alien (1979 film), 144, 154
Allan, Peter, 177
Allen, Adrianne, 141
Allender, Paul, 194
'Allo, 'Allo! (TV series), 142
Alnwick Castle Vampire (case of), 25–6
Amicus Productions, 18, 117, 129, 140–1, 143, 199, 203
Amityville Horror, The, 31
An Episode of Cathedral History, 65
'And No Bird Sings', 70
Anderson, Alexander, 170
Andrews, Barry, 123
Anne of a Thousand Days, 139
Anno Dracula, 204–6
Antinous and Other Poems, 89
Anulka (actress), 153
Apocalypse Now, 205
Archard, Bernard, 186
Are You Being Served? (TV series), 142
Argyle, Judge Michael, 177
Army Game, The, 188
Arnold, Malcolm, 105
Ash, Daniel, 196
Asher, Jack, 110
Ashton, Roy, 143
Ashurst, Sir William, 156
Astounding Stories magazine, 73
Asylum, 200
Athenaeum magazine, 58
Augustus Darvell, 187
Avalon, Frankie, 144
Avengers, The (TV series), 143, 151–2
Bacharach, Burt, 146
Back Row, 204
Badel, Alan, 103
Baden-Semper, Nina, 186
Badham, John, 153
Bain, Bill, 186
Baker, Bob, 188
Baker, Roy Ward, 127–8, 134–5, 137, 141, 153
Baker, Tom, 141, 188, 203
Baker, William, 112
Balcombe, Florence, 49, 98, 101, 108
Balderston, John, 46, 101–3, 153
Baldock, Edward, 79
Ballion, Susan (aka Siouxsie Sioux), 195

Bamu, Magalie, 78
Bamu, Kristy, 78
Barbarella, 137
Baring-Gould, Revd Sabine, 65
Bark at the Moon (music album), 194
Barker, Clive, 98, 203
Barnes, Richard, 187
Bashir, Kousar, 77
Bashir, Muhammad, 78
Bates, Ralph, 124, 129, 141, 145–6
Báthory, Erzsébet, 64, 83–4, 126, 139, 195
Bauhaus (band), 196
Bava, Mario, 193
Bayldon, Geoffrey, 117, 140, 143
Beacham, Stephanie, 129
Beasts (TV series), 185
Beaver Book of Horror, The, 29
'Bela Lugosi's Dead' (song), 196
Believer, The, 73
Bells, The (play), 49
Beltaine (music album), 196
Bennett, John, 140
Benson, E.F., 25, 66–70, 74, 104
Bérard, Cyprien, 13
Beresford, Matthew, 183
Berg, Karl, 81
Berlioz, Hector, 192
Bernard, James, 7, 99, 116, 119, 125, 152, 190, 193
Bertrand, Sgt Victor, 170
Beswick, Martine, 141
Betts, Kirsten, 137, 139
Beyond the Highgate Vampire, 161, 183
Beyond the Occult, 35–6
Beyond the Reef, 177
BFI Companion to Horror, The, 205
Bibliography of the Restoration Drama, A, 93
Bidmead, Christopher, 188
Bikubi, Eric, 78
Black & White newspaper, 57
Black, Isobel, 116
Blackburn Vampire (case of), 7, 43–4
Black Monk of Pontefract (case of), 35
Black Sabbath (band), 193–4
Black Sabbath (film), 193
Blackwood, Algernon, 18, 63
Blacula, 143
Blair, Isla, 124
Blair Witch Project, The, 107
Blashford-Snell, Col John, 38
Bloch, Robert, 73, 140
Blood, Alan, 170–1
Blood and Bone China, 45
Blood and Roses, 136
Blood Beast Terror, The, 144
'Bloodletter' (song), 194
Bloodline, 202
Bloodline: Reckoning, 202
Bloodlust, 183
Blood Merchants, The, 199
Blood of My Blood, 198
Blood of the Vampire, The (1958 film), 113
Blood of the Vampire, The (novel), 62–3
Blood on Satan's Claw, 144
Blood Suckers (see *Incense for the Damned*)
Bloody Red Baron, The, 205
Body Beneath, The, 172
Bolam, Silvester, 87
Book of Were-Wolves, The, 65
Books of Blood, 203
Books of the Beast, The, 90, 92
Boner, Charles, 55
Borley Rectory, 31–2, 36, 39, 170, 184
Bouquet of Barbed Wire, 187
Bourne, Brian (experience of), 159, 161
Bowie, David, 154
Bowie, Les, 105, 116, 150
Bowker, Judi, 186
Bradbury, Ray, 14, 143
Bram Stoker's Dracula, 102, 190, 195
Brando, Marlon, 206
Brett, Jeremy, 187
Briant, Shane, 151
Bride of Corinth, The, 9
Bride of Frankenstein, The, 91, 144
Brides of Dracula, The, 113–4, 116, 119, 126
Briggs, Ian, 189
British Occult Society (BOS), 41, 166, 169, 171, 173, 178, 180–2
British Psychic and Occult Society (BPOS), 160, 162
British Society for the Study of Sex Psychology (BSSSP), 91
Britten, Benjamin, 193
Brood, The, 203
Brooks, Mel, 142
Browning, Tod, 99–100, 102–3, 204
Brown, Murray, 153
'Brown Sugar' (song), 130
Bryan, Peter, 112, 114
Buchan, Xander, 202
Budlick, Maria, 81
Buffy the Vampire Slayer, 198
Bürger, Gottfried, 9
Buried Treasures, 48
Burrowers Beneath, The, 204

Burton, Richard, 137, 139
Burton, Sir Richard, 49
Bus Conductor, The, 104
Bush, Dick, 131
Butch Cassidy and the Sundance Kid, 146
Butler, Terence 'Geezer', 193–4
Byrne, Gabriel, 155
Byron, Lord, 10–1, 13–4, 41, 155, 187
Callan (TV series), 143
Calmet, Dom Augustin, 70, 94, 138
Cammell, Charles Richard, 96
Campbell, Ramsey, 7, 183, 203–4
Camp on Blood Island, The, 108
Camps, Prof Francis, 85
Cannon (TV series), 146
Canon Alberic's Scrap-Book, 66
Capaldi, Peter, 154–5
Captain Clegg, 115
Captain Kronos Vampire Hunter, 148, 151–2
Carew, Henry, 73
Carlson, Veronica, 123, 186
Carmel: A Vampire Tale, 202
Carmilla, 14, 18–20, 54, 64, 70, 100–1, 136–7, 139, 147, 154, 186, 187, 203
Carpenter, Edward, 91
Carradine, David, 134
Carradine, John, 134
Carreras, Michael, 104–5, 107–9, 112, 128–9, 131, 134, 147, 151–2, 190
Carreras, James, 106–7, 118, 125, 128, 136–7, 145, 148
Carrie (novel), 197
Carrington, Hereward, 36
Carry on Screaming, 127
Carson, John, 124, 151, 164
Cary, Kate, 202
Case Book of Sherlock Holmes, The, 71
Cass, Henry, 113
Casting the Runes, 186
Castle, Roy, 118
Castle Sinister, 103
Castle, William, 146
Cater, John, 151
Caton, Reginald, 93
Cavalcade of Ghosts, 72
'Cemetery and Sundown' (song), 195
Chain of Destiny, The, 48, 52–3
Chaney, Lon, 99, 101–2
Chaney Jr, Lon, 102–3, 129
Chase, The (*Doctor Who* episode), 188
Chase, Richard Trenton, 80, 87
Chetwynd-Hayes, R., 7, 142–3, 199–200
Childe Harold's Pilgrimage, 10
Cholmeley, Sir Roger, 156
Christabel, 9, 157
Christodoulou, Raymond, 142
City of the Dead, The, 117
Clairmont, Clara 'Claire', 10
Clark, Simon, 7, 203–4
Clarke, Robin, 142
Claws of Axos, The (*Doctor Who* episode), 188
Clean Sweep, 108
Clemens, Brian, 151–2
Clement, Peter James, 175–6
Clive-Ross, Francis, 29, 31
Clouzot, Henri-Georges, 105
Clyde, Jeremy, 187
Cobban, Jennie Lee, 183
Colburn, Henry, 11, 13
Cole, George, 138
Coleridge, Samuel Taylor, 9, 157
Coles, Michael, 130–3
Collins, Wilkie, 17, 52
Collinson, Mary and Madeleine, 147
Complete Works of Thomas Shadwell, The, 93
Congreve, William, 91
Connoisseur, The, magazine, 96
Connor, Kevin, 142
Conspiracy Show, The (TV programme), 183
Conversion, 203
Cooke, Christian, 189
Copper, Basil, 14, 16, 59, 87, 177
Coppola, Francis Ford, 102, 147, 190, 195, 205
Corlan, Anthony, 149
Corman, Roger, 143
Corri, Adrienne, 150
Corvinus, Matthias, 55
Count Dracula (1977 TV series), 186–7
Count Dracula Fan Club, 46
Count Dracula Fan Club Book of Vampire Stories, The, 201
Count Dracula Society, 38
Countess Dracula, 83, 126, 139, 145, 148
Count Magnus, 66, 114
Count Yorga, Vampire, 100, 128
Country Life magazine, 63
Courtney, W.L., 57
Coven of Vampires, A, 204
Coward, Arne, 82
Cowles, Frederick, 73–4
Cowper, Sir Charles, 158
Cradle of Filth (band), 140, 194–5
Craig, Michael, 141
Creature, The (TV play), 108
Crescendo, 125, 129

Criminal History of Mankind, A, 82
Cripta e l'incubo, La, 136
Croglin Grange Vampire (case of), 29–32
Crosse, Andrew F., 55
Crowley, Aleister, 88, 95–6, 199
Cruelty and the Beast (music album), 140, 195
Crypt of the Vampire (see *La cripta e l'incubo*)
Curse of Doone, The, 73
Curse of Fenric, The (*Doctor Who* episode), 189
Curse of Frankenstein, The, 106–8, 110, 112–3, 118, 137
Curse of the Crimson Altar, The, 144
Curse of the Fly, The, 115
Curse of the Werewolf, The, 193
Cushing, Peter, 107–8, 110, 112–3, 116–9, 124–5, 127–8, 131–4, 137–9, 141, 143–5, 147–8, 152, 190
Daily Express, 174
Daily Mirror, 86, 165, 174–5
Daily Telegraph, 57
Dalby, Richard, 63, 74
Dam Busters, The, 101
Damnation de Faust, Le, 192
Damned, The (band), 195
Dane, Louis, 151
Danger List, 108
Dangerous Moonlight, 116
Daniel, Jennifer, 115
Danse Macabre, 192
'Danse Vampyre' (song), 196
Dark, The, 198
Dark Eyes of London, The, 103
Dark Mysteries (comic), 170
Dashwood, Francis, 115
Davey, Daniel (aka Dani Filth), 194
David, Hal, 146
Davies, Bernard, 46
Davies, Rachel, 188
Davies, Rupert, 123
Davis, Sammi, 155
Deacon, Brian, 153
Dead Meat, 199
Dead of Night, 104, 117, 142
Deane, Hamilton, 101, 103, 153
Dear, Ian, 198
Death Box, The, 198
Dent Vampire (case of), 27–8
De Clare, Richard, 28
Defenders of the Faith (music album), 194
De Gunzberg, Nicolas, 100
Deighton, Len, 205
De Laurentiis, Dino, 137
Demon Lover, The, 62
Demons (TV series), 189
Deneuve, Catherine, 154
Denham, Maurice, 139
De nugis curialium (*Trifles of Courtiers*), 22–3, 26
De Ossorio, Amando, 135
Derby, Crispin, 177
Derleth, August, 73, 203
De Sacy, Martine, 175–6
De Sade, Marquis, 9, 88
Descendant, 202
De Souza, Edward, 115–6
De Staynton, Elizabeth, 41, 43
'Deviant' burials, 28
Devil and All His Works, The, 73
Devil Rides Out, The, 73, 121
Devil Rides Out, The (1968 film), 143
Devils, The, 154
Devil's Trill Sonata, 192
Devils of Loudun, The, 154
Diaboliques, Les, 105
Dicken, Roger, 144
Dickens, Charles, 17, 205
Dickie, James, 177
Dicks, Terrance, 133, 188, 189
Disciple of Dracula, The (unused script), 114–6
Dissertation on Apparitions (Calmet), 70
Dobkin, Harry, 86
Doctor Who, 127–8, 140–1, 148, 151, 188–9, 204
Doctors Wear Scarlet, 61, 143
Dr Terror's House of Horrors, 117–8, 140
Dodo: A Detail of the Day, 66
'Dog, The' (song), 195
Doggett, William (see Tarrant Valley Vampire)
Domain, 198
Donlevy, Brian, 105
Donner, Clive, 137, 142
Donner, Richard, 142
Donohoe, Amanda, 155
Dorabella (TV play), 187
Doyle, Sir Arthur Conan, 49, 71, 100, 190, 205
Do You Want It Good or Tuesday?, 146
Dracula (1897 novel), 7–8, 14, 35, 46–63, 65, 70, 92, 98–101, 107, 118, 134–5, 177, 186, 190, 195, 202
Dracula (1958 film), 102, 106, 109
Dracula (1968 TV series), 186
Dracula (1979 film), 153
Dracula Business, The (TV programme), 190
Dracula Cha Cha Cha, 205
Dracula Has Risen from the Grave, 7, 122–3, 145, 186

Dracula Lives (novels), 201
Dracula, My Love, 201
Dracula: Prince of Darkness, 7, 114, 119–22, 124, 130, 190
Dracula Rekindled, 202
Dracula The Undead, 202
Dracula – The Vampire Play, 101
Dracula Unborn, 201
Dracula's Brood, 63, 74
Dracula's Chair, 201
'Dracula's Daughter' (song), 193
Dracula's Feast of Blood (unused script), 125
Dracula's Guest, 70–1, 177
Dracula Society, The, 46
Dragoti, Stan, 154
Dream of Eugene Aram, The, 48
Dreyer, Carl, 100–1, 136
Driberg, Tom, 95
Drink and Ink, 95
Dr Jekyll and Sister Hyde, 141
Droomgoole, Patrick, 186
Dryden, John, 91
Dublin Evening Mail, 18, 47–8
Duffell, Peter, 140
Durand-Deacon, Mrs Olivia, 85–7
Dusk...and Her Embrace (music album), 195
Duties of Clerks of Petty Sessions in Ireland, 49
Dyall, Valentine, 145
Eastwood, Clint, 137
Eaton, Charles, 95
Ebrahim, Omar, 192
Eddy Jr, C.M., 195
Edwards, Barry, 171
Ege, Julie, 135
Elemental and Other Stories, The, 200
Eles, Sandor, 139
Ellacombe, Canon, 89
Ellis, Bill, 163, 183
Ellis, Henry Havelock, 91
Emergency Ward 10, 128
Enfield Poltergeist (case of), 35
Enter the Dragon, 134
Evans, Clifford, 116
Evans, Dame Edith, 91
Evening News (London), 170, 174
Ewers, Hanns Heinz, 62
Ewing, Barbara, 123
Exorcism!, 183, 39
Exorcist and the Possessed, 38
Exorcist, The, 107, 128, 148, 132
Extreme Hauntings, 72
Eyriès, Jean, 10
Face, The, 68, 70
Fall of the House of Usher, The, 186
Fantasmagoriana (Tales of the Dead), 10
Fanthorpe, Revd Lionel, 29
Faraday, Michael, 158
Farmer, Suzan, 119
Farrant, David, 158, 160–83
Farson, Daniel, 29–30, 45, 47, 59–60, 84, 170, 190
Fate magazine, 30
Faulkner, Sally, 153
Faust (play), 50, 192
Fear in the Night, 146
Fearless Vampire Killers, The, 138, 141
Feet Foremost, 186
Fellini, Frederico, 205
Fennell, Albert, 152
Ferenczi, Sandor, 36
Ferreira, David, 80
Ferrell, Roderick, 80
Field, Anthony, 177
Fielding, Fenella, 126
Fifteen Charlotte Street, 73
Final Edition, 67
Finch, Jon, 138
Finchley Press, 181
Finders Keepers, 139
Findlay, Arthur, 36
Fine, Harry, 137, 145–7
Finlay, Frank, 187
Firth, Violet (see Dion Fortune)
Fisher, Terence, 105, 107, 110–6, 119–22, 126–8, 130, 132–3, 135, 140, 143, 145, 154
Fisher-Rowe, Capt. Edward, 30, 31
Fist of Fury, 134
Fitzgerald, Percy, 48
Fleishman, Hy, 170
Fleming, Ian, 131, 205
Fleming, Robert, 144
Flowering of the Strange Orchid, The, 62
Fluckiger, Paul (experience of), 160
Flying Dutchman, The (opera), 48
Fodor, Nandor, 32, 36–7
Fog, The (novel), 198
Fontana Book of Great Ghost Stories, The, 200
Foot, Paul, 158
Forbes-Robertson, John, 135, 138
Forever Free (music album), 194
Fortune, Dion, 62
Fowler, Marianne, 163
Foyle, Christina, 38
Fragment of a Story, 13
Francis, Freddie, 118, 122, 125

Francis, Kevin, 125
Frank, Alan, 7, 135
Frankel, Benjamin, 193
Frankenstein, 10–1, 14, 102–3, 106, 186–7, 190
Frankenstein (1931 film), 102, 107–8
Frankenstein and the Monster (unused script), 117
Frankenstein and the Monster From Hell, 113
Frankenstein Meets the Wolfman, 103
Frankenstein Must Be Destroyed, 132
Franklyn, William, 132
Frayling, Christopher, 10–1, 14, 16, 47, 52, 155, 190
Freeman, Alan, 118
Freud, Sigmund, 36
Frewin, Kenny, 162
Friedkin, William, 128, 148
From Beyond the Grave, 141
From Demons to Dracula, 183
From the Shadow of Dracula, 48
Frost, Brian, 9, 59, 72
'Funeral in Carpathia' (song), 195
Fyfe, Sir David Maxwell, 87
Galanty Show, The, 93
Galeen, Henrik, 99, 103
Galsworthy, John, 158
Gates, Tudor, 137–8, 145, 147
Gauld, Alan, 34
Gaunt, Valerie, 111–2, 127
Gazetteer of British Ghosts, A, 38
Geography of Witchcraft, The, 91
George, Major Gwilym Lloyd, 171
George, Susan, 186
Gerard, Emily, 55, 98
Ghastly Ones, The, 172
Ghost Club, The, 38, 63, 159, 178
Ghost of Rashmon Hall, The, 103
Ghost Pirates, The, 72
Ghost Stories of an Antiquary, 65–6
Ghost Story (TV series), 146
Ghosts Over England, 72
Ghostwatch (TV programme), 155
Ghoul, The (1932 film), 103
Ghoul, The (1975 film), 125
Gibson, Alan, 129, 131, 152
Gilling, John, 104
Glasgow Herald, 57
Glenarvon, 10
Glut, Donald, 23–4, 27, 29, 83–4, 94
Gocool, Mickey, 183
God of the Labyrinth, The, 201
Godwin, Frank, 146
Goethe, Johann Wolfgang von, 9, 192
Gorbals Vampire (case of), 170, 190
Gorgon, The, 119
Gothic, 155
Gothic Quest, The, 93
Gough, Michael, 117
Gounod, Charles, 192
Gow, Capt. Neil, 34
Graham, Charles, 186
Grans, Hans, 82–3
Grant, Moray, 138
Graves, Teresa, 142
'Graveyard by Moonlight, The' (song), 195
Graveyard Vultures, The, 199
Great Catholics, 90
Green, Barbara, 42
Green, Nigel, 139
Grey, Elizabeth Caroline, 14–5
Grimoire, The, 93
Grunberg, Nava, 162
Grunewald, Fritz, 33
Guardian newspaper, 61
Guest, Val, 105, 109
Guiley, Rosemary Ellen, 183
Gwynne, Michael, 127
Haarmann, Fritz, 82–3
Haigh, John George, 84–7
Haining, Peter, 14–5, 17
Halidom, M.Y. (see Alexander Huth)
Hall Caine, Sir Thomas Henry, 56
Hall, Mike, 57
Hamer, Robert, 142
Hamlet (play), 48
Hammer Films, 104–39, 144–52
Hammer Films On Location, 163
Hammer Films: The Unsung Heroes, 137
Hammer House of Horror (TV series), 134, 152
Hammer, House of Horror, 107, 150
Hammer: The Studio That Dripped Blood, 190
Hampstead & Highgate Express newspaper, 160, 162–3, 166–7, 169–73
Hanley, Jenny, 127
Hardman, Matthew, 75–8, 87
Hardy, Robert, 187
Hare, Augustus, 30–1
Harper, Charles, 29–30
Harris, Len, 107
Harris, Sandra, 168–9
Hart, Charles, 192
Hart, James, 190
Hartford-Davis, Robert, 144
Hartley, L.P., 186
Hartmann, Dr Franz, 94
Hartnell, William, 188

Harvey, William F., 73
Haskins, Kevin and David, 196
Hassall, Imogen, 143
Haughton, Aaliyah, 76
Haunted, 198
Haunted Castle, The, 97
Haunted Churches & Abbeys of Britain, 31
Haunted Hands, 72
Haunted House of Horror, The, 144
Haunted Houses, 30
Haunted London, 158, 160
Haunted Places of Middlesex, 57
Hay, William (18th Earl of Errol), 54
Hayden, Linda, 124
Head, Anthony, 179
Hearne, Marcus, 128
Heartbeat of the Earth (music album), 196
Hellbound Heart, The, 203
Hellraiser (film series), 203
Hempel, Anouska, 126
Henderson, Dr & Mrs Archibald, 85–6
Hendry, Ian, 152
Henson, Nicky, 115
Herbert, James, 197–8
Herzog, Werner, 154
Highgate Vampire (case of), 156–184
Highgate Vampire Casebook, The, 183
Highgate Vampire Society, 159, 183
Highgate Vampire, The, 180, 182
Hill, Benny, 126
Hinchcliffe, Philip, 188
Hinds, Anthony, 105–10, 112–7, 121–2, 123–8, 134, 152, 190
Historia rerum Anglicarum (*History of English Affairs*), 24–5
History of Witchcraft & Demonology, The, 91
Hobbs, William, 152
Hobson's Choice, 101
Hodder, Reginald, 72
Hodgson, George (see Dent Vampire)
Hodgson, William Hope, 18, 72
Hogan, Bosco, 187
Holder, Geoff, 29, 31
Holly, Bernard, 188
Holly, Buddy, 193
Holmes, Robert, 188
Holt, Ian, 202
Hooper, Ewan, 123
Hopkins, Robert Thurston, 72
Horler, Sydney, 73
Hornsey Journal newspaper, 173, 181
Horror: 100 Best Books, 205
Horror of Abbot's Grange, The, 74
Horror of Dracula (see *Dracula* 1958 film)
Horror of Frankenstein, The, 126
Horror of the Heights, The, 71
Houghton, Don, 128–9, 130–5
Hound of the Baskervilles, The, 112, 190
House by the Churchyard, The, 18
House of Dracula, 102
House of Frankenstein, 102
House of the Temple, The, 204
House on the Borderland, The, 72
House That Dripped Blood, The, 129, 140
Housman, Laurence, 91
Howard, Richard, 177
Howard, Robert E., 73
Howell, Charles, 56
Huckvale, David, 116
Hudd, Roy, 144
Human Remains, 203
Humphries, Mr Justice (Haigh case), 87
Hungary in Ancient, Medieval and Modern Times, 54
Hunger, The, 154
Hunt, Marsha, 130
Hunt, Martitia, 113
Hutchings, Dr Peter, 109
Huth, Alexander, 72
Hutton, Brian, 137
Huxley, Aldous, 154
Hyæna (music album), 195
Hyman, Eliot, 106, 122
I Am Legend, 108–9
'Illicitus' (song), 195
Illustrated Police News, 170
I, Monster, 129
In a Glass Darkly, 18, 100
Incense for the Damned, 143–4
Ingrid Pitt Bedside Companion for Ghosthunters, The, 141
Ingrid Pitt Companion for Vampire Lovers, The, 141
Inhabitant of the Lake and Less Welcome Tenants, The, 203
Inkubus Sukkubus (band), 196
Inside Hammer, 118, 146
'Intercourse With the Vampire' (song), 196
International Institute for Psychical Research, 36
Interview with the Vampire, 14, 197
In the Shadow of the Highgate Vampire, 175
Iommi, Tony, 194
Iron Maiden (band), 194
Ironside (TV series), 146
Irving, Sir Henry, 48–51, 71

Jack the Ripper, 81, 100, 112, 205
'Jack the Ripper' (song), 193
Jackson, Gordon, 187
Jacobi, Carl, 177
Jagger, Dean, 105
James, Anatole (see G.E. Pickering)
James, Emrys, 188
James, M.R., 23, 65, 67, 74, 185
Janson, Horst, 151
Jarrott, Charles, 139
Jarvis, Martin, 125
Jay, Griffin, 103
Jayne, Jennifer, 118
Jefford, Barbara, 145
'Jenny wi' the Airn Teeth' (poem), 170
Jerome, Jerome K., 49
Jervis, Victoria, 176
Jewel of Seven Stars, The, 59
Johnny Alucard, 205
'Johnny Remember Me' (song), 193
Johnson, Laurie, 152
Johnson, Michael, 145
Johnson, Richard, 143
Jones, Det. Insp. Alan, 75
Jones, Freddie, 132
Jones, Stephen, 190, 199–200, 202
Jourdan, Louis, 186
Journey to the Unknown, 134
Judas Priest (band), 194
Judge's House, The, 70
Juju (music album), 195
Juliette, 9
Jürgens, Curt, 141
Justin, John, 187
Justine, 9
Kahlo, Frida, 76
Kali: Devil Bride of Dracula (unmade film), 151
Kapital, Das, 158
Kaplan, Stephen, 37
Karloff, Boris, 102–3, 105, 108, 193
Keen, Geoffrey, 124, 164
Keir, Andrew, 119
Kenilworth, 16
Keys, Anthony Nelson, 110, 119, 128
Killer Crabs, 199
Kinberg, Judson, 148
King, Stephen, 14, 46, 118, 172, 197, 199
Kinnear, Roy, 124
Kinski, Klaus, 154
Kirk, Harry, 87
Kirklees Vampire (case of), 41–3, 166
Kiss of the Vampire (aka *Kiss of Evil*), 115, 166–17
Kneale, Nigel, 105, 107–8, 185
Knighton Vampires, The, 199
Knox, Fr Ronald, 90
Kolchak: The Night Stalker, 133
Koresh, David, 114
Kung Fu (TV series), 134
Kürten, Peter, 80–2, 84
Kuttner, Henry, 14
Labyrinth, The, 200
Lady, The magazine, 199
Lady of the Shroud, The, 59
Lady Vanishes, The, 152
Laemmle, Carl, 102
Laird of Dunain, 202
Lair of the White Worm, The, 59, 70, 154
Lair of the White Worm, The (1988 film), 154
Lamb, Lady Caroline, 10, 11
Land Beyond the Forest, The, 55
Landon, Dinsdale, 189
Langella, Frank, 153
Langley, Patsy, 156, 183
Langton, Simon, 187
Larraz, José Ramón, 153
Larry's Guest, 199
Last Man on Earth, The, 109
Last of the Vampires, 62
Latham, Philip, 120
Laymon, Richard, 14
Leaky, Phil, 112
Lean, David, 101
Lecale, Erroll (aka Wilfred McNeilly), 198
Lee, Bruce, 134
Lee, Christopher, 58, 107, 110, 113, 115, 117–8, 124, 126, 131, 135–6, 145, 152, 186, 190
Le Fanu, Joseph Sheridan, 7, 14, 17–20, 25, 50, 54, 63–4, 70, 93, 100, 136–9, 147, 154, 185–6, 195, 203
Legend of the 7 Golden Vampires, The, 126, 134–5, 142, 152
Legend of the Werewolf, 125
Leiber, Fritz, 204
Leigh, Suzanna, 146
Lennox, Annie, 195
Lenore, 9
Leport, Gary, 193
Letters on Demonology and Witchcraft, 16
Levitt, S., 171
Lewis, Leopold David, 49
Leyshon, Mabel, 75–6
Leyton, John, 193
Liddell, Henry, 30
Life's a Scream, 141

Life With the Lyons, 104
Light (Spiritualist journal), 72
Lindsay, William, 188
Lippert, Robert, 109
Liszt, Franz, 192
Liveright, Horace, 101–2
Lloyd, Edward, 15
Lloyd, Jeremy, 142
London After Midnight, 100, 102
London Society magazine, 48
Looking For Something to Suck, 200
Lopez, Carmen, 77
Lord Halifax's Ghost Book, 66
Lord of Illusions, 203
Lord Ruthven ou les Vampires, 13
Loring, Frederick George, 64–5
Losey, Josef, 105
Lost Hearts, 66, 185
Lost World, The, 71
Lot No. 249, 71
Love at First Bite, 154
'Love Bites' (song), 194
Lovecraft, H.P., 11, 50, 73, 177, 195, 201, 203–4
Loved Dead, The, 195
'Lovesick for Mina' (song), 195
Loves of Count Iorga, The (unused script), 128
'Love Song For a Vampire' (song), 195
Love Thy Neighbour (TV series), 143
Lucan, Arthur, 104
Ludlum, Harry, 50
Lugosi, Bela, 74, 100–4, 106, 109–10, 143, 153, 196
Lumley, Brian, 7, 18, 204
Lumley, Joanna, 132
'Lusia' (Highgate case), 179–82
Lust for a Vampire, 145–6
Lutyens, Elisabeth, 118, 193
Lymington, John, 128
Lytton, Edward Bulwer, 17
Macbeth (play), 52
MacGregor, Scott, 131
Maclean, Keith, 178–9
Macnee, Patrick, 143
Magee, Patrick, 143
Magic Cottage, The, 198
Magpie (TV programme), 127
Mahler, 154
Mahler, Anna, 158
Mahler, Gustav, 192
Malleus Maleficarum, 92
Malory, Sir Thomas, 9
Mammoth Book of Dracula, The, 199, 203
Mammoth Book of Vampires, The, 202, 205
Manchester, Bishop Sean, 41–3, 84, 95, 166–83, 190, 202
Man-eating Tree, The, 62
Mangan, Julia, 100
Maniac, 115
Man on the Beach, A, 105
Manson, Charles, 114, 127
Man From the Bomb, The, 142
Manticore and Other Horrors, The (music album), 195
Manitou, The, 202
Man Who Could Cheat Death, The, 112
Man Who Wrote Dracula, The, 47
Map, Walter, 22–4, 26, 70
Maple, Eric, 28
Markham, Len, 42
Mark of the Vampire, 100
Marmion, 53
Marschner, Heinrich, 192
Marshall, William, 143
Marson, Ania, 187
Martell, Philip, 152
Martian Chronicles, The, 143
Martin, Dave, 188
Marquis de Sade: A Study in Algolagnia, The, 91
Marryat, Florence, 62
Marx, Karl, 158
Massey acting family, 141
Masters, Anthony, 14, 16, 22, 26, 79, 81, 84
Masterton, Graham, 202
Mastrocinque, Camillo, 136
Mathers, Samuel MacGregor, 96
Matheson, Richard, 9, 108–9, 121, 133
Matthews, Christopher, 127
Matthews, Francis, 119
Maxford, Howard, 107, 128, 150
Mayfair magazine, 202
Mayne, Ferdy, 138
Mayor, Florence, 73
Mazeppa, 13
McCallum, Neil, 118
McCarthy, Neil, 143
McConnell, Brian, 177
McCoy, Sylvester, 189
McDonald, Graeme, 188
McGavin, Darren, 133
McIlwain, David, 105
McKendrick, Thomas, 76–7
McSwann family, 85–6
Medwin, Michael, 105
Meek, Joe, 193
Megahey, Leslie, 185

Méliès, George, 97
Meller, Hugh, 157
Melrose Abbey Vampire (case of), 24–6
Melton, J. Gordon, 84, 134, 195
Menzies, Allan, 76–7, 79, 87
Mephisto Waltzes, 192
Merrow, Jane, 186
Meynell, Francis, 93
Meyrink, Gustav, 14
Midnight Meat Train, The, 203
Millais, Sir John Everett, 56
Miller, Jonathan, 185
Miller, Philip, 130
Milligan, Andy, 171–2
Mind Parasites, The, 201
Miroth family, 80
Miss Avenal, 73
Mitchell, Stacey, 78–9
Monlaur, Yvonne, 113
Monster Club, The, 200
Monster Club, The (1981 film), 143
Monsters and Vampires, 135
Monster With a Thousand Faces, The, 9, 59, 72
'Moon Over Bourbon Street' (song), 195
Moonstone, The, 52
Moontrekkers, The (band), 193
Moran, Paul and Peter, 190
More Ghost Stories of an Antiquary, 65
Morris, Marianne, 153
Morte d'Arthur, Le, 9
Moulder-Brown, John, 149
Mower, Patrick, 143
Mrs Amworth, 67
Muller, Robert, 187
Mummy, The (1959 film), 112, 114
Munro, Caroline, 130, 152
Murnau, Friedrich W., 98–9, 101, 103, 112, 185
Murphy, Peter, 196
Murray, John, 10
Murray, Paul, 48
Music Lovers, The, 154
Mykicura, Demetrious (see Vampire of the Villas)
Mystery and Imagination (TV series), 185
Mystery of the Sea, The, 54
Nadasdy, Count Ferenc, 83–4
Nanny, The, 115, 119, 128
Nathan-Turner, John, 188
National Laboratory of Psychical Research, 34, 36
Natural History of the Vampire, The, 22, 26, 81
Neame, Christopher, 129
Necros, 204
Necroscope, 204
Necroscope: The Plague Bearer, 204
Needs, James, 119
Negotium Perambulans, 67, 70
Neil-Smith, Revd Christopher, 38
Newman, Andrea, 187
Newman, Kim, 14, 52, 204–6
Nightbreed, 203
'Night Crawler' (song), 194
Night Creatures, The (see *I Am Legend*)
'Nighthunter' (song), 194
Night Land, The, 72
Nightmare, 115
Nightmare Movies, 205
Nightmare: The Birth of Horror (TV series), 190
Night of the Big Heat, 128
Night of the Crabs, 199
Night of the Living Dead, 109, 128
Night of the Vampire (instrumental), 193
'Night Shift' (song), 195
Night Stalker, The, 133
Night Wind Howls, The, 74
Nineteen Eighty-Four, 107, 205
Nineteenth Century magazine, 55
Niven, David, 142
No Common Task, 94
Nodier, Charles, 13
North London Paranormal Investigations (NLPI), 183
Nosferatu (1922 film), 98–9, 101, 185
Nosferatu (band), 196
Nosferatu the Vampyre, 154
Number 13, 185
Observer newspaper, 58
Ogden, Charles Kay, 91
Oh, Whistle and I'll Come to You, My Lad, 185
Old Dracula (see *Vampira*)
Old Godet's Ghost, 72
Oldman, Gary, 58, 102
Old Man's Story, The, 73
Old Mother Riley Meets the Vampire, 104
Olivier, Sir Lawrence, 153
O'Loughlin, Thomas (experience of), 159, 178, 180
O'Mara, Kate, 137
Omen, The (film), 202
Omen, The (novel), 202
On the Trail of the Poltergeist, 36–7
Ophelia (painting), 56
Orwell, George, 107, 205
Osbourne, John 'Ozzy', 194
Ossenfelder, Heinrich, 9

Out of the Shadows, 177
Owens, Richard, 149
Oxenberg, Catherine, 155
Oz magazine, 177
Paganini, Niccolò, 192
Page, Carol, 183
Painkiller (music album), 194
Pall Mall Gazette, 58
Pall Mall magazine, 64
Pan's Garden, 63
Paole, Arnold (case of), 27, 29
Paranoiac, 118
Paranormal Activity, 107
Paranormal Cumbria, 31
Parashumti, Valerie, 78–9
Parasite, The, 71
Parry, Michael, 203
Paul, Alexander, 139
Payne, Laurence, 149
PC 49 (radio serial), 104
Pearson, Sydney, 112
Peel, David, 113–4
Penhaligon, Susan, 186
Penrose, Valentine, 83
Penthouse magazine, 202
Perrott, Tom, 178
Personal Reminiscences of Henry Irving, 49
Pertwee, Jon, 140, 188
Peters, Luan, 148
Phantom of the Opera, The (1925 film), 99
Phantom of the Opera, The (1962 film), 115
Picethly, Laurence, 174
Pickering, Geoffrey Evans, 92
Piece of Mind (music album), 194
Pierce, Jack, 103
Pierrepoint, Albert, 87
Piper, Evelyn, 115
Pirie, David, 97, 102, 126, 128, 131, 149
Pitt, Ingrid, 117, 137–41, 146, 155, 190
Playboy magazine, 142
Play for Today (TV series), 189
Pleasance, Donald, 117, 143, 153
Plogojowitz, Peter (case of), 27, 35
Poe, Edgar Allan, 140, 186
Polanski, Roman, 128, 138, 141
Polidori, John William, 7, 10–4, 15–7, 155, 192
Poltergeist!, 35
Pope, John, 176–7, 181
Possessed, The, 177
Powell, Eddie, 121
Prest, Thomas Preskett, 16
Price, Dennis, 148
Price, Harry, 32, 34, 36, 39
Price, Vincent, 109, 143–4
Primrose Path, The, 48
Princess of Darkness, 74
Principle of Evil Made Flesh, The (music album), 195
Professionals, The (TV series), 151
Prowse, Dave, 150
Psychic Self-Defence, 62
Psycho (1960 film), 115, 117, 140
Psychomania, 115
Purcell, Mr D.J., 174
Purple Terror, The, 62
Pushkin, A.S., 93
Pye, PC John, 44–5
Quarry, Robert, 100, 128
Quatermass II, 105, 108
Quatermass and the Pit, 105
Quatermass Experiment, The, 105, 185
Quatermass Xperiment, The, 105, 108, 109
Queen of the Damned, The (film & novel), 76
Quinn, Seabury, 73
'Raindrops Keep Fallin' on my Head' (song), 146
Raising the Devil, 163, 183
Ramsey Campbell, Probably, 183
Rasputin, the Mad Monk, 115
Rath, Tina, 14, 23, 190
Rats, The, 197
Raven, Mike, 145
Raven, Simon, 61, 143
Raven's Brood, 67
Realm of Ghosts, The, 28
Recollections of Dante Gabriel Rossetti, 56
Red Flasket, The, 73
Redgrave, Corin, 186
Redgrave, Vanessa, 154
Red Reign, 205
Reed, Oliver, 154
Reeves, Michael, 144
Reptile, The, 115
Return of Count Yorga, The, 128
Return of the Vampire, The, 102
Revelations in Black, 177
Revenge of Dracula (unused script), 114
Revenge of Dracula, The (novel), 201
Revenge of Frankenstein, The, 112, 127
Rice, Anne, 14, 76, 195, 197
Richard, Cliff, 139
Richard of Bordeaux, 107
Richards, Mr Justice (Hardman case), 76
Richardson, Natasha, 155
Richardson, Sir Ralph, 158

Riddle of the Thetford Vampire, The, 72
Rigby, Jonathan, 128
Rime of the Ancient Mariner, The, 157
Ripper, Michael, 125
'Ripper, The' (song), 194
Rise (music album), 196
Ritson, Darren W., 29
Ritual in the Dark, 201
Riva, James, 77, 80, 87
Rivals, The (play), 48
Rivals of Dracula, The, 203
Roadkill, 203
Robb, David, 187
Robbins, Rossell Hope, 92
Roberts, Sarah Ellen (see Blackburn Vampire)
Roberts, Revd Dr Matthew, 31
Robinson, Bernard, 119, 122
Robinson, Harry, 138, 146
Robinson, Philip Stewart (Phil), 62
Rogers, Malcolm, 188
Rogers, Peter, 127
Rogo, D. Scott, 29–31, 88, 94
Rohmer, Sax, 205
Rolling Stones, The (band), 130
Romeo and Juliet (play), 150
Romero, George, 109, 128
Room in the Tower, The, 68–70
Rosemary's Baby, 128
Rosenberg, Max, 106, 140–1, 143
Rossetti, Dante Gabriel, 56
Round About the Carpathians, 55
Rowling, J.K., 189
Rudolph, 200
Russell, Ken, 154–5
Rymer, James Malcolm, 7, 14–8, 30, 65, 194
Rymer, Michael, 76
Sachs, Robin, 149
Saint-Saëns, Camille, 192
'Salem's Lot, 14, 118, 197, 204
Sallis, Peter, 124–5, 164
Sample, George, 160
Sanderson, Revd George, 31
Sands, Julian, 155
Sangster, Jimmy, 104–7, 110–9, 121–2, 125–6, 145–7, 190
Sasdy, Peter, 123, 126, 129, 139, 145, 148, 152
Satanic Rites of Dracula, The, 114, 132–3
Satan's Circus, 73
Saturday Night Fever, 153
Savages, The (band), 193
Saville, Philip, 186, 188
Savory, Gerald, 186
Saxon (band), 194
Scars of Dracula, 126, 128, 131, 146
Scenes from Goethe's Faust, 192
Schaffer, Anthony, 141
Schalken the Painter, 18, 185
Schmitz, Sybille, 100
Schreck, Max, 99
Schuman, Robert, 192
Schutz, Maurice, 100
Scott, Sir Walter, 16, 53
Scott, Tony and Ridley, 144, 154, 196
Scream and Scream Again, 129
Seabrook, William, 38
Secret of Crickley Hall, The, 198
Secret of the Growing Gold, The, 57, 70
Sellers, Peter, 108
Seltzer, David, 202
Sewell, Vernon, 144
Shaft No. 247, 177
Shamrock journal, 48
Sharp, Don, 115, 117, 152
Shaw, Run Run, 134
Shawcross, Sir Hartley, 87
Sheen, Martin, 205
Shelley, Barbara, 113, 119
Shelley, Mary, 10, 14, 102, 106, 108, 155, 186
Shelley, Percy Bysshe, 10, 11, 155
Sheridan, Richard Brinsley, 17
'She's Fallen in Love With the Monster Man' (song), 193
Siddal, Elizabeth, 56, 57
Silence of the Lambs, The, 107
Silver, Alain, 111–2
Simmons, Barry, 174
Simpson, Dr Keith, 85
Sinclair, Clive, 14
Singular Death of Morton, The, 63
Siouxsie and the Banshees (band), 195
Skeggs, Roy, 131, 152
Skeleton Count, The, 14–5
Skull, The, 140
Slime Beast, The, 199
Smith, Clark Ashton, 73
Smith, Edward Percy, 114
Smith, Guy N., 7, 18, 198–9
Smith, Lady Eleanor, 73
Smith, Madeline, 137
Smith, Matt, 189
Smith, Timothy d'Arch, 90–2
Smith, Tom, 139
Smith, William, 95
Society for Psychical Research (SPR), 27, 117
Some of Your Blood, 61

Songling, Pu, 134
Son of Dracula, 102, 129, 134
South Bank Show, The (TV programme), 190
Southey, Robert, 9
Space Vampires, The, 62, 200
Spaceways, 105
Spall, Timothy, 155
Spence, Lewis, 73
Spirit World, The, 62
Spuk von Talpa, Der, 33
Squaw, The, 70
SS-GB, 205
St John Passion (Bach), 79
Stark, Wilbur, 148
Starkie, Walter, 73
Stasinowsky, Jessica, 78–9
State of Decay (*Doctor Who* episode), 188
Steel Bayonet, The, 108
Steiner, Marcel, 142
Steel, Pippa, 137
Stenbock, Count Eric, 64
Stensgaard, Yutte, 145–7
Stevenson, Venetia, 117
Stewart, Roy, 148
'Still Life' (song), 194
Sting (aka Gordon Sumner), 195
Stoker, Bram (life and writings), 46–60
Stoker, Dacre, 202
Stoker, Noel Thornley, 59
Stone Chamber, The, 65
Stone, Chris, 45
Stoney, Kevin, 144
Story of My Life, The, 30
Story of the Poltergeist Down the Centuries, The, 36
Strand Magazine, The, 62, 71
Strange Case of Dr Jekyll and Mr Hyde, The, 112, 129, 190
Strange Stories From a Chinese Studio, 134
Strawberries (music album), 195
Streete, Revd Ernest, 165
Stribling, Melissa, 112
Strieber, Whitley, 154
String of Pearls, The, 16
Strøyberg, Annette, 136
Stuart-Forbes, Hector, 93, 96
Studies of Death, 64
Sturgeon, Theodore, 14, 61
Style, Michael, 137, 145–7
Subotsky, Milton, 106, 117–8, 140–3
Sucking Pit, The, 199
Summers, Montague, 8, 16, 29, 40–1, 83, 88–96, 138–9, 141, 177
Supernatural (TV series), 187
Supernatural Horror in Literature, 50
Supernatural Omnibus, The, 93
Suspended in Dusk journal, 159
Sutch, David 'Screaming Lord', 193
Sutherland, Donald, 118
'Sweetest Chill, The' (song), 195
Tabori, Paul, 105
Tales From the Crypt (comic), 170
Tales From the Crypt (film), 141
Tales of Fear and Fantasy, 200
Tarrant Valley Vampire (case of), 28
Taste of Fear, 115, 119, 128
Taste the Blood of Dracula, 123–7, 129, 148, 163
Taylor, Christine, 78
Taylor, Michael, 78
Tayman, Robert, 149
Teare, Dr Donald, 85
Telstar (instrumental), 193
Temple, William, 105
Tennyson, Alfred Lord, 49
Tenser, Tony, 144
Ten Yorkshire Mysteries, 42
Terror in the Crypt (see *La cripta e l'incubo*)
Terror of Blue John Gap, The, 71
Terry-Thomas, 141
Thalaba the Destroyer, 9
There is No Death, 62
Thesiger, Ernest, 91
Thin Ghost and Others, A, 65–6
Thomas, B.J., 146
Thomas, Damien, 147
Thorndike, Russell, 115
Thorndike, Sybil, 91
Thornography (music album), 195
Thornton Heath Poltergeist (case of), 36–7
'Thornton', Mr (experience of), 161–2
Three Cases of Murder, 103
Tieck, Johann, 9
Times Literary Supplement, The, 73
Tinderbox (music album), 195
Tingwell, Charles, 119
Today (TV programme), 168–9
Todd, Bob, 126
Tomb of Sarah, The, 64
Tomb of the Cybermen (*Doctor Who*), 148
Tombs of the Blind Dead, 135
Tomorrow journal, 31
Torture Garden, 140
To the Devil … A Daughter, 95, 152
To the Devil: A Daughter (1976 film), 152
Tractate Middoth, The, 185
Tramp, The (journal), 63

Transfer, The, 63
Transylvania, 55
Transylvanian Superstitions, 55
Travels in Central Asia, 54
Tremayne, Peter (aka Peter Beresford Ellis), 201
Trent, Martin (experience of), 182–3
Trollenberg Terror, The, 112
Troughton, Patrick, 127, 148
True Horror (TV programme), 179
True Story of a Vampire, The, 64
True Vampires of History, 23, 27, 94
Tucker, Forrest, 108
Turner, James, 177
Turn of the Screw, The (opera), 193
Twain, Mark, 49
Twenty Four Hours (TV programme), 174
Twilight, 198
Twins of Evil, 147–8
Two Roses (play), 48
Tyburn Films, 125
Unbidden, The, 200
Uncle Silas, 18
Undead, The, 177
Under the Punkah, 62
Underwood, Peter, 16, 38–40, 84, 89–90, 94–5, 138, 158–60, 177–8, 180, 183
Unleash the Beast (music album), 194
Unsolved Mysteries: Past and Present, 35
Up the Creek, 108
Ursini, James, 111–2, 114
Vadim, Roger, 136–7
Valentine, Anthony, 143
Valley of Fear, The, 115
Vambéry, Arminius, 54–5
Vampir, Der, 9
Vampira, 142
Vampire (1922 novel), 62
Vampire, Le (Nodier), 13
Vampire of the Villas (case of), 7, 44–5
Vampire, The (1913 film), 98
Vampire, The (Hodder), 73
Vampire, The (Horler), 73
Vampire Book, The, 84
Vampire Chronicles, The, 195
Vampire Cinema, The, 97, 126, 131
Vampire Circus, 148–51
Vampire Film, The, 111
Vampire: His Kith and Kin, The, 83, 88, 92, 94, 138
Vampire Hunters (unmade film), 151
Vampire Hunter's Handbook, The, 41, 167, 183
Vampire in Europe, The, 92
Vampire in Legend, Fact and Art, The, 59, 87
Vampirella (unmade film), 151
Vampire Lovers, The, 137–9, 145, 147, 153
Vampire of Kaldenstein, The, 74
Vampire of Woolpit Grange, The, 72
Vampire Omnibus, The, 14, 17
Vampire Research Centre (New York), 37
Vampire Research Society, 41–2, 180
Vampire Village, 199
Vampire Virgins, The (unused script), 147
Vampire's Bedside Companion, The, 94, 139, 177–80
Vampire's Tower, The, 98
Vampires (TV play), 190
Vampires Among Us, 183
Vampires Are, 37
Vampires at Night (amateur film), 171
Vampires of the Andes, The, 73
Vampires of the Coast, The, 98
Vampires of Venice, The (*Doctor Who* episode), 189
Vampires, Zombies and Monster Men, 29, 45
Vampyr (1932 film), 100–1
Vampyr, Der (opera), 192
Vampyre Erotica (song and music album), 196
'Vampyre Kiss' (song), 196
Vampyre of the Fens, A, 9
Vampyre, The (Polidori), 11–4, 16
Vampyres (1974 film), 153
'Vampyres Cry' (song), 196
Vampyres: Lord Byron to Count Dracula, 10, 16
Vampyrrhic, 203–4
Vampyrrhic Rites, 204
Van Eyssen, John, 112, 127
Vanian, Dave (aka David Lett), 195
Van Sloan, Edward, 101–2
Varma, Dr Devandra P., 38–9, 49
Varney the Vampyre, 15–7, 19, 30, 73, 194
Vaughan-Williams, Ralph, 193
Vault of Horror, The, 141, 203
Vault of Horror, The (comic), 170
Velliamy, Lewis, 157
Venom (band), 195
Ventham, Wanda, 144, 151
Vernon, Richard, 132
'Vesago' (vampire), 80
Victorian Ghost Stories, 93
Vignola, Robert, 98
Village of Blood, 198
Village of Vampires (unmade film), 151
Villiers, George, 91
Vincent, Fr Peter, 78
Vlad Dracu, 55
Vlad Tepes (Vlad the Impaler), 55–6

Volk, Stephen, 155
Von Vogt, A.E., 200
Wailing Well, 65
Wake Not the Dead, 9
Wallace, Edgar, 103
Wallin, Teresa, 80
Walters, Thorley, 120, 149
Warbeck, David, 148
Ward, Lalla, 149
Warner, David, 142
Warning to the Curious and Other Ghost Stories, A, 65
Wassilko-Serecki, Countess Zoë, 33
Waterhouse, Agnes, 27
Waterloo (play), 71
Waterman, Dennis, 127
Watson, H.B. Marriot, 65
Watson, Jack, 142
Waxman, Harry, 153
Wegner, Elizabeth, 164
'We Hunger' (song), 195
Weird Tales magazine, 73
Welles, Orson, 103
Wells, H.G., 62, 205
Werewolf, The, 92
Werewolf by Moonlight, 199
Whale, James, 91
Wheatley, Dennis, 73, 95, 121, 143, 152, 194, 198
Where Eagles Dare, 137
Where the Ghosts Walk, 38
Whitaker, David, 149–50
Whitby Gazette, 53
Whitby Vampyrrhic, 204
White, Frederick Merrick, 62
White, John, 175
White, Wilfred Hyde, 108
Whitelaw, Billie, 187
Whithouse, Toby, 189
Whitman, Walt, 49
Whittington-Egan, Richard, 29, 31
Wicker Man, The, 141
Wigginton, Tracey, 79
Wightman, Bruce, 46
Wild Bunch, The, 121
Wilde, Oscar, 49, 205
Wiles, Simon, 175
Wilkinson, William, 54
William of Newburgh, 22, 24–7
Williams, Dixie, 190
Williams, John (Ratcliffe Highway case), 82
Williams, Robert, 100
Williams, Roger, 42
Williamson, Revd Claude, 90
Willman, Noel, 115
Wilmer, Douglas, 138
Willows, The, 63
Wilson, Colin, 33, 35, 37, 62, 82, 133, 200
Witchfinder General, 144
Wohlbrück, Wilhelm, 192
Wojdyla, Elizabeth, 178–9
Wolfit, Donald, 105, 113
Wood, Charles Lindley, 66
Woodward, Edward, 143
Woman in Black, The (Huth), 72
Woman in White, The, 52
Women in Love, 154
Wonder Woman (TV series), 146
World Famous True Ghost Stories, 36
Wyeth, Katya, 147
Wymark, Patrick, 158
X the Unknown, 105
Yellowlees, Dr Henry, 86
Yorkshire Robin Hood Society, 42
Yorkshire Vampire (case of), 39–40, 89
Young, Aida, 123, 125, 190
Young Frankenstein, 142
Young, Robert, 148, 150–1
Zügun, Eleonora (case of), 32–4, 36